THE ROLE OF EARLY EXPERIENCE IN INFANT DEVELOPMENT

Summary Publications in the Johnson & Johnson
Pediatric Round Table Series:

1. *New Perspectives in Early Emotional Development*
   Edited by Steven P. Shelov, MD and
   John G. Warhol, PhD

2. *The Role of Early Experience in Infant Development*
   Edited by Nathan Fox, PhD, Lewis A. Leavitt, MD,
   and John G. Warhol, PhD

Series includes continuing education programs
and patient education materials.

For more information,
call 1-877-JNJ-LINK or fax 1-877-656-3299
or visit us @ jnjPediatricInstitute.com.

Table of Contents

THE ROLE OF EARLY EXPERIENCE IN INFANT DEVELOPMENT

Chaired by
Nathan A. Fox, PhD

Edited by
Nathan A. Fox, PhD, Lewis A. Leavitt MD,
and John G. Warhol, PhD

Sponsored by

Division of Johnson & Johnson Consumer Companies, Inc.

Table of Contents

Participants

Ronald G. Barr, MD
Professor of Pediatrics and Psychiatry
McGill University
Head, Child Development Program
Montreal Children's Hospital
2300 Rue Tupper
Montreal, QC, Canada H3H 1P3

C. Sue Carter, PhD
Distinguished University Professor of
  Biology
Department of Biology
University of Maryland
Room 4222 Zoology-Psychology
Building 144
College Park, MD 20742

Adele Diamond, PhD
Director, Center for Developmental
  Cognitive Neuroscience
Eunice Kennedy Shriver Center
200 Trapelo Road
Waltham, MA 02452

Nathan A. Fox, PhD
Professor, Institute for Child Study
Department of Human Development
University of Maryland
Room 4304, Benjamin Building
College Park, MD 20742

Julia Freedman
Director
Johnson & Johnson Pediatric Institute
199 Grandview Road
Skillman, NJ 08558-9418

Rick O. Gilmore, PhD
Assistant Professor of Psychology
Department of Psychology
Pennsylvania State University
643 Moore Building
University Park, PA 16802

William T. Greenough, PhD
Professor of Psychology
University of Illinois at
  Urbana-Champaign
2347 Beckman Institute, MC 251
405 North Matthews Avenue
Urbana, IL 61801

Marshall M. Haith, PhD
Director of University Research
Professor of Psychology
University of Denver
2155 South Race Street
Denver, CO 80208

Janellen Huttenlocher, PhD
Professor of Psychology
Department of Psychology
University of Chicago
5848 South University Avenue
Chicago, IL 60637

Peter R. Huttenlocher, MD
Professor of Pediatrics and Neurology
Department of Pediatrics
University of Chicago School
  of Medicine
5839 South Maryland Avenue,
  MC 3055
Chicago, IL 60637

Participants

Peter W. Jusczyk, PhD
Professor of Psychology
Department of Psychology
Johns Hopkins University
Ames Hall
3400 North Charles Street
Baltimore, MD 21218

Bryan Kolb, PhD
Professor of Psychology and
* Neuroscience*
Department of Psychology and
* Neuroscience*
The University of Lethbridge
4401 University Drive
Lethbridge, AB, Canada T1K 3M4

Patricia K. Kuhl, PhD
Chair and Professor of Speech and
* Hearing Science*
University of Washington
204 Eagleson Hall
Box 357920
Seattle, WA 98195-7920

Lewis A. Leavitt, MD
Professor of Pediatrics
Director of Developmental Pediatrics
Director, Waisman Center
University of Wisconsin
1500 Highland Avenue
Madison, WI 53705-2274

Betsy Lozoff, MD
Director, Center for Human Growth
* and Development*
Professor, Department of Pediatrics
* and Communicable Diseases*
University of Michigan
300 North Ingalls, 10th Level
Ann Arbor, MI 48109-0406

Andrew N. Meltzoff, PhD
Professor of Psychology
Department of Psychology
University of Washington
339 Guthrie
Box 357920
Seattle, WA 98195-7920

**Neena Modi, MB, ChB, MD, FRCP,
FRCPCH**
Senior Lecturer and Consultant
Department of Pediatrics and
* Neonatal Medicine*
Imperial College of Science,
* Technology and Medicine*
Hammersmith Hospital
Du Cane Road
London W12 0NN

Nora S. Newcombe, PhD
Professor of Psychology
Temple University
565 Weiss Hall
Philadelphia, PA 19122

Stephen W. Porges, PhD
Chair, Department of Human
* Development*
Director, Institute for Child Study
University of Maryland
3304 Benjamin Building
College Park, MD 20742-1131

Scania de Schonen, PhD
Director of Research
Laboratory of Cognition and
* Development*
National Center for Scientific Research
University of René Descartes – Paris V
28 Rue Serpente
F-75270 Paris Cedex 06, FRANCE

Participants (continued)

Ann C. Stadtler, MSN, CPNP
Assistant Director/Clinical Coordinator
Medical Diagnostic Programs
Boston Children's Hospital
1295 Boylston Street, Suite 320
Boston, MA 02215

Kerstin Uvnäs-Moberg, MD, PhD
Professor of Physiology
Department of Animal Physiology
Swedish University of Agricultural
  Science
171 77
Stockholm, Sweden

Carole Welp, MEd
Director
Pointe St. Charles Early Childhood
  Center
Montreal, QC, Canada H3K 2RI

Rosemary White-Traut, DNSc, RN
Associate Professor and Acting
  Department Head
Department of Maternal/Child Nursing
University of Illinois
565 North Washington Street
Hinsdale, IL 60521

Preface

Johnson & Johnson is pleased to provide this year's edition of its highly regarded Pediatric Round Table series. The goals of these conferences are to: foster the free exchange of the latest research in infant development; to discuss the clinical implications of that research; and to make those findings available to all professionals working in the field of infant health.

The faculty of this Pediatric Round Table, *The Role of Early Experience in Infant Development,* represent the world's leading researchers and clinicians working in the areas of early development of the brain, auditory and language ability, cognition, perception, and biosocial interactions. They brought to the table years of experience and unique insight into the relationship between the way an infant's experiences with his family and environment affect many aspects of early brain development.

A common theme emerging from this Round Table was that development is a process as unique as each individual child – within that spectrum, for the overwhelming majority of infants, "normal" development proceeds with routine care, without the need for developmentally aggressive toys or interventions, and extends well beyond the first 3 years of life.

Our continuing aspiration is to build and provide a library of current research and significant information on infant development that features the world's leading scientists and healthcare professionals. I hope readers of *The Role of Early Experience in Infant Development* agree that this latest volume provides a valuable resource for healthcare professionals.

Julia A. Freedman
Director, Johnson & Johnson Pediatric Institute

Introduction

Nathan A. Fox, PhD and Lewis A. Leavitt, MD

The White House Conference on Early Childhood and Brain Development in the Spring of 1995 marked a turning point in public awareness and knowledge about the effects of early experience on the developing human infant and its nervous system. At that meeting, researchers and practitioners met to discuss the important advances in our knowledge about the competencies and skills of young infants, as well as the remarkable changes that occur in infants over the first 3 years of life. Materials that were distributed at this meeting, including a special issue of *Newsweek* magazine, emphasized the importance of the first 3 years for behavioral growth and brain development. The very positive message communicated to service providers and parents was that the first 3 years of an infant's life are critical for brain development and that parents could play an important role in fostering that development. Implicitly, however, another message was communicated: once these early years were over, the window would close and opportunities for brain growth and stimulation, for enhancing cognitive and socio-emotional development, would end. Predictably, these formulations produced a flurry of excitement and concern from new parents. Parents questioned the nature of care and stimulation that they were providing their young infants. Were the environments they provided sufficient to stimulate brain growth? Could and should they be doing more to enhance cognitive and social-emotional development during these early years?

The information communicated as a result of this meeting also elicited excitement and concern from developmental psychologists and neuroscientists who study neurodevelopment. Researchers were excited that their area of interest was getting much-deserved attention. However, they were concerned about the scientific basis for many of the claims regarding the role of early experience on brain development that circulated after the meeting. Indeed, in some instances, contradictory evidence was available which called for a more balanced approach to these issues.

This background marks the starting point for the organization of a conference titled *The Role of Early Experience in Infant Development* held in January of 1999. This conference, sponsored by the Johnson & Johnson Pediatric Institute, was motivated by the divergent and often conflicting reactions that developmental psychologists, neuroscientists, and service providers for children had in response to the information that emerged after the initial White House meeting. The goal of the Johnson & Johnson meeting was to bring together developmental psychologists, neuroscientists, and practicing pediatricians and nurses who were engaged in work on the effects of early experience on infant development. Each of the participants was asked to present the current state of the art in their area of expertise, addressing the issue of early experience and the brain. The approaches represented by the faculty to these issues were diverse, and multiple areas were covered. Our aim was to achieve a balanced and comprehensive view of the issues surrounding the question of early experience and brain development. The current volume, *The Role of Early Experience in Infant Development*, presents a review of the "state of the art" written for practitioners who must do the crucial work of translating theory and research into the arena of real life.

Pediatric service providers need to consider several issues when giving advice on the effects of early experience on brain development. The most basic question can be stated rather simply: What do we know about development and the emerging competencies of the young infant in the behavioral domain and in the domain of brain development? The surprising and somewhat frustrating answer to this broad question is that, after many years of scientific research, we know quite a lot about the emerging behavioral competencies of the human infant. But we know much less about the development of the human infant's brain and even less about the manner in which behavior and brain develop and interact synchronously.

There are multiple reasons for this asymmetry in our knowledge base. First, developmental researchers have been able to test and study the behavioral competencies of the human infant for many years. They have not been hampered by lack of advances in technology or in the availability of noninvasive experimental methods. Neuroscientists who study brain development have made enormous strides in understanding the brain during the past 10 to 15 years, in part due to significant advances in technology which allow them to study brain development and activity in greater detail and precision.

Neuroscience research, however, has largely used nonhuman animal models for its work, including studies that examine brain development and the role of early experience. There is now elegant published work (for example, the chapters in this volume by Peter Huttenlocher, William Greenough and James Black, or Bryan Kolb) using data from rats or nonhuman primates which describes the natural pattern of brain growth in the first years of life and the effects of early experience on brain development. While one may utilize these data to generate hypotheses regarding brain development in the human infant and the effects of early experience on brain growth, these studies are, ultimately, no substitute for data from human infants demonstrating effects of early experience on brain development. Unfortunately, these latter data are often unavailable or are collected on populations of infants who have undergone severe trauma. It is difficult to generalize to the normal range of contexts and environments which make up the lives of most children from these extreme examples. Thus, while there are important behavioral data available on the effects of early experience on cognitive and social-emotional development over the first years of life, the parallel data on brain development is based on animal studies. The effects of early experience on brain growth are typically inferred from experiments with nonhuman species. While these data provide "best guesses" for constructing theory, they leave us with much uncertainty.

A second important question in the study of the effects of early experience is: Are there "critical periods" for human infants to be exposed to particular sensory or social inputs? There is reason to believe that certain experiences need to occur early in life in order to allow brain growth and development to proceed in a normative fashion. If these experiences are absent or occur later in development, brain growth and development are substantively altered.

The best example of this relation between timing of early experience and brain development is in work with the visual system. Research studies[1] with animals have revealed that occluding one or both eyes during the period when the brain's visual areas need stimulation impairs appropriate brain growth and development. Providing that visual stimulation after a certain age does not suffice. It is as if a window of opportunity is open during a critical age for stimulation of brain growth and differentiation in a particular region. Once a certain age is passed, the window closes and the effects of experience are no longer as effective in mediating appropriate brain growth for that region. This timing issue is known as a critical period and is obviously of great concern to those who study the effects of early experience on brain development.

A central question in this area is to which behavioral competencies and brain regions does the critical period function apply? Are there critical periods for all cognitive and socio-emotional behaviors and their underlying brain structures or only for a select few? Again, the behavioral research addresses this question by examining changes in specific cognitive and emotional competencies with maturation. The neuroscience research addresses this question by directly manipulating the type of and access to early experience in animals and then examining brain structure. There are no direct studies in humans in which such manipulations and subsequent data are available. (Refer to Neville et al[2] for effects of deafness on brain lateralization and Maurer et al[3] for effects of neonatal cataracts on visual acuity.) In this volume, the chapter by Patricia Kuhl addresses how language may be crucially affected by early experience in the human. It is important to note that even though we have evidence that early language exposure affects language skills, we do not know the limits of just how much exposure is "good enough."

A third issue in the study of the role of early experience is the notion of plasticity or flexibility of the system, particularly with regard to recovery from injury or deprivation of early stimulation. One of the questions asked by neuroscientists about the brain is: How resilient is it to insult or injury? This is of great concern due to the variety of insults that the developing brain is exposed to both in utero (eg, exposure to drugs, alcohol, smoking, or other toxins) and perinatally (due to asphyxia during labor or delivery).

Research on the developing brain[4] has detailed the processes by which nerve cells migrate to their appropriate locations and link up to create the complex infrastructure of the nervous system. These processes occur over embryological time (that is, over the course of the 9 months of gestation) and continue during the postnatal months. Timing of insult may have important consequences for the point at which interference and disruption occurs in the complex building process of the brain. Such timing may also have implications for the plasticity and recovery of the system. For example, it may be that insult late in the process of brain growth may have more severe consequences than insult early in development. The brain's developmental growth mechanisms may have the ability to compensate for early insult and work around the problem to rebuild brain structure.

The notion of plasticity also speaks to the question of when brain growth and development stops being affected by experience. The heightened emphasis on the first 3 years of life as a critical time for early stimulation may inadvertently overlook the fact that neural growth continues past age 3 and that experience continues to have a significant impact upon brain growth past this 3-year period. Indeed, recent work[5] with nonhuman primates has found that new neural growth continues in the brain throughout the life span. Some of the issues we need to grapple with when considering brain development when an infant is born prematurely and exposed to an atypical environment are addressed by Neena Modi in her chapter.

In dealing with the issues of what we know and do not know about the effects of early experience on the brain, as well as the issues of critical period effects and the notion of plasticity, the authors contributing to *The Role of Early Experience in Infant Development* were asked to address the more difficult question of boundary conditions. Both neuroscientists and developmentalists agree that conditions of extreme deprivation, malnutrition, and impoverished environmental stimulation have negative consequences for cognitive and socio-emotional growth in the young child. The effects of malnutrition on IQ, the consequences of an environment devoid of language input on language development, and the effects of rearing conditions in which infants are not provided love and responsive caregiving are well documented. These behavioral consequences have clear neural or brain changes as well. What we do not know with precision is the environmental level above which these effects do not occur. We also do not know what the upper limits may be on environmental stimulation and experience. Are there stimulus-enriched environments which have negative consequences for brain growth and development? These issues, though difficult, must be addressed if we are to advance the issue of the effects of early experience with a balanced and even-handed approach.

The Role of Early Experience in Infant Development is divided into five sections. The first section begins with a brief overview of the terminology and concepts in order to understand basic issues in neuroanatomy and its development. Chapter 2 by Peter Huttenlocher provides an overview of the timing of synaptic development, as well as descriptions of the process of synaptic pruning. This work directly addresses the issue of critical periods in brain growth as it seeks to portray neurodevelopment as a dynamic process affected by experience. This work displays the nonuniformity of development. There are periods of relatively rapid change, which are consistent with observations of "transition periods" in behavioral development. Chapter 3 by William Greenough and James Black provides an overview of their important work on the effects of early experience on brain growth and development. The models of experience-expectant and experience-dependent growth address the issue of critical periods in brain development. The final chapter in this section by Bryan Kolb and his colleagues Robbin Gibb and Agnes Dallison provides a model for understanding plasticity of the developing and mature brain. Data are presented on the effects of stimulus-rich environments and the effects of injury on brain plasticity. The work described in these chapters suggests that the sensory world of infants plays an important role in development. This is very useful for advice-givers and parents to know. However, we cannot yet directly answer the question "what stimuli are necessary or sufficient" to optimize human infant development.

The next four sections deal with four separate domains of research which directly address the issue of the importance of early experience. Section Two presents three papers on language development. Language is an ideal area for the study of early experience and the brain. The development of language has been a source of investigation for hundreds of years with philosophers, and now experimental psychologists and linguists, interested in the type and quantity of input necessary for normative language development. There is also a large body of work examining the effects of early brain injury on language development and on the pattern of brain growth and function in language production and comprehension. The papers by Janellen Huttenlocher, Peter Jusczyk, and Patricia Kuhl present an array of evidence for the impressive abilities of the young infant to extract critical information about language from the environment. The discriminative abilities of infants and their ability to find meaning in the flow of speech are molded by their language environment. In this area we have begun to piece together the interacting components of environment and neurodevelopment.

Section Three address the issue of the effects of early experience on cognitive development. The view proposed in these chapters differs greatly from the traditional one of the infant as a passive observer of the environment. Instead, infants appear to be active learners of their environment. Andrew Meltzoff, in his chapter, shows how they learn aspects of agency, control, and self-efficacy by observing and imitating adult actions in their world. Nora Newcombe shows how they learn to navigate around their world and utilize spatial cues in their environment by interaction with a rich stimulus world. In this section as well, data are presented on the development of the prefrontal cortex, the largest area of cortex in the human brain. Adele Diamond reviews the work on maturation of dorsolateral prefrontal cortex and its relation to cognitive achievements in the first and second years of life. She presents evidence for the plasticity and vulnerability of the frontal brain region as a function of deficiencies in diet (PKU). This work provides an example of how brain development and behavior could be linked.

The fourth section of this volume presents papers dealing with the development of the infant's perceptual world. Infants learn about the actions of objects on each other and in space (Rick Gilmore), about the expectations that they might have for objects appearing and disappearing as a function of the regularity of their action (Marshall Haith), and about the characteristics of people in their world from faces (Scania de Schonen). These perceptual qualities appear to be extracted from an active environment as a function of neural systems (visual and motor) which are designed to derive this information. This information, these perception-action relations provide the infant with important information about the way the world works. Additionally, they allow the infant to develop notions of self-agency with regard to the perceptual world. These chapters show how recent research places infants and their environments in an interactive model.

The final section deals with the role of neural systems in early social development. Two of the chapters, by Sue Carter and Kerstin Uvnäs-Moberg, deal directly with the influence of central neuro-hormones (oxytocin and vasopressin) on the development of mother-infant relationships in the first months of life. These chapters indicate the complex interplay of anatomy, physiology, chemistry, and behavior. The remaining chapter, by Neena Modi, provides an important look at the issue of plasticity in brain and behavioral outcomes among a population of premature infants. The three chapters provide an important view of neuroregulation of early socio-emotional behavior and the importance of early experience in reducing stress during the early post-partum period.

We have tried to emphasize in each section the importance of studying biology and behavior in an integrated fashion. In some areas our knowledge of one domain surpasses the other. Yet it is clear that the past two decades have provided us with a clearer picture of how neuroscience can inform our understanding of infant and early child behavior. Although there are significant gaps in our ability to translate laboratory work into advice for parents, we have made great strides in our basic knowledge of visual, auditory, and language development as well as in confirming the influence of the environment on nervous system development. Practitioners can use the material presented here to give scaffolding to their pediatric advice. They will as well learn about the areas we are more and less confidant in the strength of our data.

The conference on *The Role of Early Experience on Infant Development* could not have taken place without the intellectual support of Julia Freedman, director of the Johnson & Johnson Pediatric Institute. Julia was uncompromising in her desire to identify the critical issues for discussion and to select the individuals whose work best addressed the areas of concern for the meeting. Her energy and commitment to a balanced, even-handed program and approach to the problem of studying the effects of early experience motivated the organization of the program and ultimately this volume. It is our hope that this collection of papers will be of use to pediatricians and service providers of children as well as parents and of course researchers in the ongoing debate about the importance of early experience for healthy and normative growth and development. Pediatricians and parents need to know what is known and what we do not know about the effects of early experience on different domains of development so that they might make informed decisions regarding the health and positive growth of their children.

References

1. Hubel DH, Wiesel TN. Ferrier lecture: Functional architecture of macaque monkey visual cortex. *Proceedings of the Royal Society of London.* 1977;198:1-59.

2. Neville HJ, Bavelier D, Corina D, et al. Cerebral organization for language in deaf and hearing subjects: biological constraints and effects of experience. *Proceedings of the National Academy of Science, USA.* 1998;95(3):922-929.

3. Maurer D, Lewis TL, Brent HP, Levin AV. Rapid improvement in the acuity of infants after visual input. *Science.* 1999;286:108-110.

4. Sidman RL, Rakic P. Neuronal migration with special reference to developing human brain: a review. *Brain Research.* 1973;62:1-35.

5. Gould E, Reeves AJ, Graziano MSA, Gross CG. Neurogenesis in the neocortex of adult primates. *Science.* 1999;286:548-552.

Section 1:
Brain Development

Abstracts From Section 1. Brain Development

Neuroanatomy and Development Overview

Bryan Kolb, PhD

Within 5 months of conception, all of the 80 billion neurons that will form the mature cerebral cortex have been created; during the period of peak production some 250,000 neurons are "born" each minute. These cells then embark on a process of growth, migration, maturation, and selective ablation that allows the brain of an infant to develop into the complex, fully integrated, reasoning brain of an adult. This introductory chapter briefly summarizes the process of brain development and reviews its major anatomical structures to establish a context for the more in-depth discussions in subsequent chapters.

Synaptogenesis in Human Cerebral Cortex and the Concept of Critical Periods

Peter R. Huttenlocher, MD

Synapses are the points of communication between neurons that primarily develop postnatally in a process characterized by overproduction in infancy followed by "pruning" throughout childhood and adolescence. Pruning may be tempered by experience, which tends to preserve more active synapses and neural pathways. The age at which synapse number is high (about adult level) coincides with so-called critical periods during which certain types of learning, including language learning, are enhanced.

Experience, Neural Plasticity, and Psychological Development

William T. Greenough, PhD, James E. Black, MD, PhD

The brain employs two strategies for learning and retaining information – experience-expectant storage is often associated with critical periods in development; experience-dependent storage generally occurs unconstrained by critical periods. Both strategies result in the formation of new synaptic connections, but simply having an abundance of synapses is neither normal nor desirable. Mental retardation associated with the fragile X syndrome, for example, is distinguished by a synaptic profusion that may result from ineffective pruning due to an underlying biochemical/genetic defect.

Early Experience, Behavior, and the Changing Brain

Bryan Kolb, PhD, Robbin Gibb, Agnes Dallison

Experience can alter the brain by modifying existing neural circuits or creating new ones, usually through proliferation of synapses. A complex, stimulus-rich environment produces a wealth of experiences that generally lead to increased dendritic branching and synaptic density. Injury, age, and gender affect the impact of experience on cortical development, and raise the possibility that behavioral therapies may be helpful in reversing the effects of prenatal brain injury.

Neuroanatomy and Development Overview

Bryan Kolb

Introduction

This introductory chapter is designed to review, highlight, and condense particular aspects of neuroanatomy and neurodevelopment that are directly related to the manuscripts presented in *The Role of Early Experience in Infant Development,* rather than to provide an exhaustive review of neural systems and their origins. Neurologists and those with similar training may wish to skip this section – others should find that the figures and text create a framework for understanding features of the more technical papers. Because most of the research discussed in this volume deals with the cerebral cortex, this review focuses on the cortex while progressing from the outside inwards, from the macroscopic to the microscopic; the remainder of the brain and its structures are then addressed from the bottom up.

Major Features of the Brain

An external view of an intact healthy human brain reveals three predominant structures shown in Fig 1. The largest by far, covering the surface of the brain is the gray, wrinkled, fissured cerebrum. Tucked at the base of the brain is another reticulated structure, the cerebellum. Leading to the brain is the stalk-like brainstem.

Cerebrum/Cerebral Cortex

Macroscopic view. The cerebrum is the gray convoluted outermost layer of the brain that one sees when the skull and meninges are removed. The cerebrum is frequently referred to as the "cerebral cortex" or simply the "cortex" (after Latin for "cover"). Although more specialized textbooks use more precise and restrictive definitions for cortical tissue (for example limbic cortex, cingulate cortex, allocortex), all of the articles in *The Role of Early Experience*

Fig 1. Major features of the brain.

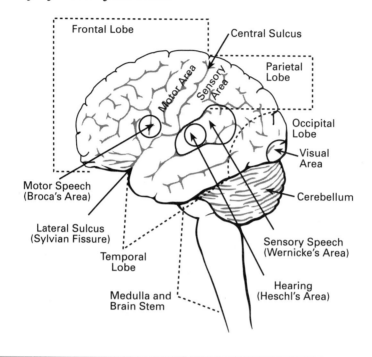

in *Infant Development* use "cortex" generically to refer to the neocortex of the cerebrum.

The folding and convolutions of the cortex effectively increase its surface area, an evolutionary adaptation that has enabled humans to fit more cortex within their skulls. Rats, for example, lower on the evolutionary tree, do not have a folded cortex, and the convolutions of nonhuman primates are less extensive than humans. The folding has enabled the human cortex to become the largest structure of the human brain, comprising 80% of its volume. More remarkably, the cortex is less than one eighth of an inch thick, a size disproportionate to its importance in all forms of cognitive behavior.

The in-folded creases are known as sulci (or fissures, if very deep) and the out-folded bumps are known as gyri. The larger fissures provide functional and anatomic landmarks that divide the brain. The longitudinal fissure (also known as the sylvian fissure) divides the cortex into distinct left and right hemispheres. Lying under both hemispheres is the corpus callosum, a tract of approximately 20 million nerve fibers that connect the left and right halves of the cortex. Within each hemisphere deep sulci divide the cortex into lobes (from front to back): the frontal, parietal, and occipital; below these is the temporal. The central sulcus divides the frontal and parietal lobes; the lateral fissure borders the temporal lobe; however, the occipital lobe is not clearly defined by a fissure. Unfortunately, the names were assigned to each lobe long ago, and reflect only the identity of the bones in the skull that cover them – not functional features.

Functional mapping of the cortex has revealed that certain areas have specific functions. Several are described below. The prefrontal cortex is involved in the "executive functions" of higher-level problem solving and creative thought. It occupies about one fourth of the cortex and is located behind the forehead and in the front of the motor area. The motor area (immediately in front of the central sulcus) controls deliberate motion. The sensory area (immediately behind the central sulcus) integrates information flowing in from all the senses. Wernicke's area (or the sensory speech area) is the region thought to be essential for understanding and formulating coherent speech; it is located behind and below the sensory area. Broca's area (or motor speech area) is involved in the motor mechanisms that govern articulated speech; it is located in front of and below the motor area. The visual cortex is located at the back of the brain in the occipital lobe.

Microscopic view. A thin section of the cortex prepared for the light microscope reveals six fairly distinct layers (I–VI) characterized by different cell types (Fig 2). The exact appearance and thickness of the layers vary throughout the cortex and have made it possible to create cytoarchitectural maps that help relate cortical structures and functions. The layers are described as follows in their most general, classical terms. Layer 1, also known as the molecular layer, is topmost; virtually no neuron cell bodies are present, giving it a clear "molecular" appearance. Layer 2 is the outer granular layer. Layer 3 is the pyramidal cell layer, named for the characteristic shape of the neurons residing therein. Together, layers 1, 2, and 3 integrate and provide connections between sensory and motor functions. Layer 4, also called the inner granular layer, receives sensory input and has densely packed neurons; this layer is relatively thick in sensory areas of the cortex. Layer 5, the inner granular layer, sends outgoing signals to muscles; this layer is relatively thick in the motor area of the cortex. Layer 6, the multiform layer, is also involved in motor output.

Fig 2. Microscopic anatomy of the sensory cortex and motor cortex.

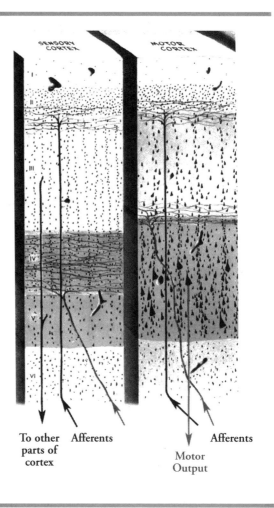

Courtesy of B. Kolb.

More Microscopic Anatomy

Neurons and glia. Despite its intricacy, the brain is composed predominantly of two cell types, neurons and glia – it is the way these cells are arranged and connected that create the ability to learn, adapt, and reason. There are approximately 100 billion glial cells in the brain. They support, nourish, and modulate the activity of neurons. Neurons number about 80 billion, they are the fundamental hardwiring of the nervous system that conduct information in the form of bioelectric impulses. A typical neuron has a large cell body containing the nucleus. Extending from the cell body are thin fibers, either axons or dendrites. By convention dendrites are efferent fibers that carry information toward the nucleus; axons are afferent fibers that carry information away from the nucleus. Dendrites are highly branched ("arborized") and most often localized near the nucleus; this branching is a very effective way to increase the surface area of the cell (increased surface area leads to potentially more neural connections). An axon extends some distance from the nuclear area and terminates in branches, although much fewer than a dendrite. Neurons connect with each other at specialized junctions, synapses, at the tips of axons and dendrites. At the synapse, the bioelectric impulse is transferred from axon to dendrite via chemical neurotransmitters.

Visualizing neurons. In a whole section of the brain, at a gross level, neuronal cell bodies appear gray, creating the characteristic color of the cerebral cortex, our own "gray matter." Axons, because they are wrapped in a fatty, electrically insulating sheath, appear white, hence "white matter." When the cortex is prepared for the light microscope (up to about 1000x magnification), basic histology stains reveal only the positions of the cell bodies (together with capillaries and glia), but nothing of the axons or dendrites. Thanks to a fortunate laboratory accident, a silver stain (or Golgi's stain) that specifically colors the entire neuron was discovered. Silver staining has made it possible to measure a neuron's length, interconnections, and extent of branching. Even more fortunate, Golgi's stain affects only about 10% of the neurons present in any histologic section: if all the neurons were stained, the section would be entirely black. At higher magnifications available in the electron microscope (2500x and beyond), smaller neural structures can be visualized, including subcellular organelles and fine details of synapses. The electron microscope has made it possible to enumerate "dendritic spines" where synapses are likely to occur.

Other Brain Structures

Because the cerebral cortex integrates and modulates the activities of the rest of the brain, a brief review of other brain structures is in order, this time from the bottom up.

Brainstem. The brainstem is, in evolutionary terms, the oldest area of the brain. A reptile's brain, for example, is limited to the brainstem. Appearing as an enlargement of the spinal cord, the brainstem is concerned with control of breathing and heart rate, and determining the general level of alertness. It receives afferent neural fibers from all of the senses and sends efferent fibers to control movement (except for fine movements of the fingers and toes). The brainstem communicates incoming information with the cortex through a "reticular activating system." The brainstem is composed of three substructures: the medulla, pons, and part of the midbrain. The midbrain receives information from the optic nerve (via the superior colliculus) and auditory nerve (via the inferior colliculus) to produce movement to orient the head to sights or sounds.

Cerebellum. The cerebellum is the striated and folded structure attached to the rear of the brainstem. It maintains and adjusts posture, coordinates complex muscular movement, and stores memories of learned responses.

Limbic System. Located between the brainstem and the cortex, this "system" is highly developed in mammals. It helps maintain homeostasis – body temperature, blood pressure, heart rate, blood sugar levels, emotional responses, sleep/wake cycles, and reproduction. Two noteworthy components of the limbic system are the hypothalamus and pituitary gland. Hormones controlled by the pituitary – testosterone, oxytocin, vasopressin – play crucial roles in mating, attachment, and reproductive behavior.

Thalamus. Located just over the hypothalamus (hence the name), the thalamus may be considered the sensory gateway to the cortex. For example, the optic nerve passes through the lateral geniculate nucleus of the thalamus, which processes some visual information before passing it on to the visual cortex.

Basal Ganglia. On either side of the limbic system, the basal ganglia (caudate nucleus and lentiform nucleus) participate in control of motor activities. Failure in the basal ganglia is associated with conditions such as Parkinson's Disease and Gilles de la Tourette's Syndrome.

Development of the Brain

Our brains make each of us uniquely human; we are each, in many ways, the sum total of our synapses, dendrites, and neurotransmitters. Understanding how these parts come together over time to form an individual human brain is the crux of developmental research; ensuring that these parts come together in an optimal fashion is the goal of clinicians and parents alike. These issues are addressed in great detail in *The Role of Early Experience in Infant Development,* particularly with regard to the development of language, cognition, and perception, as well as how the brain itself develops pre- and post-natally. A good starting point when discussing development, and perhaps infants and children in general, is provided by a simple clinical observation – 2-month-olds behave differently than 2-year-olds because their brains are different. The same holds true for behavior at 12 years and 24 years. How these differences arise, and what differences constitute "good" or "bad" development, is the subject of intense research and debate.

This brief review introduces the basics of neurodevelopment that are elaborated upon in subsequent chapters.

Prenatal Development

The brain, like the rest of the body, develops from a single fertilized cell into a complex network of billions of interconnected cells. The generation of cells that eventually form the cortex begin on embryonic day 42 and continue until about day 138. All of the 80 billion neurons that will form the mature cortex are therefore present by approximately 4.5 months of gestation. At the peak of neuron production it is estimated that 250,000 are created each minute. These cells are "born" deep within the brain and migrate upwards to their proper positions using glial cells as a scaffolding; thus, the lower layers of the cortex are older than the upper layers. Neuron migration continues until about 7 months gestation. Once in place, neurons begin a process of maturation that involves production of axons, dendrites, and synapses that continues for years, even into adulthood.

Looking at the surface, the brain takes on a characteristically human shape with a prominent cortex, by approximately 100 days, although the cortex has not yet begun folding to form gyri and sulci. These convolutions begin to develop at approximately 7 months and reach an adult-like configuration by 9 months. At this stage, although its gross appearance may resemble a mature adult, the brain is still immature and has yet to undergo considerable cellular growth.

Postnatal Development

Following birth, the mass of the brain increases in predictable growth spurts. Between 3 and 18 months the weight of an infant's brain increases 30%. This is followed by 5% to 10% increases for each period between ages 2 to 4 years, 6 to 8 years, 10 to 12 years, and 14 to 16 years. This increased mass is not due to the birth of new neurons (which stopped at about 4.5 months gestation). Rather it is due to the growth of synapses, the increased metabolic demands of the neurons, and the expansion of glial cells and blood vessels needed to support and nourish the neurons. For example, synapses themselves are unlikely to add much weight to the brain. However, the growth of synapses is correlated with increased metabolic demands that are met by larger blood vessels. Overall, this increase in complexity of the cortex is accompanied by increased complexity in behavioral functions.

Synapse development. Synapse formation is a central feature of brain development. It has been estimated that the number of *possible* interconnections between neurons in the brain is greater than the number of atoms in the universe[*]; the number of *actual* connections is on the order of 10^{14} (originating from close to 10^{11} neurons). How synapses form and why they persist or perish depends on the confluence of biochemistry, genetics, and experience.

[*]There are an estimated 10^{78} to 10^{80} atoms in the observable universe. The number of ways to connect N objects is N factorial (N!). A mere 60 neurons creates more than 10^{81} possible connections.

For example, the number of synapses exceeds the possible amount of genetic information required to code for them. Consequently, other mechanisms of achieving a fully connected neural network are active. Perhaps the most important mechanism is that of synaptic pruning (undoing synaptic arborization) coupled with neuronal death, a model that accounts for the overproduction and subsequent loss of neurons and synapses observed in all vertebrates (described in detail in this volume by P. Huttenlocher, Greenough, and Kolb).

By analogy, synaptic pruning creates the brain in much the same way as a sculptor carves away marble to create a work of art. Beginning with an overabundance of synapses and neurons, those that are not energetic are "pruned" away, leaving only functional synapses. The selection process for pruning or persistence is thought to involve competition among neurons for growth factors and nutrients that depend on synaptic activity: if the synapse is active regularly, it persists – if it is never active, it is pruned. Experience plays a role in the development of stable synaptic networks by providing an opportunity for consistent and regular synaptic activity at specific sites, but not at others. For example, animals raised in enriched environments have more synapses than those reared in standard laboratory cages because the enriched environment consistently stimulates more neurons. Conversely, blindness due to congenital cataracts occurs in part because of insufficient stimulation of the optic nerve, which leads to pruning of the synapses necessary to process visual information.

Because pruning is necessary for the normal, healthy growth of the brain and body, the extent of synaptic elimination has been carefully studied to determine "normal" levels of synapse loss. In general, after about 1 year of age synaptic density begins to decline as the brain begins to delete unnecessary or incorrect synapses. The extent and rate of this loss can be quite impressive. It has been estimated that at the peak of synaptic loss in humans up to 100,000 synapses may be lost per second. As large as this may seem, it is only about one ten-millionth of a percent of our final 10^{14} synapses. Other estimates suggest that about 40% of the cortical synapses present in infancy are eliminated by adulthood.

Behavior, Experience, and Brain Development

Brain maturation, encompassing synaptic arborization, pruning, and increased metabolic capacity, proceeds at different rates in different areas of the brain. With maturation comes the development of specific behaviors and capacities, such as speech, object grasping, and problem-solving. Yet these behaviors only emerge after specific neural connections have been made. Once these links have been tentatively established, behaviors develop quickly and are influenced significantly by the infant's experience – repeating similar actions and exploring new ones. Repetition of the successful behaviors leads to a stable neural network with persistent synapses.

Throughout *The Role of Early Experience in Infant Development* the consequences of this interplay between experience, behavior, and brain development are explored in detail. One example that briefly illustrates this phenomenon is the development of grasping motor behavior in infants. Soon after birth, infants develop the ability to use both arms in a scooping motion that could bring an object towards its body, but it is uncertain to researchers if the infant actually directs its arm movements toward any specific target. By about 3 months, an infant can orient its hands toward and grasp a specific object using a "whole hand" grip. Later, this grip is refined to a "scissors" grip using the sides of the thumb and index finger. By about 8 months, a very precise "tweezer" grip (using the tips of the thumb and index finger) develops that enables the infant to manipulate very small objects. At the neural level, the development of the whole hand grip coincides with myelination of a group of axons in the motor cortex that affect hand motion. Development of the tweezer grip coincides with myelination of another group of motor cortex neurons that control finger movements.

Critical periods. The step-wise or sequential maturation of the cortex gives rise to the concept of "critical periods" of development, in which there are particular times that certain experiences have the greatest impact on normal development. Consider, for example, language acquisition, as detailed in this volume by J. Huttenlocher, Jusczyk, and Kuhl. The critical period for learning a second or third language and speaking accent-free extends up to puberty. Even earlier, 9-month-old infants prefer hearing speech in their native language, whereas infants at 6 months show no preference, suggesting a critical period for distinguishing native from nonnative speech. Another example is the critical period for reversing strabismus. In many cases, strabismus can be reversed before the age of 5 years, but not afterwards. This is due to the ongoing process of synaptic pruning in the visual cortex – while a synaptic abundance still exists, the weaker eye can be trained to track appropriately. However, after a certain number have been pruned, the neural circuits are locked in place along with the lack of eye control.

Summary

The study of human neural systems can occupy hundreds of hours of research, thousands of pages of text (as in classic reference works such as *Human Neuroanatomy* by Carpenter), and fill a lifetime of scientific inquiry. Sometimes, a few short pages are all that is needed to refresh memories that will help improve understanding of a larger body of work such as *The Role of Early Experience in Infant Development*. While this overview section has been intentionally brief, readers are encouraged to explore the suggested reference list for more in-depth coverage, as well as all the references cited by authors throughout this volume.

Suggested References

Parent A, ed. *Carpenter's Human Neuroanatomy*. Media, Pa: Williams & Wilkins; 1996.

Ornstein R, Thompson RF. *The Amazing Brain*. Boston, Mass: Houghton Mifflin Company; 1984.

Zeki S. *A Vision of the Brain*. Cambridge, Mass: Blackwell Scientific Publications; 1993.

Littel EH. *Basic Neuroscience for the Health Professions*. Thorofare, NJ: Slack Incorporated; 1990.

Kolb B, Whishaw IQ. *Fundamentals of Human Neuropsychology*. 4th ed. New York, NY: Freeman; 1996.

Kolb B, Whishaw IQ. *Concepts of Behavioral Neuroscience*. New York, NY: Worth/Freeman; In press.

Synaptogenesis in Human Cerebral Cortex and the Concept of Critical Periods

Peter R. Huttenlocher, MD

Introduction

The cerebral cortex is an extremely complex information-processing system. Histologically, it consists of six fairly distinct horizontal layers, each with unique functions. These include information processing (layers II and III), receiving information from subcortical and other cortical systems (layer IV), and transmitting information to other cortical or subcortical areas (layers V and VI). The cerebral cortex goes through several distinct developmental phases, starting with formation of neurons in the subventricular (germinal matrix) area, followed by neuronal migration to the cortical plate, then by growth of axons and dendrites. By the time a human infant becomes viable, neuronal migration is nearly complete and axon and dendrite growth has started. Synapses, the points of communication between neurons, are the last components to develop. Most synapses are made between branches of axons and spines on the dendrites. These dendritic spines are demonstrable by light microscopy in sections prepared by the Golgi method, but synapses themselves are seen only in electron micrographs.

Synaptic activity is essential for a neural system to function. Therefore, the appearance of synapses provides a measure of the earliest possible age at which a nervous system can function. In humans the first synapses in the cerebral cortex appear near the end of neuronal migration to the cortical plate, at about conceptual age (CA) 23 weeks. However, the great majority of synapses are formed postnatally.

Our understanding of cortical development has improved dramatically in recent years. Many of the developmental steps, especially the early ones, such as neuronal birth and migration, are now known to be genetically determined. Some years ago, Beatrice Garber, Louis Larramendi and I showed that several late developmental events in the cerebral cortex are most likely also under genetic control because they are determined by information present in individual cortical neurons.[1] These developmental events include pyramidal cell shape, formation of dendritic branches, and the proper alignment and orientation of neurons in a "cortical plate." In a tissue culture system, cortical neurons formed aggregates that reproduced cerebral cortical anatomy to a remarkable degree. Synapses formed, apparently randomly, at points where axons and dendrites came into contact. These data indicate that at least some synapses can form in a self-contained neural system without environmental input. In vivo, most synapses in the developing cerebral cortex apparently are also made randomly, at points where growing axons and dendritic branches happen to meet.

The steps involved in synaptogenesis are well described in a recent review by Haydon and Drapeau.[2] Synaptogenesis is thought to depend on chemical signals produced by growing immature axons that promote contact with nearby dendritic branches. The signaling agent may be a substance that will act as a neurotransmitter after the synapse has been formed. At the point of axon-dendrite contact, the axonal membrane becomes specialized to form the presynaptic area of neurotransmitter synthesis and release, and the dendritic membrane becomes the postsynaptic area that contains neurotransmitter receptors.

Less random mechanisms for synapse formation also exist. One involves both antegrade signaling by the growing axon and retrograde signaling by the dendrite, which lead to synapse formation only if the two signals are both properly matched. This method of signaling ensures that a specific group of axons will make synaptic contact with a specific population of dendrites. Exact specification of more than a small minority of synapses is not possible. The human genome is much too small for genetic determination of the huge number of synapses in human cerebral cortex, which is estimated to be on the order of 10^{14}.

Changeux was first to theorize clearly how a collection of random connections could develop into an integrated, functioning neural system. This process involves input initially from sense organs and later from other regions of the neural system.[3,4] Environmental input is therefore likely to be important in development of the cerebral cortex. Signals related to environmental changes are transmitted from the sense organs to the cerebral cortex, where they lead to formation of neural circuits that use some of the randomly formed synapses. Synapses persist if they are incorporated into functioning circuits – those that are not eliminated or "pruned." This theory predicts that there should be initial overproduction of synapses followed by synapse elimination.

Changeux based this theory on observations in relatively simple systems, such as developing neuromuscular junctions. We found similar developmental changes in the human cerebral cortex. There is an initial period of rapid synapse formation, in which maximum synaptic density (up to twice the adult value) is reached in late infancy. This is followed by synapse elimination during childhood.[5-8] These findings have been replicated in other mammalian species, most extensively in the rhesus monkey.[9,10]

Synaptogenesis in Human Cerebral Cortex

Prefrontal cortex. My colleagues and I first established normal control values for synaptic density in a project designed to document abnormal synaptogenesis in the cerebral cortex of mentally retarded persons. Paradoxically, in our early studies, the findings in the normal population were more interesting than the abnormal population.

The initial study was carried out in the middle frontal gyrus, part of the large region of human prefrontal cortex that is concerned with reasoning and judgment, the so-called executive functions.[5] We used an electron microscopic method that stained presynaptic proteins selectively (Fig 1),[11,12] which enabled rapid recognition and quantitation of synapses. Synapses were counted in layer III only.

The results showed a number of surprising findings: 1) *Synaptogenesis in human cerebral cortex, while prenatal in onset, is mostly a postnatal event.* This makes it possible to consider the existence of a causal relationship between *synapse* formation and the emergence of cortical functions. 2) *Synaptic density is greatest in infancy and declines during childhood, reaching adult values by midadolescence.* Developmental changes in the organization of cortical connections occur later than had been expected. 3) *There was an initial increase in number of synapses per neuron; this was followed by a decline in the mean number of synapses per neuron.* This indicates pruning of synapses during normal development. Additional data on synaptogenesis in the middle frontal gyrus were obtained in a later study, in which synapse quantitation was extended to all six cortical layers.[6]

*Fig 1. Synaptic profiles in prefrontal cortex (middle frontal gyrus),
age 3½ years, as demonstrated with the phosphotungstic acid method.
Magnification x 20,000.*

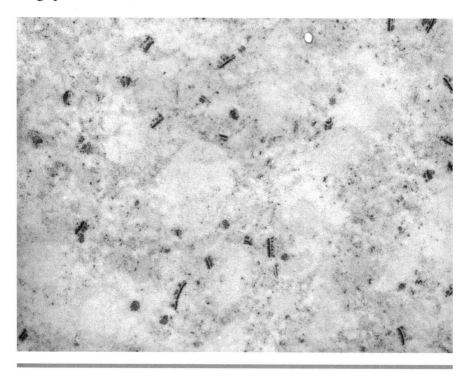

Combined data for layer III are presented in Fig 2. The graph shows four distinct phases of synaptic density: 1) an infancy period of rapid synapse proliferation between birth and age 1 year; 2) an early childhood period during which synaptic density is at a high plateau, nearly double the adult value; 3) a period of decreasing synaptic density or synaptic pruning, extending from about age 8 years to adolescence; and 4) adulthood, with relatively stable synaptic density.

Visual cortex. The results of synaptogenesis in the prefrontal cortex were confirmed and extended in a study of the primary visual cortex, in which I collaborated with Drs de Courten, Garey, and Van der Loos.[7,8] In the visual cortex, it was possible to measure total cortical volume, since this region is marked by the presence of a large fourth cortical layer, transected by a prominent horizontal fiber system, the line of Gennari. Estimates of the total num-

Fig 2. Synaptic density in layer III of middle frontal gyrus expressed as percent of maximum, as a function of age.

Data from two separate studies. ○ = data points from Huttenlocher[5]; x = data from Huttenlocher and Dabholkar.[6] In the Huttenlocher study, synaptic density was determined in neuropil exclusive of cell bodies, blood vessels, and empty spaces; in the Huttenlocher and Dabholkar study, synaptic density was obtained in whole cortex. This difference affects absolute values, which are higher in neurophil than in whole cortex. Data expressed as percent of maximum are not affected by the different methods, except for fetal and early infancy tissue, where neurophil makes up a smaller percentage of total cerebral cortex than it does later in development or in adults. This probably accounts for somewhat higher values for the percent of maximum in the neonatal samples from the earlier study.

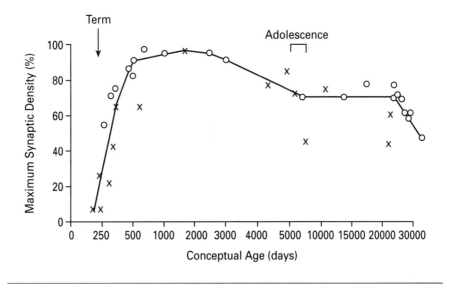

ber of synapses in the visual cortex were obtained at various ages. These showed a burst of rapid synapse formation between birth (when the total number of synapses was about 6x10[11], or 17% of maximum) and 4 months (when the total number of synapses was about 33x10[11], or 95% of the maximum). Both synaptic density and total synapse number stayed at a plateau of 32 to 35x10[11] between ages 4 months and 8 months; they began to decrease gradually from about age 11 months to 10 years, when they reached an adult value of about 20x10[11].

These data clearly indicate a substantial loss of synapses prior to age 10 years. As in the prefrontal cortex, this was due to pruning of synapses rather than loss of neurons. No evidence of cortical neuron loss or apoptosis was found during the period of synaptic pruning. The cell counts necessary for the calculation of neuronal density were carried out by Leuba and Garey.[13] While there have been more recent claims of apoptosis in human visual cortex, this was not confirmed in a follow-up study of a large number of brains by Leuba and Krafsik.[14]

The loss of synapses during maturation was associated with some shrinkage in visual cortex volume. The volume of primary visual cortex increased rapidly between birth and age 4 months, remained stable at 6.11 to 6.82 cm³ between ages 4 months and 5 years, and reached the adult range of 5.6 to 5.9 cm³ by age 10 years. The age when cortical volume decreases correlates well with the age during which synaptic pruning occurs. These results also agree with data on the volume of human visual cortex published by Sauer et al.[15] Furthermore, two quantitative MRI studies have documented shrinkage of the prefrontal cortex (amounting to 6% to 7%) between age 13 to 18 years.[16,17] These results correspond with data on the timing of synaptic pruning, which occurs later in the prefrontal cortex than in the visual cortex. Although shrinkage of the cerebral cortex that occurs during childhood or adolescence appears to be quite sizable, up to 10% of total gray matter volume, it is not reflected in decreased total brain weight. This is because myelination occurs concurrently and increases the weight and volume of the white matter.

Within the visual cortex there are some differences in the timing of synapse formation between cortical layers: Maximum synaptic density is reached at age 4 months in layers I to IVb, at 8 months in layer IVc, and at 11 and 19 months in layers V and VI.[8] It therefore appears that in the visual cortex, afferent and information-processing systems develop prior to the efferent system that is localized in layers V to VI. This layer-specific difference was not seen in a less complete data set from auditory and prefrontal cortex.[6]

Recent data in rhesus monkeys suggest that synaptogenesis is simultaneous in all neocortical areas.[9,10] In contrast, synaptogenesis in the human neocortex occurs at different times in different cortical regions, with earlier development of primary sensory (visual and auditory) than prefrontal cortex.[6] This agrees with the association between anatomical development and the development of function, because functional development is hierarchical. Reading, for example, can emerge only after basic visual and language functions have developed.

Ongoing studies. Arun Dabholkar and I recently examined the time course of synaptogenesis in cortical areas that are concerned with motor, cognitive, and language functions. This is ongoing work, and the results need to be extended and confirmed by the addition of more data at several crucial ages. A few tentative conclusions can already be drawn, however. *In motor cortex (hand area), synaptic density in layers V to VI is lower than in any other cortical region at all ages examined.* This raises the question of whether the motor-efferent system of the cerebral cortex may be more "hard-wired" than other cortical areas. This would be consistent with the clinical observation that voluntary finger and hand movements show little or no recovery after early (pre- or perinatal) damage to motor cortex.

We are in the process of collecting and comparing data from three speech-related areas: primary auditory cortex (Heschl gyrus), Wernicke's area in the left temporal cortex (concerned with receptive language), and Broca's area in lateral frontal cortex (concerned with speech or expressive language). *Data collected up to now suggest earliest synapse formation in auditory cortex, followed by Wernicke's area, with Broca's area last (Fig 3).* There are as yet insufficient data for comparison of the ages of synaptic pruning.

Fig 3. Density of synaptic profiles plotted against age in three language-related areas: primary auditory cortex, Wernicke's area in superior temporal gyrus, and Broca's area in lateral frontal lobe. Data obtained in layer II, a region specified for information processing.

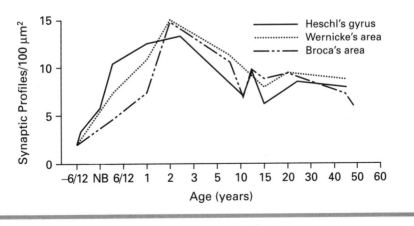

It appears that there is a difference in development between human frontal and more posterior (parietal, occipital, and temporal) cortical areas. This is reflected even in the motor cortex, the most posterior section of the frontal cortex, which has rather late synapse formation. This late neurologic development correlates with a well-known aspect of human infant behavioral development – the emergence of sensory (visual and auditory) alertness several months prior to the development of voluntary hand and finger movements.

Synaptogenesis in Other Mammalian Species

It is interesting to compare the time course of synaptogenesis in humans with that of other mammals. The most extensive animal data have been reported by Rakic et al in rhesus monkeys.[9,10] These primates show the same general pattern of synapse formation as do humans: There is an early period of rapidly increasing synaptic density, followed by a high plateau during early childhood, followed by synapse pruning in late childhood and adolescence. In contrast, however, brain development in the monkey is much more rapid, most of the cortical synaptogenesis occurs prenatally, and synapse formation appears to be synchronous in all cortical regions. Additionally, the late development of the frontal cortex in humans is not evident in rhesus monkeys. Another species difference is the larger size of the human prefrontal cortex, which controls the "executive functions" of planning, judgment, and reasoning that are not well developed in subhuman primates. The fact that these executive functions develop slowly during childhood and adolescence may be reflected by the slower rate of development in the prefrontal cortex.

Some data on synaptogenesis in subprimate mammalian species are available. Overproduction of synapses during development has been shown to exist in kittens, but appears of smaller magnitude than in primates.[18] In general, the decrease in synaptic density that occurs during development becomes less prominent as one descends the phylogenetic scale. Data in the rat show only about a 10% decrease of synaptic density during development.[11] It is not clear whether this is due to less dendritic pruning in the simpler, less-plastic brain or to other factors, such as the simultaneous occurrence of synaptogenesis and of synaptic pruning in species with very rapid brain development.

Synaptogenesis and the Development of Function

Structure-function relationships are most clear in the visual cortex, where much is known about both anatomical development and the emergence of function. At birth, there is little evidence of information processing by the human visual cortex. Brief visual fixation and following are present in neonates, but it is not clear whether this is due to cortical or subcortical activity. Preferential fixation on a face and imitation of lip and tongue movements have been described in human neonates, but we have no information about the cerebral representation of these responses. Developments in the visual cortex undoubtedly contribute to the marked increase in visual alertness that occurs between ages 2 and 4 months. Functions that involve binocular interactions that can only be carried out at the cortical level, such as stereopsis and stereoacuity, also develop rapidly during this period.[19] Anatomically, this is the period of rapid growth of dendrites and synapses, as well as expansion of visual cortex volume. It therefore appears likely that the basic functions of a cortical area emerge at the time of rapid synaptogenesis. This development of basic functions appears to be relatively unaffected by differences in environmental stimulation. *Every normal infant develops basic visual functions, including visual alertness and stereopsis, without special training.* In monkeys, early visual stimulation, brought on by premature delivery, has no effect on the time course of synaptogenesis in the visual cortex.[20]

Unilateral visual defects. Soon after birth, exposure to light and images becomes necessary to develop and maintain cortical synaptic circuits in both animals and humans. Infants with unilateral congenital cataracts develop near-normal vision in the affected eye only if the cataract is removed prior to about age 4 months.[21] After that age, strabismus or unilateral visual deprivation, as for example by unilateral cataract, leads to loss of vision (amblyopia) in the deprived eye. More surprising, strabismic amblyopia may be reversed by forcing the child to use the deprived or squinting eye, either by patching the good eye or by wearing an opaque lens over the dominant eye that blurs the image. After about 5 to 6 years, patching of the dominant eye becomes less effective, and amblyopia becomes permanent. Development of strabismus at a later age results in diplopia (double vision) but not in visual loss. Strabismic amblyopia and its reversibility represent important examples of plasticity in developing visual cortex. Animal experiments by Hubel and Wiesel have proven that these effects are due to changes in the synaptic organization in layer IV of the visual cortex, the layer that receives afferent input from the eyes.[22] It appears that in the developing visual cortex, there is competition between the two eyes for synaptic sites on cortical neurons. Normally, the inputs are balanced, but when afferent activity from the two eyes is asymmetric, the dominant eye wins out. These observations provide powerful evidence of the importance of sensory input in the development and maintenance of synaptic connections in cerebral cortex.

Bilateral visual deficits. Curiously, the long-term effects of bilateral visual deprivation are less severe than those of unilateral deprivation.[23] Similar to the unilateral situation, vision tends to be good if bilateral cataracts are removed prior to age 4 months, and impaired if removal occurs after age 4 months. There is, however, considerable subsequent recovery of visual acuity. This may be because bilateral visual deprivation avoids the negative effects of competition between the two sides.

Language systems. Evidence for enhanced responsiveness to the environment during childhood has been found in auditory and language systems. Cochlear implants for the treatment of congenital sensory-neural hearing loss work best when they are inserted during early childhood.[24] Adults who became deaf before they learned to speak are still unable to speak after they receive cochlear implants. In general, decrease in the ability to learn language occurs around puberty. This is also the age at which second-language learning in normal persons becomes more difficult and less perfect. In particular, accent and grammar are likely to be affected.

Although we know little about the underlying anatomy of language plasticity, it is a remarkable human capacity. Some evidence suggests that language is processed in both cerebral hemispheres in children, but becomes restricted to the dominant hemisphere during late childhood and adolescence.[25] In adults, only limited aspects of speech, specifically recognition of prosody or the music of language, are represented in the nondominant hemisphere.[26] Plasticity in language functions begins to decrease at about the time of synapse elimination in the language areas of the brain. Synapse elimination and decreased functional plasticity occur synchronously in visual, auditory, and language areas, which suggests but does not prove a causal relationship between structure and function in these systems.

Synaptogenesis, Critical Periods, and Windows of Opportunity

Critical periods during which a developing system is especially vulnerable to injury are thought to correspond to periods of rapid growth.[27,28] Such critical periods are difficult to delineate in the cerebral cortex because of its complexity and because its components have growth spurts at different times. For example, neuronal birth occurs between conceptual age (CA) 7 and 16 weeks, neuronal migration between CA 10 and 20 weeks, dendritic and axonal growth from CA 20 weeks to age 2 years, synapse formation from CA 25 weeks to age 3 years, and synaptic pruning between ages 2 and 14 years (all dates approximate). Furthermore, at least some of the growth spurts occur at different times in different cortical regions. It therefore is not possible to define a single critical period for the development of the cerebral cortex. Instead, there are different critical periods for different developmental events.

An interesting question arises: Is it possible to influence the development of the cerebral cortex by changing the environment? Recently, there has been special interest in "windows of opportunity" – age periods during which learning ability is enhanced – that might be exploited in training and teaching. The existence of such windows is supported by the developmental anatomy of the cerebral cortex in that there are periods during which exuberant synapses may be available for the formation of new neuronal circuits. The time windows differ for different cortical areas and for different functions. For example, synapse elimination in the visual cortex occurs early. It begins at about age 1 year and is completed by age 10 years. Correspondingly, enhanced plasticity of visual cortex functions, such as the ability to reverse strabismic amblyopia, ends early, at about age 5 years. The window for perfect learning of second languages ends later, in early adolescence, when synaptic density in language areas approaches the adult range.

It must be stressed that the age-related decrease in synaptic density and functional plasticity is gradual; that a good deal of cortical plasticity persists in adult life; and any decreases will display individual variability. It is also important to realize that our knowledge of the development and function of the cerebral cortex provide no information about what should be taught at any given age. For example, the fact that a 5-year-old child has the capacity to learn a second – or third or fourth – language effortlessly and more completely than an adult should be only one of several deciding factors regarding early second-language teaching. If parents do decide to teach their child a second language, available information about critical periods would favor early exposure, at a time when the language can be learned perfectly with normal grammar and accent. Such learning can be achieved more reliably in young children than in teenagers or adults.

There also is a lower age limit for "windows of opportunity," but this is not well characterized. For language development, it must be at or above the age for native-language learning, which usually occurs between ages 1 and 2 years. At present, we have no evidence that enhanced environmental input during early infancy designed to teach skills such as a second language imparts special benefit to the child.

While the presence of exuberant synapses early in life appears to be a factor in the plasticity of the child's brain, there is no evidence that we can train a child to maintain this high synapse number as an adult or that this would impart any functional superiority. Synaptic pruning is a normal developmental event. It may be necessary for the removal of redundant connections that decrease the efficiency of the system and decrease the signal-to-noise ratio. Recent data reported by Mills et al suggest that children with high verbal ability begin to use their dominant cerebral hemisphere for language processing earlier than those with slow language development.[25] This is accompanied by loss of language processing in the nondominant hemisphere, which may be due to early pruning or by inhibition of "dormant" neural pathways. Such inhibition seems prominent in normal somatosensory cortex in the adult brain and is likely to occur in other systems as well.[29] When it comes to the anatomical and physiologic basis of plasticity in the cerebral cortex, it is evident that multiple mechanisms are involved, only one of which is synaptic exuberance and pruning. There is also much that is as yet unknown.

References

1. Garber BB, Huttenlocher PR, Larramendi LH. Self-assembly of cortical plate cells in vitro within embryonic mouse cerebral aggregates. Golgi and electron microscopic analysis. *Brain Research.* 1980;201:255-278.

2. Haydon PG, Drapeau P. From contact to connection: early events during synaptogenesis. *Trends in Neuroscience.* 1995;18:196-201.

3. Changeux J-P, Danchin A. Selective stabilization of developing synapses as a mechanism for the specification of neural networks. *Nature.* 1976;264:705-712.

4. Changeux J-P, Heidmann T, Patte P. Learning by selection. In: Marler P, Terrace HS, eds. *The Biology of Learning.* New York, NY: Springer Verlag; 1984:115-137.

5. Huttenlocher PR. Synaptic density in human frontal cortex: developmental changes and effects of aging. *Brain Research.* 1979;163:195-205.

6. Huttenlocher PR, Dabholkar AS. Regional differences in synaptogenesis in human cerebral cortex. *Journal of Comprehensive Neurology.* 1997;387:167-178.

7. Huttenlocher PR, de Courten C, Garey LJ, Van der Loos H. Synaptogenesis in human visual cortex: evidence for synapse elimination during normal development. *Neuroscience Letters.* 1982;33:247-252.

8. Huttenlocher PR, de Courten C. The development of synapses in striate cortex of man. *Human Neurobiology.* 1987;6:1-9.

9. Rakic P, Bourgeois J-P, Eckenhoff MF, Zecevic N, Goldman-Rakic PS. Concurrent overproduction of synapses in diverse regions of the primate cerebral cortex. *Science.* 1986;232:232-235.

10. Rakic P, Bourgeois J-P, Goldman-Rakic PS. Synaptic development of the cerebral cortex: implications for learning, memory and mental illness. *Progress in Brain Research.* 1994;102:227-243.

11. Aghajanian G, Bloom FE. The formation of synaptic junctions in developing rat brain. *Brain Research.* 1967;6:716-727.

12. Bloom FE, Aghajanian G. Fine structural and cytochemical analysis of the staining of synaptic junctions with phosphotungstic acid. *Journal of Ultrastructural Research.* 1968;22:361-375.

13. Leuba G, Garey LJ. Evolution of neuronal numerical density in the developing and aging human visual cortex. *Human Neurobiology.* 1987;6:11-18.

14. Leuba G, Krafsik R. Changes in volume, surface estimate, three-dimensional shape and total number of neurons of the human primary visual cortex from midgestation until old age. *Anatomy and Embryology.* 1994;190:351-366.

15. Sauer B, Kammradt G, Krauthausen I, Kretschmann H-T, Lange HW, Wingert F. Qualitative and quantitative development of the visual cortex in man. *Journal of Comparative Neurology.* 1983;214:441-450.

16. Jernigan TL, Trauner DA, Hesselink JR, Talal PA. Maturation of human cerebrum observed in vivo during adolescence. *Brain.* 1991;114:2037-2049.

17. Pfefferbaum A, Mathalon DH, Sullivan EV, Rawles JM, Lim KO. A quantitative MRI study of changes in brain morphology from infancy to late adulthood. *Archives of Neurology.* 1994;51:874-887.

18. Cragg BG. The development of synapses in the visual system of the cat. *Journal of Comparative Neurology.* 1975;160:147-166.

19. Wilson HR. Development of spatiotemporal mechanisms in infant vision. *Vision Research.* 1988;28:611-628.

20. Bourgeois J-P, Jastreboff P, Rakic P. Synaptogenesis in the visual cortex of normal and preterm monkeys: evidence for intrinsic regulation of synaptic overproduction. *Proceedings of the National Academy of Sciences of the United States of America.* 1989;86:4297-4301.

21. Horton JC, Hocking DR. Timing of the critical period for plasticity of ocular dominance columns in macaque striate cortex. *Journal of Neuroscience.* 1997;17:3684-3709.

22. Wiesel HR. Postnatal development of the visual cortex and the influence of environment. *Nature.* 1982;299:583-591.

23. Mohindra I, Jacobson SG, Held R. Binocular visual form deprivation in human infants. *Documenta Ophthalmologica.* 1983;55:237-249.

24. Bonn D. Tune in early for best results with cochlear implants. *Lancet.* 1998;352:1836.

25. Mills DL, Coffey-Corina S, Neville HJ. Language comprehension and cerebral specialization from 13 to 20 months. *Developmental Neuropsychology.* 1997;13:397-445.

26. Voeller KK. Right-hemisphere deficit syndrome in children. *American Journal of Psychiatry.* 1986; 143:1004-1009.

27. Flexner LB. The development of the cerebral cortex: a cytological, functional and biochemical approach. *Harvey Lectures, Series.* 1953;47:156-179.

28. Dobbing J. Prenatal nutrition and neurological development. In: Buchwald NA, ed. *Brain Mechanisms in Mental Retardation.* New York, NY: Academic Press; 1975:401-420.

29. Buonomano DV, Merzenich MM. Cortical plasticity: from synapses to maps. *Annual Review of Neuroscience.* 1998;21:149-186.

Acknowledgement

The work described in this chapter has been supported by grants from the National Institutes of Health (Grant # 5RO1-NS28726) and from the McCormick-Tribune Foundation.

Experience, Neural Plasticity, and Psychological Development

William T. Greenough, PhD, James E. Black, MD, PhD

Introduction

How is information from experience incorporated into the structure and function of the developing brain? Conceptually, information is stored in the brain by one of two processes that are either considered species-typical "experience-expectant" or idiosyncratic "experience-dependent." Recent experiments have shown that nonneural as well as neural tissues of the brain are changed by experience. Other investigations have revealed that protein synthesis underlies neural plasticity. In particular, the fragile X mental retardation protein (FMRP) has a crucial role in determining the persistence or removal of synapses, and that this may affect information storage. Disrupted experience or impaired neural plasticity can have clinical implications such as dysfunctional development and mental retardation. Fortunately, our growing knowledge of neural plasticity suggests possible paths to treatment or corrective experience.

Two Basic Categories of Neural Plasticity

A great deal of brain development occurs independently of experience, and other aspects of development depend on neural activity that is not experience driven. Tens of thousands of genes unique to brain development are expressed during gestation and early life, resulting in an enormously complex structure that is primed for obtaining and organizing experience. These intrinsically originating processes interact with other genetic mechanisms to use additional information for brain development and refinement. Many species have found adaptive value in using neural plasticity to incorporate information from experience (eg, sea slugs, honeybees, and fish),[1] but mammals, especially primates, seem to have particularly elaborated such systems. For example, the human brain acquires more than two thirds of its mass after birth, much of it associated with the addition of synapses to the cerebral cortex. Two seemingly different forms of brain information storage from experience have been observed.[2]

The first of these, **experience-expectant** information storage, is often associated with critical or sensitive periods in behavioral development. It is a neurobiological process whereby the brain becomes organized by experience in a way that would be shared by all members of the same species. One could hypothesize that such "expected" experiences common to most human infants include aspects of early parental attachment, social experience, eye-hand coordination, and language.

The most frequently described example of experience-expectant information storage is development of the visual system. Here, the latticelike arrangement of axon terminals (the "transmitting" part of the neuron) from the left and right eyes in the visual cortex emerges through the "pruning" of axons that have grown to improper locations. Accurate pruning depends on experience – if one eye is deprived of patterned visual input, its axons will be over-pruned, while the other eye's axons will be under-pruned and therefore extensive.[3]

Similarly, axons representing each of the large facial whiskers of a mouse terminate in the centers of cylindrical "barrels" in cortex. In adult mice, most dendrites (the "receiving" part of the neuron) of these barrel neurons are oriented toward the interior of the cylinder, termed the barrel "hollow." In young mice, however, the dendrites initially grow in all directions. As development proceeds, the outwardly oriented dendrites are pruned, and those that are properly oriented inward add additional branches.[4] As these examples illustrate, a characteristic of experience-expectant information storage is that synaptic connections are put into place in excess of the number that will survive, such that experience determines which ones **do** survive. Thus, **the loss of some synapses is a normal part of development.** Another important conclusion is that different brain regions overproduce synapses and prune them back on a staggered schedule (as described by P. Huttenlocher in the previous chapter). The early development of visual cortex, for example, may set the stage for experience used by the later-developing prefrontal cortex.

Experience-dependent information storage is usually not tied to critical or sensitive periods in behavioral development and continues to occur throughout life, although it may operate more efficiently earlier for some kinds of learning. These mechanisms store "idiosyncratic" information unique to the individual, such as knowledge about food sources or shelter in the immediate environment. In humans this might include specific items such as vocabulary, cultural behaviors, or complex motor skills.

An experimental example of experience-dependent information storage occurs when rats housed individually (IC) in standard laboratory cages are compared with rats living in a large, object-filled "enriched cage" (EC). Behaviorally EC rats typically outperform IC rats in complex, challenging learning tasks such as mazes.[5] The brains of EC rats develop thicker cerebral cortex,[6] have neurons with larger dendritic fields, and have more synapses per neuron in various brain regions than do IC rats.[7]

Experience-dependent information storage is typically characterized by the net addition of synapses to a brain region, although selective synapse loss may be part of the addition process. One of the most important results of this research is that this form of neural plasticity persists into old age, offering the opportunity for lifelong learning and for lasting therapeutic results.

Effects of Experience on Nonneural Tissues

It is important to note additional effects of experience that may influence development. Not only do EC rats have more synaptic connections, they have more capillaries supplying each neuron and more supportive glial cell material per neuron.[8,9] In a sense, this effect is analogous to the effect of exercise on a muscle. Blood vessels supply oxygen and nutrients to the brain which, unlike many other bodily tissues, cannot store much fat or sugar to provide cellular energy. Presumably, the higher demand for neuronal activity in the complex environment causes the vasculature to hypertrophy, as occurs in an exercised muscle. Glial cells called astrocytes maintain the environment near neurons and their synapses in a manner that is optimal for their functioning. The additional astrocyte material in EC rat visual cortex may support both the added synapses and their increased level of activity. In any case, it appears that the brain of an EC rat is more "ready for action" because of these experience-stimulated modifications. Thus, while much neural-plasticity research focuses on synapses, it appears that the brain operates as an "organ" with interdependent tissue components.

This raises the issue of whether the synaptic and associated changes are primarily due to information storage or to increased neural activity. To do this, we compared four groups of rats[10]:

1) rats that **learned** motor skills traversing a complex elevated obstacle course several times each day (the acrobat condition, AC) – these animals obtained relatively little exercise

2) rats that exercised at their own discretion in an exercise wheel attached to their cage (voluntary exercise, VX) – these rats had very little opportunity for learning (rats seem to have learned to run by a fairly early age)

3) rats forced to exercise on a treadmill (forced exercise, FX) – these rats also had little opportunity for learning

4) inactive-condition (IC) rats housed in cages and handled daily for a time period equal to the athletic activities of the other groups but without opportunity for either learning or exercise

We examined the cortex of the cerebellum, an elaborate structure in humans that appears to play a major role in motor performance as well as in aspects of language and higher cognition. The results were straightforward: Animals that exercised, whether freely or forced, increased the density of their capillaries, while animals that learned motor skills increased the number of synapses per neuron. It thus appears that synapse formation encodes motor skill learning and that capillary formation supports increased metabolic activity. It should also be noted that very similar results were observed in the motor cortex of other similarly trained animals, so it appears that these effects are distributed across multiple brain areas involved in performing the learned or practiced behavior.[11]

In an animal model of the effect of alcohol on fetal brain, acrobatic training seemed very effective at "rehabilitating" both motor behavior and cerebellar cortex.[12] Glia exhibited a two-phase response. At the end of training, the increased amount of glia was proportionate to the increase in synapse numbers in the AC rats.[13,14] If training was suspended for a few weeks, however, the changes in synapse number persisted, but the glial changes faded away relatively quickly.[15] It appears, then, that the activity-associated astrocytes require neuronal and synaptic activity for their continued enlargement.

To summarize, when animals (and presumably also people) learn, their memories appear to take the form of new synaptic connections added to multiple interrelated regions of the brain. There is evidence that existing synapses also may be altered in structure and in physiological properties when learning takes place. In addition, recent data suggest that complex experience or exercise can result in formation of new neurons in a discrete brain region, and such neurogenesis may be small but lifelong in humans.[16-18] New synapses are associated with increased glial astrocyte material, which requires continued activity to persist. The blood supply to affected brain areas supports cortical expansion and increased brain activity as a result of the experience.

Protein Synthesis Underlies Neural Plasticity

A second set of findings may provide insight into the cause of these changes and lead to a better understanding of a major form of inherited mental retardation. Some time ago, Steward observed that when the brain was constructing new synapses in response to damage, polyribosomal aggregates involved in protein synthesis formed on the "receiving" side of synapses.[19] In addition, protein synthesis at synapses was more common during developmental periods of synapse addition and stabilization. Subsequently, we noted that synapses were more likely to contain polyribosomal aggregates in rats raised in enriched conditions than in inactive conditions.[20] This suggests that protein synthesis at the synapse might be involved in synapse addition. In a series of studies using a preparation of synapses purified from rat cerebral cortex, we determined that protein synthesis at synapses was triggered by the neurotransmitter glutamate at a particular type of receptor termed a "metabotropic receptor."[21-26]

The next major finding concerned *which* proteins were synthesized and why they were synthesized at synapses far from the cell body (where most protein synthesis takes place). So far, we have identified one protein that is specifically synthesized in our purified synapse preparation in response to glutamate or chemicals that mimic glutamate: the fragile X mental retardation protein (FMRP). The absence of this protein is responsible for fragile X mental retardation syndrome, the leading cause of inherited mental retardation. In fragile X syndrome, the protein cannot be synthesized because of a genetic defect that suppresses the gene that codes for the protein.[27] Affected individuals (possibly as many as 1 in 2000 males[28]) typically exhibit mild to severe mental retardation, often exhibit some of the symptoms of attention deficit disorders and of autism, often have difficulty in social relationships, and may exhibit a characteristic pattern of facial features.[29]

We obtained a "knockout" mouse model of the human disorder in which the gene that encodes FMRP (called FMR-1) has been inactivated such that it cannot produce its mRNA, the necessary intermediary between the gene and the protein it encodes.[30] When we prepared purified synapses from these mice, we found that they did not synthesize protein in response to neurotransmitter stimulation, in contrast to those from genetically normal mice.[31] Moreover, there were fewer polyribosomes at the synapses of knockout mice than in normal mice. This may be because FMRP is the only protein synthesized at the synapse, and without the gene for FMRP there could be no protein synthesis. This is unlikely, however, because we have recently found that more than additional proteins are synthesized in our purified synapse preparations. Thus, our working hypothesis is that FMRP may be required for the synthesis of itself and/or other proteins at the synapse.

We have discovered several other details about FMRP and the knockout mice that are beginning to illuminate its role in synapse development. We confirmed the findings of others that FMR-1 expression is developmentally regulated, with higher levels of expression generally occurring during developmental periods when synapses are forming.[32-34] We also found, however, that the level of expression of mRNA, and hence the capacity to make FMRP rapidly, remains relatively elevated at 1 year of age (rat adulthood) in regions of the brain that retain their plasticity postdevelopmentally – that is, areas in which synapses have been shown to form spontaneously or in response to experience in adulthood: the cerebellar cortex, cerebral cortex, hippocampal formation, and olfactory bulb.[34] This finding suggests that FMRP expression may continue to play a role in experience-dependent neural processes, including learning and memory, across the lifespan.

We also observed that the expression of FMRP may be driven by behavior, a finding compatible with the increased presence of polyribosomal aggregates at synapses of rats raised under enriched conditions compared with those raised under inactive conditions.[35] In EC rats, expression of FMRP is elevated in the visual cortex (the region of greatest difference from IC rats) after 20 days of postweaning exposure to the complex environment. In adult AC rats, FMRP expression is similarly elevated in the motor cortex after 7 days of training. These results support the suggestion that FMRP expression may be involved in the experience-dependent information storage of later development and adulthood.

How FMRP Is Related to Neuroanatomy

Studying the pathologic changes in the brain that underlie the mental retardation and developmental delay in fragile X syndrome should provide clues to the role of FMRP in the formation of normal neural architecture. Previous work on human cerebral cortex autopsy tissue indicated that adult fragile X patients had an excess of elongated, thin, postsynaptic dendritic spines, a morphology typical in developing humans and animals.[36,37] We confirmed this basic finding in the knockout mice; remarkably, we also found that the knockout mice had *more* spines, and presumably more synapses, than genetically normal wild-type mice.[38] We subsequently confirmed both of these results in autopsy cerebral cortical tissue from subjects with fragile X syndrome.

This pattern contrasts with most other mental retardation syndromes, in which there are typically *fewer* synapses in the retarded population (if synapse numbers differ at all). It is possible that FMRP expression at the synapse is an essential component of the overproduction and subsequent pruning of synapses in experience-expectant development of the nervous system. Without FMRP neither maturation of dendritic spines (from the thin, elongated shape characteristic of early development into the short, stubby shape characteristic of adulthood) nor synapse pruning can take place normally. The developmental pattern of initial outgrowth of long, thin processes that subsequently become shorter, thicker mature spines was described recently by Maletic-Savatic, Malinow, and Svoboda.[39] We are currently testing this hypothesis both by manipulating experience during development and by examining the developmental patterns of spines and synapses.

The clear implication of both experience-expectant development and the fragile X syndrome results is that having more synapses is not always better. While synapses added in response to experience during experience-dependent neural processes correlate with improved behavioral performance, synapses left behind when a pruning process was operating might actually add "noise" to the operation of the system. The elimination of synapses during development, in other words, is often a good thing that is necessary to proper neurobehavioral development.

Conclusions and Clinical Implications

Brain development in infants and children can be affected by problems with neural plasticity in at least three ways: 1) illness breaks down the neural mechanisms used to store information; 2) illness symptoms interfere with the ability to extract "expected" information from the environment; 3) the child's experience is severely impoverished or abusive. Some genetic or acquired disorders of early brain development (eg, Rett's syndrome, Tay-Sach's disease, or untreated phenylketonuria) may cause brain damage that impairs a child's ability to learn. Until recently, quality-of-life issues for these children could be addressed with behavior therapy, but little could be done to restore aspects of brain development that use experience. Recent advances in neuroscience offer hope that medical treatments could halt some diseases or restore neural plasticity. For example, as we learn more about the molecular mechanisms of FMRP synthesis and its activity at the synapse, the possibility exists to design drugs that can compensate for its absence. Future therapies may also involve insertion of an active FMR-1 gene to restore its function.

Other disorders are associated with symptoms that interfere with the quality and amount of early experience. Children with autism, for example, have relatively subtle neuropathology, but their symptoms interfere with learning language and social skills. If experience-expectant processes are activated when these symptoms disrupt the child's experience (as they almost certainly are with regard to language), a cascade of events in neural development may be disrupted.[40] From this line of reasoning, an intervention may be created to provide the child with suitably adaptive experiences – some promising results have been found with intensive, early intervention in autism.[41,42] Computers have been used successfully to adapt learning to the individual disabilities of children.[43] Although not often described this way, many special-education techniques for attention deficit or learning disabilities effectively adapt the environment to the child's developmental needs.

Many questions remain about fragile X syndrome, such as: If there is a partial deficiency in encoding experiential information, might afflicted children be less responsive to normal experience, resulting in mental retardation? Might enrichment of the available experience help them compensate? This question can be asked, at least initially, in animal studies using the knockout mouse fragile X model; if they are successful, perhaps clinical trials in human subjects will be warranted. Therapies for humans with fragile X might well include some of the approaches discussed in other chapters of this publication.

It should be noted that neural plasticity, as developmentalist J. McVicker Hunt liked to say, "cuts both ways." That is, just as developmentally "positive" experiences can influence development in desirable directions, "negative" experiences may have negative developmental consequences. In animal studies, severe stress can cause certain axons to retract from cortex.[44] In an animal model of depression, previous complex experience appears to protect against this axon retraction.[45] Although the literature is complicated, it appears that stress can sometimes lead to hippocampal damage, with the effects ameliorated or worsened by early experience.[46] A history of severe abuse in childhood is associated with certain regions of the brain being abnormally small; early abuse is associated with stronger effects.[47] Early adverse experiences can have effects lasting for decades, such as vulnerability to depression and personality disorders.[48,49] The terribly impoverished conditions of Romanian orphans led to lasting cognitive and emotional impairment.[50] Clearly, the best approach to this sort of problem is prevention.

With justifiable emphasis on the importance of early experience and the possible negative effects of experience,[51] it is sometimes easy to overlook many children's resilience in the face of adversity and the possibilities of corrective experience.[52,53] Children actively extract information that interests them, and caretakers play active roles in the structuring of experience.[54] We want to emphasize that even when development "goes wrong," humans apparently have the capacity to benefit from experience throughout their lives, whether that experience is self-generated, facilitated by caretakers, or provided by therapy.

References

1. Capaldi EA, Robinson GE, Fahrbach SE. Neuroethology of spatial learning: the birds and the bees. *Annual Review of Psychology.* 1999;50:651-682.

2. Black JE, Greenough WT. Induction of pattern in neural structure by experience: implications for cognitive development. In: Lamb ME, Brown AL, Rogoff B, eds. *Advances in Developmental Psychology.* Vol 4. Hillsdale, NJ: Lawrence Earlbaum; 1986:1-50.

3. LeVay S, Wiesel TN, Hubel DH. The development of ocular dominance columns in normal and visually deprived monkeys. *Journal of Comparative Neurology.* 1980;191(1):1-51.

4. Greenough WT, Chang F-LF. Dendritic pattern formation involves both oriented regression and oriented growth in the barrels of mouse somatosensory cortex. *Developmental Brain Research.* 1988;43:148-152.

5. Greenough WT, Madden TC, Fleischmann TB. Effects of isolation, daily handling, and enriched rearing on maze learning. *Psychonomic Science.* 1972;27:279-280.

6. Rosenzweig MR, Bennett EL, Diamond MC. Chemical and anatomical plasticity of brain; replications and extensions. In: Gaito J, ed. *Macromolecules and Behavior.* 2nd ed. New York, NY: Appleton-Century-Crofts; 1972:205-278.

7. Black JE, Jones TA, Nelson CA, Greenough WT. Neural plasticity. In: Alessi N, ed. *The Handbook of Child and Adolescent Psychiatry. Vol IV. Varieties of Development.* New York, NY: John Wiley & Sons; 1998:31-53.

8. Black JE, Sirevaag AM, Greenough WT. Complex experience promotes capillary proliferation in young rat visual cortex. *Neuroscience Letters.* 1987;83:351-355.

9. Sirevaag AM, Greenough WT. A multivariate statistical summary of synaptic plasticity measures in rats exposed to complex, social and individual environments. *Brain Research.* 1988;441:386-392.

10. Black JE, Isaacs KR, Anderson BJ, Alcantara AA, Greenough WT. Learning causes synaptogenesis, while motor activity causes angiogenesis, in cerebellar cortex of adult rats. Proceedings of the National Academy of Sciences (US). 1990;87:5568-5572.

11. Kleim JA, Lussnig E, Schwarz ER, Comery TA, Greenough WT. Synaptogenesis and Fos expression in the motor cortex of the adult rat following motor skill learning. *Journal of Neuroscience.* 1996;16:4529-4535.

12. Klintsova AY, Matthews JT, Goodlett CR, Napper RMA, Greenough WT. Therapeutic motor training increases parallel fiber synapse number per Purkinje neuron in cerebellar cortex of rats given postnatal binge alcohol exposure: preliminary report. *Alcoholism: Clinical and Experimental Research.* 1997;21:1257-1263.

13. Anderson BJ, Li X, Alcantara AA, Isaacs KR, Black JE, Greenough WT. Glial hypertrophy is associated with synaptogenesis following motor skill learning, but not with angiogenesis following exercise. *Glia.* 1994;11:73-80.

14. Jones TA, Hawrylak N, Greenough WT. Rapid laminar-dependent changes in GFAP immunoreactive astrocytes in the visual cortex of rats reared in a complex environment. *Psychoneuroendocrinology.* 1996;21:189-201.

15. Kleim JA, Vij K, Ballard DH, Greenough WT. Leaning dependent synaptic modifications in the cerebellar cortex of the adult rat persist for at least four weeks. *Journal of Neuroscience.* 1997;17:717-721.

16. Eriksson PS, Perfilieva E, Bjork-Eriksson T, et al. Neurogenesis in the adult human hippocampus. *Nature Medicine.* 1998;4:1313-1317.

17. Kempermann G, Kuhn HG, Gage FH. Experience-induced neurogenesis in the senescent dentate gyrus. *Journal of Neuroscience.* 1998;18:3206-3212.

18. van Praag H, Kempermann G, Gage FH. Running increases cell proliferation and neurogenesis in the adult mouse dentate gyrus. *Natural Neuroscience.* 1999;2(3):266-270.

19. Steward O. Polyribosomes at the base of dendritic spines of central nervous system neurons – their possible role in synapse construction and modification. *Cold Spring Harbor Symposium on Quantitative Biology.* 1983;48(Pt 2):745-759.

20. Greenough WT, Hwang H-M, Gorman C. Evidence for active synapse formation, or altered postsynaptic metabolism, in visual cortex of rats reared in complex environments. Proceedings of the National Academy of Sciences (US). 1985;82:4549-4552.

21. Weiler IJ, Greenough WT. Potassium ion stimulation triggers protein translation in synaptoneurosomal polyribosomes. *Molecular and Cellular Neurosciences.* 1991;2:305-314.

22. Weiler IJ, Greenough WT. Metabotropic glutamate receptors trigger postsynaptic protein synthesis. Proceedings of the National Academy of Sciences (US). 1993;90:7168-7171.

23. Weiler IJ, Wang X, Greenough WT. Synapse-activated protein synthesis as a possible mechanism of plastic neural change. *Progress in Brain Research.* 1994;100:189-194.

24. Weiler IJ, Hawrylak N, Greenough WT. Morphogenesis in memory formation: synaptic and cellular mechanisms. *Behavioral Brain Research.* 1995;66:1-6.

25. Weiler IJ, Childers WS, Greenough WT. Calcium ion impedes translation initiation at the synapses. *Journal of Neurochemistry.* 1996;66:197-202.

26. Angenstein F, Greenough WT, Weiler IJ. Metabotropic glutamate receptor-initiated translocation of protein kinase p90rsk to polyribosomes: a possible factor regulating synaptic protein synthesis. Proceedings of the National Academy of Sciences (USA). 1998;95:15078-15083.

27. Warren ST, Nelson DL. Advances in molecular analysis of fragile X syndrome. *Journal of the American Medical Association.* 1994;271:536-542.

28. Brown WT. The FRAXE Syndrome: is it time for routine screening? *American Journal of Human Genetics.* 1996;58:903.

29. Hagerman RJ, Cronister A, eds. *Fragile X Syndrome: Diagnosis, Treatment, and Research.* Baltimore, Md: Johns Hopkins University Press; 1996.

30. Consortium, Dutch-Belgian Fragile X. FMR1 knockout mice: a model to study fragile X mental retardation. *Cell.* 1994;78:23-33.

31. Spangler CC, Weiler IJ, Oostra B, Greenough WT. Studies of protein translation at synapses in fragile X knockout and wild type mice. *Society for Neuroscience.* Abstracts. 1998;24:1374.

32. Abitbol M, Menini C, Delezoide AL, Rhyner T, Vekemans M, Mallet J. Nucleus basalis magnocellularis and hippocampus are the major sites of FMR-1 expression in the human fetal brain. *Nature Genetics.* 1993;4:147-153.

33. Hinds HL, Ashley CT, Sutcliffe JS, et al. Tissue specific expression of FMR-1 provides evidence for a functional role in fragile X syndrome. *Nature Genetics.* 1993;3:36-43. [Published erratum appears in *Nature Genetics.* 1993;5:312.]

34. Cohen M, Smith SS, Weiler IJ, Greenough WT. Fragile X mRNA is enriched in highly plastic structures of the developing and adult rat brain. *Society for Neuroscience.* Abstracts. 1997;23:233.

35. Irwin SA, Swain RA, Christmon CA, Chakravarti A, Greenough WT. Altered expression of the fragile-x mental retardation protein in response to behavioral stimulation. *Neurobiology of Learning and Memory.* In press.

36. Rudelli RD, Brown WT, Wisniewski K, et al. Adult fragile X syndrome. Clinico-neuropathologic findings. *Acta Neuropathol.* 1985;67(3-4):289-295.

37. Hinton VJ, Brown WT, Wisniewski K, Rudelli RD. Analysis of neocortex in three males with the fragile X syndrome. *American Journal of Medical Genetics.* 1991;41(3):289-294.

38. Comery TA, Harris JB, Willems PJ, et al. Abnormal dendritic spines in fragile-X knockout mice: maturation and pruning deficits. Proceedings of the National Academy of Sciences (US). 1997;94:5401-5404.

39. Maletic-Savatic M, Malinow R, Svoboda K. Rapid dendritic morphogenesis in CA1 hippocampal dendrites induced by synaptic activity. *Science.* 1999;283(5409):1923-1927.

40. Yeung-Courchesne R, Courchesne E. From impasse to insight in autism research: from behavioral symptoms to biological explanations. *Developmental Psychopatholology.* 1997;9:389-419.

41. McEachin JJ, Smith T, Lovaas OI. Long-term outcome for children with autism who received early intensive behavioral treatment. *American Journal of Mental Retardation.* 1993;97(4):359-372.

42. Ozonoff S, Cathcart K. Effectiveness of a home program intervention for young children with autism. *Journal of Autism and Developmental Disorders.* 1998;28(1):25-32.

43. Merzenich MM, Jenkins WM, Johnston P, Schreiner C, Miller SL, Tallal P. Temporal-processing deficits of language-learning impaired children ameliorated by training. *Science.* 1996;271:77-81.

44. Kitayama I, Yaga T, Kayahara T, et al. Long-term stress degenerates, but imipramine regenerates, nora-drenergic axons in the rat cerebral cortex. *Biological Psychiatry.* 1997;42:687-696.

45. Black J, Kodish I. Are depression and its treatment related to structural changes in brain anatomy? Some lessons from animal models. Presented at the Society for Research in Child Development, Albuquerque, New Mexico. April 17, 1999.

46. Francis DD, Meaney MJ. Maternal care and the development of stress responses. *Current Opinions in Neurobiology.* 1999;9(1):128-134.

47. De Bellis MD, Keshavan MS, Clark DB, et al. Developmental traumatology part II: brain development. *Biological Psychiatry.* 1999;45:1271-1284.

48. Weiss EL, Longhurst JG, Mazure CM. Childhood sexual abuse as a risk factor for depression in women: psychosocial and neurobiological correlates. *American Journal of Psychiatry.* 1999;156:816-828.

49. Johnson JG, Cohen PC, Brown J, Smailes EM, Bernstein DP. Childhood maltreatment increases risk for personality disorders in early adulthood. *Archives of General Psychiatry.* 1999;56:600-606.

50. Kaler SR, Freeman BJ. Analysis of environmental deprivation: cognitive and social development in Romanian orphans. *Journal of Child Psychology & Psychiatry.* 1994;35:769-781.

51. Karr-Morse R, Wiley MS. *Ghosts From the Nursery: Tracing the Roots of Violence.* New York, NY; Atlantic Monthly Press; 1997.

52. Bruer JT. The brain and child development: time for some critical thinking. *Public Health Reports.* 1998;113:388-397.

53. Greenough WT. We can't focus just on ages 0-3. *APA Monitor.* 1997;28:9.

54. Rogoff B, Baker-Sennett J, Lacasa P, Goldsmith D. Development through participation in sociocultural activity. *New Directions in Child Development.* 1995;67:45-65.

Early Experience, Behavior, and the Changing Brain

Bryan Kolb, PhD, Robbin Gibb, Agnes Dallison

Introduction

An assumption underlying the study of the relationship between brain and behavior is that the structure of the brain is directly related to its functioning. It follows that if behavior changes, then structure must also change. Conversely, if the structure changes, the behavior will also change. The goal of this paper is to illustrate some of the general principles underlying experience-dependent change in the cerebral cortex during development.

In theory, experience could alter the brain in two ways: by modifying existing circuitry or by creating novel circuitry. It is reasonable to suppose that the brain makes use of both strategies, although the details of the particular strategy will likely vary with the age of the subject. Indeed, during development of the brain all circuitry is, by definition, novel.

Changes in neural circuitry can occur in several ways. The consensus among neuroscientists has been that changes occur at the synapse, partly because this is where neurons influence one another. This idea dates back to the work of the Spanish anatomist Ramon y Cajal, who in 1928 postulated that the process of learning might produce prolonged morphologic changes in synapses that were activated in the learning process.[1] Twenty years later a Canadian psychologist, Donald Hebb, proposed a mechanism for Cajal's synaptic change,[2] but it was 30 years before his proposed mechanism could be studied directly. There is now considerable evidence that behavioral change is correlated with synaptic change.[3]

It recently became apparent that there is another previously unsuspected way that experience can influence brain structure: Experience can influence the genesis and survival of neurons and glial cells.[4] Although research on the role of experience in cell generation and survival is still in its infancy, the implications for understanding the effects of experience on the brain are far-reaching.

In particular, early experience may have the capacity to significantly influence the number of neurons in certain parts of the cerebral hemispheres.

Assumptions

Several assumptions are necessary for a cohesive discussion of structure-function changes in the developing brain. First, the structural properties of the brain are important in understanding its function. Although such an assumption is self-evident to most neuroscientists, it is not as ubiquitously assumed by psychologists who study behavior rather than the brain itself.[5,6] An important corollary of this assumption is that changes in the structural properties of the brain reflect changes in the function of neural circuits.

Second, changes in neural circuit structure can be inferred from neuronal changes that are visible through a light microscope. Although final verification of the structural modification must be at the electron microscopic level, ultrastructural studies are impractical on a large scale, as they are time (and money)-consuming. Practically, therefore, our studies are conducted in tissue that is stained with a Golgi-type stain for neurons, or with other specialized histochemical procedures that identify the presence of new neurons (Fig 1).

Third, although there are many ways to examine experience-dependent changes in the nervous system,[7,8] our group looks at the effects of different experiences on neuronal structure and function. Thus, either our animals are placed in differential environments (such as "complex environments" versus "impoverished environments") or our animals are trained in specific types of tasks (such as mazes). In either paradigm, the experience is correlated with some measure of structure such as brain weight or dendritic extent. The latter can be expressed almost interchangeably as dendritic length or dendritic arborization. These experiments generally show that experiences embellish neural circuitry relative to the absence of experience, which fails to do so. Although such studies have obvious limitations, the study of these experience-dependent changes has provided a rich broth of information that is relevant both to basic neurobiological theories of brain function and to general theories of behavioral organization.

Fig 1. Left: Photograph of layer III pyramidal neuron from parietal cortex. The cell is stained with a variant of the Golgi-Cox procedure. Right: Higher-power photograph illustrating dendritic spines.

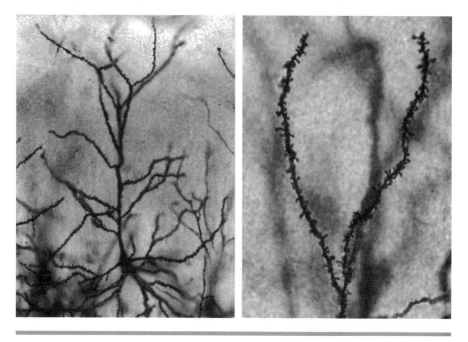

Finally, because most work on cortical plasticity and behavior is done using rats, we have assumed that changes in cortical structures are likely to be largest, and thus easiest to study, in those structures that play a central role in somatosensory and motor function. Rats are nocturnal animals that rely heavily on tactile sensitivity, especially in the representation of the face and snout, and they have well-developed forelimb-manipulatory abilities. In fact, rats are skilled climbers and jumpers and are able to use their forelimbs in ways that are strikingly similar to those seen in primates.[9] Thus, our complex environments are organized to allow considerable motor activity and feature many tunnels, the opportunity to climb, and the opportunity to manipulate objects with both the forelimbs and the mouth (Fig 2).

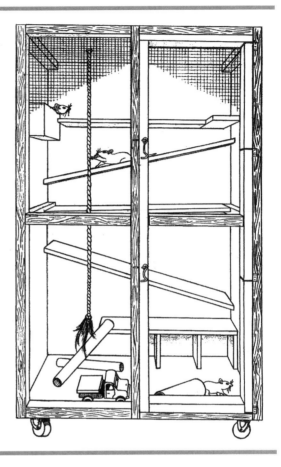

Fig 2. Schematic illustration of rat condominiums used in studies of the effects of complex housing on behavioral and neuronal change.

Neuronal Changes During Development

The mammalian brain follows a general pattern of development, beginning as a hollow tube in which a thin layer of presumptive neural cells surrounds a single ventricle. The development of the brain from the neural tube involves several stages, including cell birth (mitosis), cell migration, cell differentiation, dendritic and axonal growth, synaptogenesis, cell death, and synaptic pruning (Fig 3). The order of these events is similar across species, but because gestation time varies dramatically among different mammalian species, the timing of the events relative to birth varies considerably. This is borne out by the common observation that whereas kittens and puppies are born helpless and blind (their eyes do not open for about 2 weeks), human babies are born somewhat more mobile and with their eyes open, and calves

Fig 3. Top: Main cellular events related to cortical plasticity. Bottom: Summary of the time-dependent differences in cortical plasticity.

Bars mark the approximate beginning and ending of different processes. The shading reflects the intensity of the phenomenon.

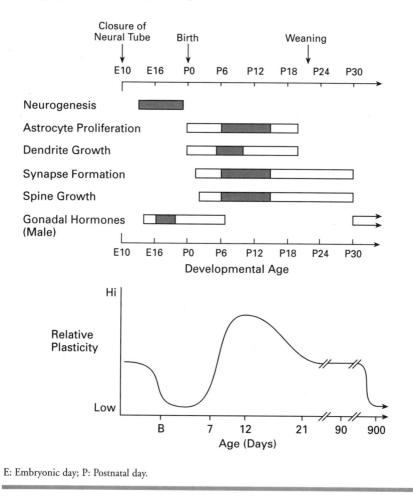

E: Embryonic day; P: Postnatal day.

at birth are able to stand, walk about, and of course, have their eyes open. It is worth noting here that rats, the subject of choice in most plasticity and recovery studies, are born even less mature than kittens and their eyes do not open until about postnatal day (P) 15. They are weaned around P21, reach adolescence about P60, and can be considered adults by about P90.

In the rat, neuron birth in the cortex begins on about embryonic day (E) 12 and continues until about E21.[10] (Birth occurs on about E22.) Neuron migration begins shortly after neuron birth and continues in the cortex until about P6. The development of dendrites, axons, and synapses begins once cells arrive at their final destination and differentiate into particular cell types. The peak rate of this growth is probably around P10 to P15, although it continues for some time afterward. Glial development takes place later than neural development, with astrocyte growth reaching its peak in the cortex around P7 to P10.

In cortical development, there are several key elements that contribute to cortical plasticity. *First, there is the genesis of neurons.* Although the genesis of cortical neurons in the rat is normally complete by birth, neurons are generated postnatally; they are generated throughout life, for the olfactory bulb and dentate gyrus of the hippocampus. Furthermore, the stem cells for neurons remain active in the subventricular zone throughout life. This implies that neurogenesis throughout life is possible for the cortex. *Second, there is the genesis of glial cells,* especially astrocytes. Astrocytes play a special role in plasticity because they manufacture various chemical messengers, including some neurotrophins. As a result, an increase in astrocyte production facilitates plasticity; an absence of astrocytes, such as during the first days after birth, retards plasticity. *Third, there is the production of synapses,* which likely requires dendritic changes. This can occur throughout life, but the most active time is from about P7 to P15, which implies that this might be an especially plastic time for the cortex. *Finally, there is the cell death and synaptic pruning,* which provides a mechanism for fine-tuning the connectivity of the cortex. This is likely most active from about P15 to P30, although it will continue throughout life.

From this, we can make some predictions.

- The period immediately following birth (say P1 to P6) is likely to be a time of limited plasticity, because there are few cortical astrocytes. There is also limited synapse formation.

- The period from P7 to P15 may be a time of maximal plasticity, because the cortex is actively making connections and astrocytic activity is high.

- The period from about P15 to P30 may be more plastic than later in life, because there is the unique period of neuron death and pruning. It is possible that experience would influence the rate, and perhaps the extent, of neuron death.

- As rats reach puberty, around P60, there may be a special period of plasticity as gonadal hormones are known to influence cell structure and connectivity.

- After puberty, there may be a slow diminution of plasticity as the brain ages.

It is difficult and perhaps even hazardous to try to identify a precise human analogue to the plastic phases in rats. Nonetheless, the plastic embryonic period will theoretically be sometime in the second trimester of gestation. In the third trimester, the end of neurogenesis is probably equivalent to the period of poor plasticity in newborn rats. It is uncertain just how long this period continues, but based on the effects of birth injury on subsequent brain functioning, it seems likely that it includes the early postnatal period. The human brain then enters a period of maximum dendritic and synaptic growth in the cortex, continuing until somewhere around 2 years of age. This marks the highly plastic period. After age 2, there is a gradual decline in plasticity until adulthood. As in rats, there is an adolescent period that is characterized by remodeling of neural circuits by gonadal hormones. Finally, in senescence, there is a rapid decline in plasticity.

Dendritic Correlates of Early Experience

To examine the effects of early experience on brain development, we placed rats in complex environments for 3 months beginning at either weaning (P21), young adulthood (4 months of age), or senescence (2 years or older). After this period of housing we harvested their brains, stained them using a modified Golgi-Cox procedure,[11] and compared them to animals that lived in groups of four in standard laboratory cages. The morphology of the dendritic fields of cortical pyramidal neurons was analyzed in two ways: Using a camera lucida procedure, we traced the neurons and estimated the dendritic length. Because dendritic length is correlated with the number of synapses on a given cell,[12] we could then get a rough estimate of synapse numbers. Next, using a higher magnification, we drew selected parts of the dendritic field and determined the density of dendritic spines. Dendritic spines are the site of most of the excitatory synapses on pyramidal cells, and the spine density is known to vary with experience.

We discovered that there were qualitative differences in dendritic structure depending on the age at which animals were placed in the enriched environments. Rats placed into the complex environments in young adulthood showed a large increase in dendritic length and an increase in spine density relative to cage-housed control animals (Fig 4). Parallel results were seen in senescent animals. In contrast, animals that were placed in the condominiums as juveniles displayed an increase in dendritic branching but a consistent decrease in spine density. That is, the young animals showed a qualitatively different change in the distribution of synapses on pyramidal neurons compared with older animals.[13]

Fig 4. Summary of the effects of housing in condominiums beginning at weaning (young), in young adulthood (adult), or in old age (old).

Enriched housing led to an increase in dendritic branching in all groups. In contrast, spine density was decreased in the young group and increased in the adult and old groups.

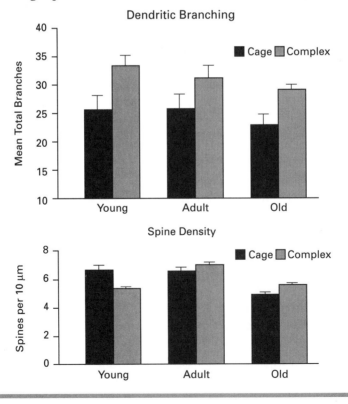

The differential effect of enrichment in younger versus older animals led us to look at the effects of environmental manipulation even earlier in the animals' lives. It has been shown that tactile stimulation of premature human babies with a brush leads to faster growth and earlier hospital discharge.[14-16] In addition, studies in infant rats have shown that similar treatment alters the structure of olfactory bulb neurons and has effects on later behavior.[17-19] We therefore stroked infant rats with a camel-hair paintbrush three times daily from P7 to P21. Animals were subsequently raised in standard lab cages and their brains were analyzed in adulthood. Golgi analysis revealed that the stroking had no effect on dendritic length in adulthood, but there was a significant drop in spine density.[13]

These results were unexpected and led us to wonder if these morphologic changes might influence behavior in adulthood. We therefore repeated the experiment, but this time the animals were tested as adults on two behavioral tasks, a place-learning task (Morris water task) and a skilled reaching task (Whishaw reaching task).[9,20] The Morris water task requires animals to learn the location of a hidden platform in a large swimming pool, and the Whishaw reaching task requires animals to learn to reach through bars to obtain food. Performance of the Morris task is influenced by the integrity of various cortical regions including the prefrontal, posterior parietal, and hippocampal cortex.[21] Cage-reared laboratory rats learn this task so efficiently that it would be difficult for them to show much improvement in response to experience. However, if decreased spine density were a negative consequence of the stroking, we might expect impaired performance. Performance of the Whishaw task depends on many motor structures, especially the corticospinal tract, which originates in various frontal cortical regions. Cage-reared laboratory rats benefit from extended training on this task, so the early stroking experience could either improve or impair performance.

Results of the water-task performance test revealed that stroked animals did as well as unstroked control animals. In contrast, the stroked animals learned the skilled reaching task faster and performed it more efficiently than unstroked control animals. This result is remarkable, because it shows that 2 weeks of tactile stroking in infancy significantly enhanced motor learning in adulthood. Although it is difficult to prove, it appears that the decreased spine density resulting from tactile stimulation may have had a beneficial effect on adult behavior.

It has long been assumed in the psychological literature that experiences in early childhood have greater effects on later behavior than similar experiences in adulthood. Our analysis of behavioral and dendritic effects of experiences during development suggests that there is a structural basis for the differential effect of early experience on behavior. Our results led us to several conclusions: *"Enriched" experience can have very different effects on the brain at different ages.* Additionally, *experience not only leads to "more" but can also lead to "less."* That is, although there is a temptation to assume that experiences lead to increased numbers of synapses (and probably to increases in glia), it appears that there may be either increases or decreases, depending on when the subject experiences the stimuli. Furthermore, *changes in dendritic length and dendritic spine density are clearly dissociable.* It is not immediately clear what the differences mean in terms of neuronal function, but it is clear that experience can alter these two measures independently and in different ways at different ages.

Sex, Experience, and Cortical Structure

Juraska and colleagues reported that neurons in the occipital cortex of male rats show significant dendritic growth with 30 days of enriched experience, whereas neurons in the occipital cortex of female rats do not.[22-24] In contrast, they noted that hippocampal neurons show a greater response to enriched rearing in the female brain than in the male brain. Although we found these experiments intriguing, they were also puzzling, because it seemed reasonable to suppose that experience was altering the cortex of both males and females. We hypothesized that perhaps Juraska's sex differences were at least partly due to differences in the sensitivity of the cortex to experience. In other words, we wondered what would happen if animals were given more prolonged exposure to the enriched environments.

We therefore placed adult male and female rats in complex environments for 5 months. Analysis of the pyramidal cells in layer III of both parietal and occipital cortex revealed an unexpected result: Although the dendritic arborization of both males and females increased with 5 months of living in the condominiums, the increases were greater in females! Thus, in contrast to Juraska's studies, we found a larger increase in dendritic arborization in the cells in female cortex than in male cortex (Table 1). Unexpectedly, however, when we examined spine density, we found a larger increase in spine density in males than in females.[25]

Table 1. Effects of Enriched Experience on Cortical Neurons.

	30 Days Experience[22-24]		5 Months Experience[25]		
	Dendritic Growth and/ or Arborization				Spine Density
	Occipital Cortex	Hippocampus	Occipital Cortex	Parietal Cortex	
Male	+	−	+	+	++
Female	−	+	++	++	+

These results led us to two conclusions: Both males and females show experience-dependent changes in the pyramidal neurons of the cortex. Males, however, appear to be more sensitive to experience and show morphologic changes sooner. This may account for the apparent difference between the results of Juraska and colleagues and our results. Also, there is a sex difference in the details of the structural changes in cortical neurons: Males show a greater increase in spine density, whereas females show a greater increase in dendritic length.

Because we had shown that experience has qualitatively different effects at different ages, we wondered whether these effects might be sexually dimorphic. Our initial studies had not considered gender as a variable, so we reanalyzed our studies in which juvenile rats were placed in the condominiums or infant rats were given tactile stimulation.[25] The results showed that the sex-dependent differences in the effects of enrichment varied with age. At birth females showed greater response to tactile stimulation than males and had a greater increase in spine density. At weaning, when placed in enriched condominium environment, both sexes showed an increase in dentritic arborization and a decrease in spine density. Thus, it appears not only that gender differences in the effect of experience are influenced by the length of the enrichment experience but that the details of the environment-responsive changes vary with age.

Neurogenesis and Early Experience

It has been known for a long time that fish, amphibians, and reptiles are capable of regenerating neurons.[26,27] The idea that neurogenesis might be possible in adult birds or mammals has been slower to take hold. There have been hints that neural proliferation might be possible in adults, but for the most part these hints have been treated as curiosities. This was partially because neurogenesis in bird brains appeared limited to areas involved in song[28]; in mammals the number of new neurons seemed rather small; and the new neurons were functional.[29,30] Furthermore, until recently, the work of Rakic was influential in its assertion that there was no postnatal neurogenesis in primates.[31]

In the past several years, evidence has accumulated to refute Rakic's conclusion. It is now clear that both rodents and primates (including humans) generate new neurons postnatally and likely throughout life.[32,33] Although these spontaneously generated neurons were presumed to be destined for the hippocampus and the olfactory bulb, recent work has suggested that they may also migrate to the cortex in the frontal and temporal lobes.[57] Importantly, the stem cells giving rise to new neurons are continuously, albeit slowly, dividing throughout adult life. The brain thus appears capable of generating new cortical neurons throughout life when the right stimulus is present.

It is known that the stem cells from the subventricular zones (SZ) of mammals are capable of producing progenitor cells that, in turn, can produce both neurons and glia.[34,35] In vitro studies have shown that cells taken from the SZ can be stimulated by epidermal growth factor (EGF) to give rise to neurons with various neurotransmitter phenotypes, such as γ-aminobutyric acid and Substance P.[36] Infusion of EGF into the ventricle of mice increases the population of dividing SZ cells 17-fold, leading to a subpopulation of new neurons and glia in the striatum.[37,38] Using a similar procedure in rats, we have also seen small numbers of newly formed neurons in the neocortex, especially in the prefrontal cortex.

The fact that a neurotrophic factor such as EGF can stimulate neurogenesis in postnatal mammals is exciting, because it is known that experience can stimulate growth factor production.[39] It is therefore plausible to suggest that experience might influence the brain by stimulating the generation of new neurons. Kempermann and colleagues showed that placing mice in complex environments leads to a 15% increase in hippocampal granule neurons.[4,34] These researchers did not look in the neocortex, but it is likely that there will be changes in cortical neuron numbers as well. This possibility is exciting and might help explain some age-related dendritic changes. For example, it is possible that decreased spine density in animals with early tactile stimulation or complex-environment housing may result from an increase in the number of neurons in the cortex. Thus, even though spine density is reduced, which implies a reduction in synapse number, it may be that the total number of synapses is increased, because the animals actually have more neurons. We are actively pursuing this possibility.

Neuronal Change After Early Brain Injury

One of our consistent findings in the past decade has been that the anatomical sequelae of cortical injury vary with precise developmental stage (Table 2). In brief, when the cerebral cortex of rats is damaged in the first few days of life (a time just after neural proliferation is complete but while neural migration and differentiation are still ongoing), there is a marked generalized atrophy of dendritic arborization and a decrease in spine density throughout the cortical mantle.[40,41] This is correlated with a miserable functional outcome and is reminiscent of the marked abnormalities in the brains of retarded children.[42] In contrast, when the frontal, cingulate, or visual cortex of rats is damaged in the second week of life (a period of rapid dendritic growth and synaptic formation), there is a generalized enhancement of dendritic arborization and/or spine density throughout the remaining cortex.[40,41] This is correlated with dramatic functional recovery. For some reason, damage to the posterior parietal cortex at 10 days of age does not lead to much functional recovery and there is no associated dendritic growth.[43] Similar damage to the adult brain produces little dendritic reaction and little functional recovery, although dendritic growth and functional recovery can be stimulated with infusion of trophic factors such as nerve growth factor.[44] Thus we see that if a cortical injury is followed by dendritic proliferation, there is a good functional outcome, whereas if the injury leads to retarded development of dendritic material, there is a poor functional outcome. It was our expectation, therefore, that if we could potentiate dendritic growth in damaged cortex, we would enhance functional recovery.

Table 2. Effects of Frontal Cortical Injury at Different Ages.

Age at Injury	Result	Reference
E18	Cortex regrows with odd structure Functional recovery	Kolb, Cioe, Muirhead[45]
P1–P6	Small brain, dendritic atrophy Dismal functional outcome	Kolb, Gibb[40]
P7–P12	Dendrite and spine growth Cortical regrowth Functional recovery	Kolb, Gibb[40] Kolb et al[46]
P120	Dendritic atrophy, then growth Partial return of function	Kolb[47]
P120+NGF	Dendritic and spine growth Enhanced functional recovery	Kolb et al[44]

NGF=nerve growth factor.

Experience and the Injured Infant Brain

Because young brains respond to experience or injury differently at different ages, we predicted there might be an interaction between brain injury and postinjury experience. We anticipated that animals with a cortical lesion in the first days of life would benefit the most from early experience because they are functionally devastated in adulthood, and have atrophied cortical neurons. Animals were given frontal or posterior parietal lesions at P4, followed by tactile stimulation (stroking) until weaning. They were group housed in laboratory cages and then tested on various tasks to measure frontal or parietal function.[48]

Rats that received tactile stimulation recovered remarkable amounts of their cerebral function (Table 3 and Fig 5). In fact, rats with frontal lesions now performed nearly as well on the skilled reaching task as control rats. Their brains did not show the atrophy of cortical neurons normally associated with such early lesions. More interestingly, the decrease in spine density that is normally associated with the tactile stimulation was reversed. In other words, stroking leads to a decrease in spine density in normal animals but to an increase in spine density in the lesion animals.

Table 3. Effects of Experience on the Injured Brain.[48,49]

Experience	Spine Density	Dendritic Atrophy	Behavior/Cerebral Function
Stroking	↑	↓	↑
No stroking (control)	↓	↑	↓
Rat condominium	↑	↓	↑
Control	↓	↑	↓

Fig 5. Summary of Morris water task behavior and Whishaw reaching task behavior of rats that did and did not receive tactile stroking during the first 2 weeks of life.

Rats with frontal lesions on P4 show a dramatic recovery of function in adulthood. Note also that tactile stimulation of unoperated rats also improved skilled forelimb performance in adulthood.

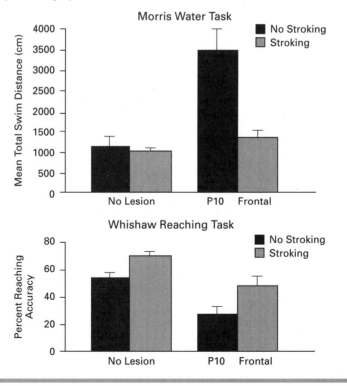

In another series of experiments we placed animals who had lesions on P4 in our "rat condominiums" for 3 months beginning at the time of weaning.[49] Once again there was reversal of the behavioral impairments, reversal of the dendritic atrophy, and reversal of the decreased spine density in the normal animals that was associated with the recovery. Thus it is clear that environmental events can have different effects on the normal and the injured brain. A plausible explanation is that the lesion differentially affects the production of astrocytes, growth factors, or other substances, and these in turn influence the effect of experience on the remaining brain. Whatever the explanation, it is clear that environmental stimulation has profound effects on recovery from perinatal cortical injury.

Gender and the Injured Infant Brain

We had seen that frontal lesions in adulthood had different effects in males and females[50]; we therefore anticipated that there might be similar differences after early injuries. Our initial studies revealed that animals with cortical injury at P7 to P10 displayed extensive functional recovery, regardless of gender.[51,52] Quite surprisingly, although males and females had similar functional outcomes, the anatomical changes varied with gender. In particular, we found that cortically injured males showed greater increases in dendritic spine density than did females, whereas females showed larger increases in dendritic arborization[52] (Table 4). Thus it appears that males and females show different plastic changes in the brain to support functional recovery.

Table 4. Gender and Cortical Injury.[48,51,52]

	Behavior/ Cerebral Function	Spine Density	Dendritic Arborization
No intervention			
Male*	extensive recovery	↑↑	↑
Female*	extensive recovery	↑	↑↑
Complex environment			
Male**	↑↑	↑	↑
Female**	↑	↓	↑

*Cortical injury on day P7 to P10.
**Frontal cortical removal on day P7.

The fact that males and females with infant cortical injuries responded differently led us to wonder whether experience might also influence the injured cortex differently. We therefore placed rats that had undergone frontal cortical removal on P7 into complex environments on P22.[48] Three months later, the animals were tested in the Morris water task and the Whishaw reaching task. We found that environmental stimulation enhanced recovery, but the effect was larger in males. Complex housing increased dendritic arborization in both the control and cortically injured groups equivalently in both sexes. Curiously, however, whereas control groups and the cortically injured female group showed a decrease in spine density, males with frontal lesions showed an increase. Thus the enriched environmental experience apparently had a different effect on the brains of males than females, which correlated with better functional recovery in the males. This suggests that other experiences, such as early tactile stimulation, might also differentially affect cerebral morphology in brain-injured infants. These studies are in progress.

It appears that there is a gender-related difference in the response of the infant brain to early cortical injury: Males show a greater increase in spine density than females, and females show a greater increase in dendritic length. This difference interacts with experience after the injury: Males continue to show a large increase in spine density, whereas females show a decrease.

Neurogenesis After Early Brain Injury

During our studies on behavioral change after cortical lesions in infancy, we made the unexpected observation that if the lesion was restricted to the midline frontal cortex, the lesion cavity appeared to fill in with cortical tissue.[51,53] Although the cavity's disappearance may be due to collapse of adjacent tissue, we reasoned that it was also possible for new neurons to "regrow" the lost tissue.[46] This is, in fact, the case. If the midline frontal cortex is removed on P7 to P12, the lesion cavity is filled with neurons and glia that are born after the injury (Fig 6). Removals before or after this time do not fill.[51] We observed that the tissue volume is only about 65% of normal and that the cortex is thinner. The dendritic growth of the neurons in the filled-in area is retarded relative to normal frontal cortex, as would be anticipated if the cells were younger.[53] Regrowth of lost tissue (and recovery of function) can be blocked by embryonically pretreating animals with a mitogenic marker, bromodeoxyuridine.[54,55] Furthermore, as shown in Fig 7, we have removed the regrown tissue in adulthood and also blocked recovery.[56]

Fig 6. Photographs of brains of adult animals that had a sham treatment (A), medial frontal lesion on P10 (B), or removal of the olfactory bulb on P10 (C).

Similar removals on P1 or in adulthood do not result in regrowth of the tissue.

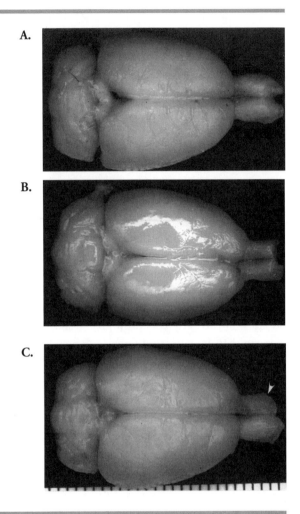

We noted earlier that environmental stimulation appears capable of generating new neurons. We also noted that tactile stroking has a spectacular effect on the functional recovery of rats that experienced cortical injuries in the first few days of life. One possibility that must be explored is that tactile stimulation contributes to the generation of new neurons and that these neurons participate in functional recovery.

Fig 7. Summary of performance of rats in the Morris water task.

Rats received either sham surgery or medial frontal removals on P10. In adulthood they received either control or medial frontal removals on about P160. The P10 rats that received sham treatments in adulthood performed nearly as well as controls, whereas rats with removal of the regrown frontal tissue performed very poorly, suggesting that the regrown tissue was supporting performance.

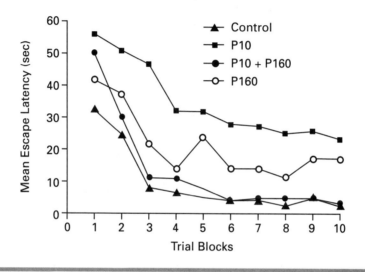

Conclusions

It has long been assumed in the psychological literature that experiences early in life have greater, and perhaps different, effects on later behavior than do experiences in adulthood. It follows that experiences can have age-dependent effects on the brain. Experience can modify the brain either by altering existing circuitry or by creating novel circuitry. We studied the age-dependent changes in cortical structure by exposing rats to specific experiences at different times in their lives and then examining the changes in the gross structure of cortical neurons. From these studies we can reach the following conclusions.

1. *Experience alters the synaptic organization of the cortex.* It is possible to visualize with a light microscope morphologic changes in the cortex that reflect synaptic modification. The neuronal changes can be quantified as

increases or decreases in the amount of dendritic arborization as well as in the density of dendritic spines.

2. *There are clear qualitative differences in the effects of experience on cortical neurons at different ages.* For example, when rats are placed in complex environments as juveniles, cortical neurons show a <u>decrease</u> in spine density, which implies a decrease in synapses, whereas adults show an <u>increase</u> in spine density, which implies an increase in synapses. Changes in the infant brain have significant effects on the way the brain responds to experience in adulthood. For example, tactile stimulation in infancy changes cortical neurons and the way they respond to experience in adulthood. Age-dependent changes in cortical plasticity are likely very important and reflect the differential sensitivity of the child's brain to experience during development. What is not yet known is how different experiences at different times in life might interact and to what extent the absence of particular experience might be compensated for later in life.

3. *Changes in synaptic organization are correlated with changes in behavior.* Animals with more dendritic growth than untreated animals show enhanced performance on many types of behavioral measures, especially of cognitive activity.

4. *There is preliminary evidence that experience alters the structure and connectivity of existing cells and stimulates the generation of new neurons.* This is likely to be a focus of intense research over the next decade, particularly because the stimulation of new neurons also appears to be a route to recovery from cortical injury.

5. *Compensatory changes in the brain following injury are similar to those observed when animals learn from experience.* These injury-induced changes are age dependent. For example, animals with cortical injuries in the first week of life show decreased dendritic arborization and poor functional outcome. In contrast, animals injured in the second week of life show increased dendritic arborization and a good functional outcome.

The similarity between the changes in the cortex following injury or experience suggests that there may be common mechanisms of synaptic plasticity. This is an encouraging possibility, because it offers hope for improved recovery from cerebral injury by taking advantage of the innate mechanisms that the brain uses for other forms of plasticity. To offer a more speculative hypothesis, it may also be possible to reverse the effects of impoverished experience by using pharmacologic treatments that are effective in improving recovery from brain injury.

6. *Injury-induced changes in cortical structure are modified by experience.* Brains that show the least change following a cortical injury appear to be the most responsive to experience. For instance, animals with neonatal brain injuries have a poor functional outcome and atrophied cortical neurons, but these animals show dramatic functional recovery and marked synaptic growth in response to environmental manipulation. This is encouraging, because it suggests that behavioral therapies should be especially helpful in reversing some of the devastating consequences of prenatal brain damage in human infants.

7. *Gonadal hormones influence the synaptic organization of the cortex throughout life.* Males and females have brains that are, at least in some regions, fundamentally, morphologically different. Gender, as well as age, may influence the morphologic changes in the brain following experience.

References

1. Ramon y Cajal S. *Degeneration and Regeneration in the Nervous System.* London, UK: Oxford University Press; 1928.

2. Hebb DO. *The Organization of Behavior.* New York, NY: McGraw-Hill; 1949.

3. Kolb B, Whishaw IQ. Brain plasticity and behavior. *Annual Review of Psychology.* 1998;49:43-64.

4. Kempermann G, Kuhn HG, Gage FH. Experience-induced neurogenesis in the senescent dentate gyrus. *Journal of Neuroscience.* 1988;18:3206-3212.

5. Pylyshyn ZW. Computation and cognition: issues in the foundations of cognitive science. *Behavioral and Brain Sciences.* 1980;3:11-69.

6. Skinner BF. *The Behavior of Organisms.* New York, NY: Appleton-Century-Crofts; 1938.

7. Greenough WT, Black JE, Wallace CS. Experience and brain development. *Child Development.* 1987;58:539-559.

8. Kolb B. Brain plasticity and behavioral change. In: Sabourin M, Craik FIM, Robert M, eds. *Advances in Psychological Science, Vol 2: Biological and Cognitive Aspects.* London, UK: Psychology Press; 1998: 115-144.

9. Whishaw IQ, Pellis SM, Gorny BP, Pellis VC. The impairments in reaching and the movements of compensation in rats with motor cortex lesions: an endpoint, videorecording, and movement notation analysis. *Behavioural Brain Research.* 1991;42:77-91.

10. Uylings HBM, van Eden CG, Parnavelas JG, Kalsbeek A. The prenatal and postnatal development of rat cerebral cortex. In: Kolb B, Tees R, eds. *The Cerebral Cortex of the Rat.* Cambridge, Mass: MIT Press; 1990:35-76.

11. Gibb R, Kolb B. A method for Golgi-Cox staining of Vibratome cut tissue. *Journal of Neuroscience Methods.* 1998;79:1-4.

12. Schanberg SM, Field TM. Sensory deprivation stress and supplemental stimulation in the rat pup and preterm human neonate. *Child Development.* 1987;58:1431-1447.

13. Kolb B, Gibb R. Experience and the changing brain. I. Experience-dependent changes in dendritic growth vary with age. Manuscript in submission, 1999.

14. Field T, Schanberg SM, Scafidi F, et al. Tactile/kinesthetic stimulation effects on preterm neonates. *Pediatrics.* 1986;77:654-658.

15. Purves D. *Neural Activity and the Growth of the Brain.* Cambridge, Mass: Cambridge University Press; 1994.

16. Solkoff N, Matuszak D. Tactile stimulation and behavioral development among low-birthweight infants. *Child Psychiatry and Human Development.* 1975;6:33-37.

17. Leon M. The neurobiology of filial learning. *Annual Review of Psychology.* 1992;43:377-398.

18. Sullivan RM, Leon M. Early olfactory learning induces an enhanced olfactory bulb response in rats. *Developmental Brain Research.* 1986;27:278-282.

19. Woo CC, Leon M. Sensitive period for neural and behavioral response development to learned odors. *Developmental Brain Research.* 1987;36:309-313.

20. Morris RGM. Spatial localization does not require the presence of local cues. *Learning and Motivation.* 1980;12:239-261.

21. Kolb B, Sutherland RJ, Whishaw IQ. A comparison of the contributions of the frontal and parietal association cortex to spatial localization in rats. *Behavioral Neuroscience.* 1983;97:13-27.

22. Juraska JM. Sex differences in dendritic responses to differential experience in the rat visual cortex. *Brain Research.* 1984;295:27-34.

23. Juraska JM. The structure of the cerebral cortex: effects of gender and the environment. In: Kolb B, Tees R, eds. *The Cerebral Cortex of the Rat.* Cambridge, Mass: MIT Press; 1990:483-506.

24. Juraska JM, Fitch J, Henderson C, Rivers N. Sex differences in the dendritic branching of dentate granule cells following differential experience. *Brain Research.* 1985;33:73-80.

25. Kolb B, Gibb R, Gorny G, Forgie M. Experience and the changing brain. III. Sex-dependent changes in dendritic growth following enriched rearing at different ages. Manuscript in submission, 1999.

26. Harrison RG. Wound healing and reconstitution of the central nervous system of the amphibian embryo after removal of parts of the neural plate. *Journal of Experimental Zoology.* 1947;106:27-84.

27. Nicholas JS. Results of inversion of neural plate material. Proceedings of the National Academy of Science, USA. 1957;43:253-283.

28. Nottebohm R, Alvarez-Buylla A. Neurogenesis and neuronal replacement in adult birds. In: Cuello AC, ed. *Neuronal Cell Death and Repair.* New York, NY: Elsevier; 1993:227-236.

29. Altman J. Are new neurons formed in the brains of adult mammals? *Science.* 1962;135:1127-1128.

30. Altman J, Bayer S. Are new neurons formed in the brains of adult mammals? A progress report, 1962-1992. In Cuello AC, ed. *Neuronal Cell Death and Repair.* New York, NY: Elsevier; 1993:203-225.

31. Rakic P. Limits of neurogenesis in primates. *Science.* 1985;227:1054-1056.

32. Okano HJ, Pfaff DW, Gibbs RB. RB and Cdc2 expression in brain: correlations with 3H-thymidine incorporation and neurogenesis. *Journal of Neuroscience.* 1993;13:2930-2938.

33. Shankle WR, Landing BH, Rafii MS, Schiano A, Chen JM, Hara J. Evidence for a postnatal doubling of neuron number in the developing human cerebral cortex between 15 months and 6 years. *Journal of Theoretical Biology.* 1998;191:115-140.

34. Kempermann G, Kuhn HG, Gage FH. More hippocampal neurons in adult mice living in an enriched environment. *Nature.* 1997;386:493-495.

35. Weiss S, Reynolds BA, Vescovi AL, Morshead C, Craig CG, van der Kooy D. Is there a neural stem cell in the mammalian forebrain? *Trends in Neuroscience.* 1996;19:387-393.

36. Reynolds B, Weiss S. Generation of neurons and astrocytes from isolated cells of the adult mammalian central nervous system. *Science.* 1992;255:1710-1727.

37. Craig CG. In vivo growth factor expansion of endogenous subependymal neural precursor cell populations in the adult mouse brain. *Journal of Neuroscience.* 1996;16:2649-2658.

38. Morshead CM, Reynolds BA, Craig CG, et al. Neural stem cells in the adult mammalian forebrain: a relatively quiescent subpopulation of subependymal cells. *Neuron.* 1994;13:1071-1082.

39. Bonhoeffer T. Neurotrophins and activity-dependent development of the neocortex. *Current Opinion in Neurobiology.* 1996;6:119-126.

40. Kolb B, Gibb R. Sparing of function after neonatal frontal lesions correlates with increased cortical dendritic branching: a possible mechanism for the Kennard effect. *Behavioral Brain Research.* 1991; 43:51-56.

41. Kolb B, Gibb R, van der Kooy D. Neonatal frontal cortical lesions in rats alter cortical structure and connectivity. *Brain Research.* 1994;645:85-97.

42. Purpura DP. Dendritic spine 'dysgenesis' and mental retardation. *Science.* 1974;186:1126-1128.

43. Kolb B, Cioe J. Absence of recovery or dendritic reorganziation after neonatal posterior parietal lesions. *Psychobiology.* 1998;26:134-142.

44. Kolb B, Cote S, Ribeiro-da-Silva A, Cuello AC. NGF stimulates recovery of function and dendritic growth after unilateral motor cortex lesions in rats. *Neuroscience.* 1997;76:1139-1151.

45. Kolb B, Cioe J, Muirhead D. Cerebral morphology and functional sparing after prenatal frontal cortex lesions in rats. *Behavioural Brain Research.* 1998;91:143-155.

46. Kolb B, Gibb R, Gorny G, Whishaw IQ. Possible regeneration of rat medial frontal cortex following neonatal frontal lesions. *Behavioural Brain Research.* 1998;91:127-141.

47. Kolb B. Brain *Plasticity and Behavior.* Mahwah, NJ: Lawrence Erlbaum; 1995.

48. Kolb B, Gibb R, Gorny G. Experience and the changing brain. IV. Therapeutic effects of enriched rearing after frontal lesions in infancy. Manuscript in preparation, 1999.

49. Kolb B, Elliott W. Recovery from early cortical damage in rats. II. Effects of experience on anatomy and behavior following frontal lesions at 1 or 5 days of age. *Behavioural Brain Research.* 1987;26: 47-56.

50. Kolb B, Cioe J. Sex-related differences in cortical function after medial frontal lesions in rats. *Behavioral Neuroscience.* 1998;110:1271-1281.

51. Kolb B, Petrie B, Cioe J. Recovery from early cortical damage in rats. VII. Comparison of the behavioural and anatomical effects of medial prefrontal lesions at different ages of neural maturation. *Behavioural Brain Research.* 1996;79:1-13.

52. Kolb B, Stewart J. Changes in neonatal gonadal hormonal environment prevent behavioral sparing and alter cortical morphogenesis after early frontal cortex lesions in male and female rats. *Behavioral Neuroscience.* 1995;109:285-294.

53. de Brabander J, Kolb B. Development of pyramidal cells in medial frontal cortex following lesions of anterior midline cortex. *Restorative Neurology and Neuroscience.* 1997;11:91-97.

54. Kolb B, Gibb R, Pedersen B, Whishaw IQ. Embryonic injection of BrdU blocks later cerebral plasticity. *Society for Neuroscience Abstracts.* 1997;23:677.16.

55. Kolb B, Pedersen B, Ballermann M, Gibb R, Whishaw IQ. Embryonic and postnatal injections of bromodeoxyuridine produce age-dependent morphological and behavioral abnormalities. Manuscript in submission, 1998.

56. Temesvary A, Gibb R, Kolb B. Recovery of function after neonatal frontal lesions in rats: function or fiction. *Society for Neuroscience Abstracts.* 1998;24:518.5.

57. Gould E, Reeves AJ, Graziano SA, Gross CG. Neurogenesis in the neocortex of adult primates. *Science.* 1999;286:548-552. (Added in proof.)

Acknowledgements

This research is supported by grants from the Natural Science and Engineering Research Council of Canada and the Medical Research Council of Canada.

Section 2:
Auditory/Language Development

Abstracts From Section 2. Auditory/Language Development

Language Input and Language Growth

Janellen Huttenlocher, PhD

Language acquisition is important in a child's intellectual development – it creates the ability to communicate intentions and share thoughts with others. A young child's language skills are influenced by parental input: the more a parent speaks to his or her child, the greater the child's vocabulary and language ability. This input effect has also been documented during kindergarten and first grade, but not the intervening summer; the language-rich school environment contributed positively to language growth.

One Step at a Time

Peter W. Jusczyk, PhD

Infants are able to detect a number of subtle distinctions among speech sounds, even among those outside of their native language. Between the ages of 7 and 11 months of age, the ability to segment words from speech develops considerably, using a variety of auditory cues. This discriminative capacity is important for learning language because it provides infants with the means to distinguish one word from another in the flow of normal speech.

The Role of Experience in Early Language Development: Linguistic Experience Alters the Perception and Production of Speech

Patricia K. Kuhl, PhD

Infants throughout the world achieve certain milestones in language development at approximately the same time, regardless of the language to which they are exposed. They begin life producing a universal set of utterances that cannot be distinguished, but by the end of the first year they produce sounds that reflect the ambient language to which they have been listening. The transition from universal to specific utterances involves both linguistic input and social interaction; the result is a developmental change characterized by the creation of a complex mental map that actually warps acoustic dimensions and alters perceptions that highlight language differences.

Language Input and Language Growth

Janellen Huttenlocher, PhD

Introduction

The acquisition of language is of great importance in children's intellectual development. Language underlies the most distinctive of human characteristics – the ability to exchange information about past or recent events, to share feelings, to formulate explanations and conjectures, and so forth. The role of an infant's native ability has figured prominently in studies of language development involving both vocabulary and syntax. Native endowment is clearly critical, yet recent studies have shown that language input (not just native ability) plays a substantial role in the development of both vocabulary and syntax.

Two factors are prominent in studies of whether language input affects the development of language skills in children. First, among the children tested, there must be variability in *language skills*. Second, their *language environments* must also vary substantially. If these two conditions hold, one can determine whether variations in language input are correlated with the skill levels of children and whether the relation is a causal one.

Variability Among Language Skills in Children

For vocabulary, it is well known that there is variability among individuals. The size of a person's vocabulary is often regarded as a measure of his or her intelligence. In fact, vocabulary tasks are very widely used on IQ tests, and, on short IQ tests, vocabulary is sometimes the only task. The use of vocabulary tasks to assess IQ assumes that the *ability to learn* from incoming speech, not the *amount of exposure* to incoming speech, is critical to vocabulary size. Vocabulary tasks were first included in IQ tests long ago without an assessment of whether vocabulary size actually reflects a biologically determined ability.

For syntax, it is widely believed that skill levels do not vary substantially among people, because they depend on dedicated innate mechanisms that yield uniform competence in all normal humans. Several facts support the view that innate mechanisms play a major role in syntactic development. It is not just that humans have a syntax; it is acquired rapidly early in life, and there is great similarity among children in the course of its development, notably in the order in which various grammatical forms appear.

Actually, however, there is considerable variability in the ages when various syntactic forms appear. In the four children originally studied by Roger Brown,[1] there was extensive variability in mean length of utterance at particular ages. Such variability also was reported in later studies with larger samples of children. Miller and Chapman studied 123 middle-class children aged 17 to 59 months and found large differences in the lengths of their utterances at particular ages.[2] Fenson et al also found extensive variability in the syntactic development of 1800 children aged 8 to 30 months.[3]

Variability in the syntax produced by individual children persists into school age. After age 5, there are differences in the frequency of complex constructions, such as expanded noun phrases, adverbial clauses, and subordinate clauses.[4] Loban found variability in the extent to which complex structures such as dependent clauses are incorporated into sentences through grade 12.[5] There are also individual differences in syntactic comprehension. For example, the ability to understand coreference relations varies up to 10 years of age.[6,7]

Is There Variability in Language Input?

The language input children receive can vary with their home environments. Several studies of lower-socioeconomic status (SES) mothers show that they talk less to their children and spend less time engaged in mutual activities where language is used than do middle-SES mothers. Lower-SES mothers more often use speech to direct children's behavior than to engage them in conversation; their speech is less frequently contingent on the child's speech, including fewer instances where they improve on children's expressions (expansions).[8-12]

Is Language Input Related to Language Growth?

Individual differences in language development might be due to biological factors, to variations in input, or both. There is some evidence from behavioral genetics that biological factors play only a small role in vocabulary. And, surprisingly, the effects of variations in language input on vocabulary had not been systematically explored until we began our own studies a few years ago.

With respect to syntax, Pinker and Bloom pointed out that syntax should show variability if it is genetically determined and shaped by evolutionary forces because variability allows for selection of adaptive forms of a skill.[13] Alas, the possibility of biologically based variability in syntactic skills in normal populations has not been explored systematically. There is a relationship, however, between the nature of syntactic input and syntactic growth in children. Frequent use of imperatives in parent speech ("Come here!" "Stop it!") is associated with slow syntactic growth.[14,15] Frequent use of expansions of what children say, and of yes/no questions ("Did you eat your food?"), are associated with rapid growth in their use of auxiliary verb forms[14-18] that have been corroborated in experimental studies.[19]

Does Input Play a Causal Role in Language Growth?

It is difficult to tell whether or not the relationships between language input and language growth are causally connected. For example, there are data that show that children who receive different language input exhibit differential language growth. Interpreting this finding is not so simple for several reasons. First, in studies of poorest-child dyads, the child's ability level might determine the type of input their parents provide. Given the one-to-one interaction in families, it is reasonable that a child's ability might influence how parents behave rather than vice versa. Second, biological similarities between caregivers and children may contribute to the observed connections. While these alternatives are obviously possible in studies of parents and their own children, there are also problems with studies in day-care centers and schools. That is, although the caregivers are not biologically related to the children, children with smarter or better-educated parents may attend better centers or schools.

Current Studies on Vocabulary and Syntax

In the last several years, my colleagues, students, and I have done a series of studies of early language growth, examining both vocabulary and syntax (J. Huttenlocher, unpublished data).[20,21] These studies show there are large differences in the language to which children are exposed; there is a striking relationship between language input and language skills; there is a causal relationship of language input to language skills.

Early Vocabulary

In our initial study of language input,[20] we examined vocabulary growth in 22 middle-class children over the initial period of word learning, from 16 to 26 months of age. We obtained samples of the verbal interactions of mothers and their children for several hours each month. The number of different words each child used served as our estimate for vocabulary size.

At 16 months, the children's vocabularies were small, but over the next months all children had accelerated vocabulary growth, the well-known "vocabulary spurt." Individual differences in vocabulary growth over this age period were striking, as shown in Fig 1. Note that at 26 months one of the children spoke less than 200 words, whereas another of the children spoke more than 800 words.

The difference in the amount of speech among parents was striking and consistent over time. The most talkative mother talked about 10 times as much as the least talkative mother – that is, about 7000 words during a 3-hour period versus about 700 words. The number of words they used when their children were 16 months old was highly correlated with the number of words they used when their children were 24 months old. Volubility seems to be a relatively permanent personal characteristic.

There was obviously a substantial relationship between vocabulary growth in children and the amount their caregivers spoke. We evaluated this relationship for the most – and least – talkative parents using hierarchical linear modeling to provide a measure of the input effect. The differences in child vocabulary were about 30 words at 16 months, 130 words at 20 months, and 300 words at 24 months.

Fig 1. Vocabulary size in three children from 14 to 26 months of age.

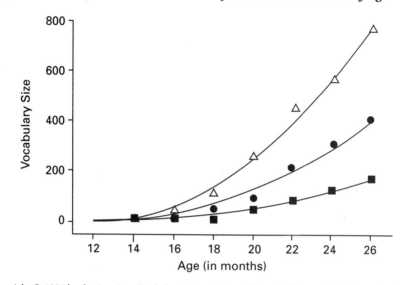

These results suggest that children learn words from exposure to speech. Can we conclude that the amount of parent speech is causally related to vocabulary growth? Our study provides reason to believe that parent speech *does* play a causal role in vocabulary growth. First, it was the *amount* of parent speech, not the *size* of parent *vocabulary*, that was related to children's vocabulary size. In fact, the words all the parents used were words everyone knows regardless of their vocabulary size, not the rare words that differentiate people with different vocabulary sizes.

Second and most important, we found evidence that the effects of the frequency of word use were not mediated by biological similarity between mother and child. That is, the relative frequency of particular words was highly conserved across parents. Not only did all mothers use the same words, they used them in the same order of frequency, reflecting the daily activities of families with young children – baby, bottle, bath. We found that the mothers' input frequency was highly related to the age of language acquisition in children, with a correlation coefficient of about 0.7. This clearly indicates that the age of vocabulary acquisition is (at least partly) due to input – the frequency of incoming speech. The observed early age of language acquisition was not simply due to differing ability levels among families, because all the mothers in the study had similar verbal IQ scores.

There was an additional aspect of the child data we did not report in the original study – a very high correlation between the length of children's multi-word utterances and their vocabulary size. Work by Fenson and colleagues also showed a very high correlation of utterance length and vocabulary size in a huge sample of children up to 2½ years of age.[3] Given the relationship in our data between utterance length and vocabulary size, as well as vocabulary size to the amount of parent speech, the relationship of utterance length to amount of parent speech also must have been strong.

Syntactic Development

In two recent studies, we examined the relationship of parents' language input to the level of syntactic skill in older children (Cymerman et al, unpublished data). Both studies measured the use of complex sentences in which simple sentences are conjoined or embedded in one another. The possible effects of parental input on this aspect of syntactic development had not been studied previously.

In our first study, we determined the proportion of sentences with more than one grammatical clause in parent and child speech. (Multiclause example: "Pretend you saw this break apart" and "I'm up here because I want to wait." Single-clause example: "Give me that" and "That's my truck.") We used an existing database from Hall and Nagy, who had transcribed several hours of parent and child speech, which is available on Child Language Data Exchange System (CHILDES). We used the data to examine syntax at home and at school in 34 low- and middle-income children.

Children's speech at home and at school was very similar. For some children, there were very few complex sentences. For others, as much as one fourth of the sentences were complex. There also were substantial differences in the proportions of complex sentences spoken by caregivers. Most importantly, there was a striking correlation between the proportion of complex utterances in parent and child. Furthermore, the high parent-child correlation was not due to the common conversational context at home because children used similar speech patterns at home and at school.

How should the correlation between parent and child speech be interpreted? Why do some children use complex sentences only rarely? Maybe children acquire syntactic skills by hearing particular language forms frequently, and those who rarely hear complex sentences have only a limited command of recursive devices. Alternately, children's speech may not display their syntactic knowledge because conversational habits in particular families or groups may obscure a higher level of syntactic knowledge. On the other hand, apparently complex speech in children whose parents use complex speech may reflect use of a few frozen forms rather than formulations of new complex ideas.

There are two ways to examine these issues. One is to look more carefully at the complex sentences children produce to determine if these relate to complex aspects of situations (such as causal or temporal relations) or if they involve mainly habitually used ("frozen") language. Another approach is to determine the relationship between speaking complex sentences and understanding such sentences. If speech production is controlled by underlying syntactic knowledge rather than by conversational habits, the complexity of the children's sentences should be related to their level of comprehension.

These issues are being explored in a new study, in which we recorded our own collections of parent and child speech from 48 parent-child pairs. As in the initial study, there were equal numbers of lower- and middle-class families. In addition to obtaining language production data, we obtained language comprehension data using a comprehension scale of our own design for complex sentences. We found a substantial correlation, over 0.6, between the complexity of the sentences children produced and that of the sentences they comprehended. Not surprisingly we found, as in the first study, a substantial correlation between complexity of parent speech and of child speech.

We are currently examining the extent to which a child's use of complex utterances involves fixed expressions vs newly constructed sentences. Thus far, it seems that children with high comprehension scores are more likely to produce newly constructed complex sentences. These findings suggest that syntactic skills vary across children, not simply cultural habits of conversation. Children who hear complex sentences more frequently are more skilled in understanding and producing them. It is possible that a gradual learning process is at work because children seemed to vary in skill levels in ways that were related to input variations. Finally, it is also possible that the effects we observed were because children and their parents are genetically similar with the same gift for language. Unfortunately, correlational studies such as ours cannot reveal a genetic component.

Input Variation Over Time

Our final study established the causal role of input in language growth among kindergarten and first-grade children.[21] Previously, several study designs attempted to eliminate the ambiguity about the relationship between input and skill levels in natural environments. One design, not often used, randomly assigns children to experimental and control groups. An example is Campbell and Ramey's work,[22,23] which compared impoverished preschool children randomly assigned to an intervention group and a control group. The investigators found long-lasting effects of their intervention on verbal IQ.

Another design compares children who fall on different sides of school cutoff ages – children who are in different grades even though they are almost the same age. The assumption here is that such children are equal in ability, and any differences in their performance must be due to differences in the input provided at school. This design has been used in a set of studies by Fred Morrison and his colleagues. Questions have been raised as to whether this design provides a fully effective control against differences in ability. For example, the smartest children in a grade tend to be the youngest.[24]

Our study was designed so that ability *cannot* be a confounding factor on the effects of naturally occurring variations in input. We studied a single group of children at different points in time, and compared language growth over periods that differed in language input. A similar design was used in earlier studies, notably by Entwistle and Alexander, who looked at growth in mathematical skills.[25] We used this design to evaluate whether skills commonly believed to reflect ability levels might be input sensitive.

Four large groups of children were tested at four time points 6 months apart – October and April of kindergarten; October and April of first grade. Children's activities differ over these periods: from October to April they are at school and for the next 6 months there is an extended summer vacation; there are periods of starting up activities in the fall and winding down in the spring. Because the same children are measured at different time periods, language growth should clearly reflect input differences. For example, if the growth of a skill is maturationally regulated, reflecting an individual's ability, it should grow as in Fig 2a. On the other hand, if a skill is regulated by relevant input, and that input is greatest at school, it should grow as in Fig 2b.

Fig 2. Developmental growth curves.

Growth reflecting maturation is depicted in A. Growth reflecting input is depicted in B.

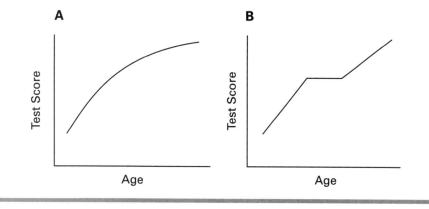

To assess language growth, we developed separate syntax and vocabulary tasks. The tasks involved pointing to a picture to indicate the meaning of a word ("Show me 'the steeple,'" as shown in Fig 3) or a sentence ("Show me 'The flowers are being watered by the girl,'" as shown in Fig 4). The vocabulary tasks varied widely in difficulty and involved only object names, the least syntactic of words. The syntactic structures we used also varied widely in difficulty. Scores for both syntax and vocabulary were merged into a single language scale.

Fig 3. Vocabulary test item (steeple).

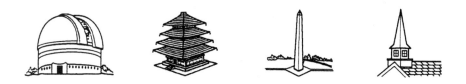

Fig 4. Syntax test item "The flowers are being watered by the girl."

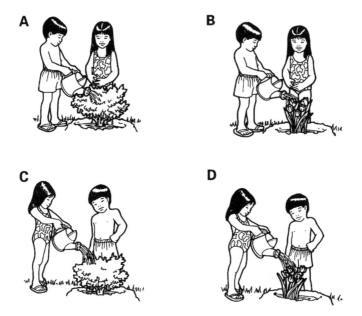

Reproduced with permission of The McGraw-Hill Companies, Inc. Huttenlocher J, Levine SC. *Primary Test of Cognitive Skills. California Test Bureau.* Monterey, Calif: Macmillan-McGraw-Hill; 1990.

The results for language development over the four time periods are shown in the cumulative performance graph (Fig 5). The horizontal axis represents language scores, and the vertical axis indicates the percent of children receiving *up to* those scores. Notice that the range of scores at the end of the school years is higher in first grade than in kindergarten (as would be expected with normally developing children). More importantly, there is a negligible difference in the range of scores measured at the end of kindergarten and the start of first grade. This may be interpreted simply as "the kids did not learn much during the summer," or, more eloquently, that the environment at school contributed positively to language growth.

Fig 5. Growth scores of language (vocabulary and syntax combined) for four age groups.

Each curve shows the cumulative proportion of children receiving various scores.

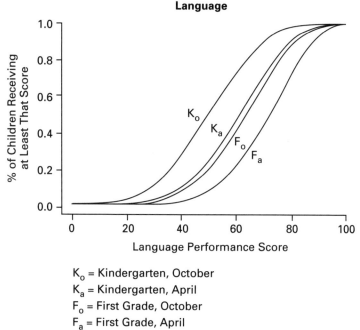

Language

% of Children Receiving at Least That Score

Language Performance Score

K$_o$ = Kindergarten, October
K$_a$ = Kindergarten, April
F$_o$ = First Grade, October
F$_a$ = First Grade, April

When the language growth that occurred during the 2 school years was averaged and compared with summer growth, the difference was statistically significant (P=.001). In a further analysis of the data, syntax and vocabulary were examined separately and found to grow mainly during the school year.

Also note that the language curves are *parallel* – school affected children at the lower percentiles as much as it did children at the higher percentiles. That is, the gain from input was similar for children whose starting skill levels were very different.

When intervention has parallel effects, the interpretation often given is that the *change* is affected by input but that the *start level* is determined by biological factors. However, in this and other studies, we have found large home-input effects in younger children that may contribute to the baseline scores. Children with higher starting scores might not gain more during the summer because they have already learned most of the words parents use in daily conversation at home where talk mainly concerns the same matters over the years. Most later words and forms of expression may be acquired in school, where new information is being imparted.

It is unlikely that the apparent difference in language growth could be an artifact due to improved test-taking skills in the children. We found no school year-summer difference in an associative memory test using the same testing format. In fact, there was uniform growth during the entire age period.

Conclusions

There is considerable variability among children, both in vocabulary and in syntax. There is also considerable variability in children's language environments. A substantial relationship exists between naturally occurring variations in children's language environments and their skills in both vocabulary and syntax. Such a relationship is found during the earliest stages of language development (between 16 and 26 months of age) and later, at 5 and 6 years of age.

There are many studies that show correlations between language input and language growth in natural environments, but most are subject to alternative interpretations. For example, parents and children are genetically related, children's skill levels may influence parental input, and the quality of input can vary with the quality of schools in different neighborhoods. Our study of language input at school minimized the effects of these confounding factors. The study design was able to isolate input effects by evaluating the same group of children at 6-month intervals that bracketed the school year. Under these conditions, language input was found to have a significant impact on language growth. While it is clear that differences in language input within the normal range lead to particular patterns of language growth in the early years of life, much more work remains to develop a model of the acquisition process that properly incorporates the role of input.

References

1. Brown R. *A First Language: The Early Stages.* Cambridge, Mass: Harvard University Press; 1973.

2. Miller JF, Chapman RS. The relation between age and mean length of utterances. *Journal of Speech and Hearing Research.* 1981;24:154-161.

3. Fenson L, Dale PS, Reznick JS, Bates E, Thal DJ, Pethick SJ. Variability in early communicative development. *Monographs of the Society for Research in Child Development.* 1994;59:Serial No. 242.

4. Scott CM. Adverbial connectivity in conversations of children 6 to 12. *Journal of Child Language.* 1984;11:423-452.

5. Loban W. *Language Development: Kindergarten Through Grade Twelve.* Urbana, Ill: National Council of Teachers of English; 1976.

6. Chomsky C. *The Acquisition of Syntax in Children From 5 to 10.* Cambridge, Mass: MIT Press; 1969.

7. Goodluck H. Children's grammar of complement-subject interpretation. In: Tavakolian SL, ed. *Language Acquisition and Linguistic Theory.* Cambridge, Mass: MIT Press; 1981.

8. Bee HL, Van Egeren LF, Streissguth AP, Nyman BA, Leckie MA. Social class differences in maternal teaching strategies and speech patterns. *Developmental Psychology.* 1969;1:726-734.

9. Farian DC, Haskins R. Reciprocal influence in the social interaction of mothers and three-year-old children from different socioeconomic backgrounds. *Child Development.* 1980;51:780-791.

10. Heath SB. *Ways With Words: Language, Life and Work in Communities and Classrooms.* Cambridge, Mass: Cambridge University Press; 1983.

11. Hess RD, Shipman VC. Early experience and the socialization of cognitive modes in children. *Child Development.* 1965;36:859-886.

12. Schachter FF. *Everyday Mother Talk to Toddlers: Early Intervention.* San Diego, Calif: Academic Press; 1979.

13. Pinker S, Bloom P. Natural language and natural selection. *Behavioral and Brain Sciences.* 1990;13:707-784.

14. Barnes S, Gotfreund M, Satterly F, Wells G. Characteristics of adult speech which predict children's language development. *Journal of Child Language.* 1983;10:65-84.

15. Newport EL, Gleitman H, Gleitman L. Mother, I'd rather do it myself: some effects and noneffects of maternal speech style. In: Snow CE, Ferguson CA, eds. *Talking to Children: Language Input and Acquisition.* Cambridge, Mass: Cambridge University Press; 1977.

16. Furrow D, Nelson K, Benedict H. Mothers' speech to children and syntactic development: some simple relationships. *Journal of Child Language.* 1979;6:423-442.

17. Hoff-Ginsburg E. Some contributions of mothers' speech to their children's syntactic growth. *Journal of Child Language.* 1985;12:367-385.

18. Hoff-Ginsburg E. Maternal speech and the child's development of syntax: a further look. *Journal of Child Language.* 1990;17:337-346.

19. Nelson KE, Carskaddon G, Bonvillian JD. Syntax acquisition: impact of experimental variation in adult verbal interaction with the child. *Child Development.* 1973;44:497-504.

20. Huttenlocher J, Haight W, Bryk A, Seltzer M, Lyons T. Early vocabulary growth: relation to language input and gender. *Developmental Psychology.* 1991;27:236-248.

21. Huttenlocher J, Levine SC, Vevea J. Environmental effects on cognitive growth: evidence from time period comparisons. *Child Development.* 1998;69:1012-1029.

22. Campbell FA, Ramey CT. Effects of early intervention on intellectual and academic achievement: a follow-up study of children from low-income families. *Child Development.* 1994;65:684-698.

23. Campbell FA, Ramey CT. Cognitive and school outcomes for high-risk African-American students at middle adolescence: positive effects of early intervention. *American Educational Research Journal.* 1995;32(4):743-772.

24. Gottfried AW, Gottfried AE, Bathurst K, Guerin DW. *Gifted IQ: Early Developmental Aspects. The Fullerton Longitudinal Study.* New York, NY: Plenum Press; 1994.

25. Entwistle DR, Alexander KL. Summer setback: race, poverty, school composition and mathematics achievement in the first two years of school. *American Sociological Review.* 1992;52:72-84.

One Step at a Time

Peter W. Jusczyk, PhD

Introduction

Young infants come into the world with an array of perceptual capacities that are well adapted for perceiving speech and acquiring language. Early investigations of these capacities revealed that infants are able to detect a number of subtle distinctions among speech sounds,[1-5] even among ones that do not occur in their own native language.[6-8] These discriminative capacities are important for learning language, because they provide infants with the means to distinguish one word from another.

Although words that differ in their meanings often differ in their acoustic patterns, not every acoustic difference carries a difference in meaning. Consider the fact that there are acoustic differences between two different talkers' productions of exactly the same word. Sensitivity to such acoustic differences is helpful for identifying who said the word but not for understanding the word's meaning. Rather, a listener must be able to ignore these kinds of acoustic differences to recognize the word's meaning. Thus, one potential difficulty for a language learner is knowing exactly which kinds of acoustic differences are relevant for signaling differences between meanings and which ones are not. Fortunately, young language learners seem to possess capacities that allow them to recognize when the same speech sound is uttered by different talkers.[9-11] They also seem able to compensate for the kinds of acoustic variation that occur when the same word is spoken at different rates of speech.[12,13]

These capacities for discriminating speech sounds are in place and functioning within the first half year of life. They allow infants to begin to categorize the speech sounds that occur in their home environments. Such abilities are clearly a *necessary* foundation for learning the words of one's native language, but they are not *sufficient* for this purpose. Among the other important capacities needed for acquiring a vocabulary (or lexicon) are the ability to: segment words from fluent speech; represent and remember the sound patterns of different words; and correctly link sound patterns to particular meanings.

To an adult user of a particular language, it might not be obvious why an ability to segment words from speech is so important. When listening to our own native tongue, we seldom have difficulty telling where one word leaves off and another word begins. Thus, we have the impression that words are separated from each other in the acoustic signal in much the same way that written words on a page are separated by blank spaces. This illusion is shattered, however, when we experience someone speaking in an unfamiliar foreign language. Then we often have the impression that the speech stream is continuous and that one word runs into another. In fact, the same holds for our own native language when heard by foreigners. Why, then, do we seem to experience little difficulty in segmenting words from native-language utterances? The answer is that we have learned to pick up certain cues in the acoustic signal that indicate where the word boundaries are. The cues that are present in the acoustic signal depend very much on how the sound structure of a particular language is organized. This explains why we have difficulty in segmenting foreign languages; we are unfamiliar with their particular sound structures and have not learned which kinds of cues are used to mark word boundaries. Notice that infants are in the same position with respect to their native language, they too need to learn what cues are used to indicate the boundaries between words in speech. Thus, infants will require some knowledge of the sound structure of their native language before they can successfully segment words.

The Beginnings of Word Segmentation

There are a number of indications that infants begin to learn about the specific sound organization of their native language around the middle of their first year. The first demonstration that native-language structure has an impact on infants' speech-perception capacities came in an investigation of English learners' abilities to perceive nonnative speech contrasts.[14] Werker and Tees reported that although English-learning 6- to 8-month-olds could discriminate contrasts from Hindi and Nthlakapmx (a Native American language), English-learning 10- to 12-month-olds failed to discriminate the same contrasts. Werker and Tees argued that this decline in discriminative ability to the nonnative contrasts could be traced to infants' growing sensitivity to which sounds appeared regularly in the speech input. Similar declines in discriminative sensitivity have been found to occur for some but not all nonnative contrasts.[15-17]

Development of Language Perception in Infants.

Perception Test	Age (months)	Outcome
Perceive nonnative speech contrasts[14]	6-8	Yes
	10-12	No
Prefer hearing native speaker[18]	6	No
	9	Yes
Prefer native stress pattern[19]	6	No
	9	Yes
Recognize familiar words[20]	6	No
	7.5	Yes
Recognize segmented words embedded in sentences[20]	7.5	Yes
Identify real words[20]	7.5	Yes
Recognize complete word match[23]	7.5	Yes
Deal with talker variability[29]	7.5	No
	10.5	Yes
Recognize words in context from different speakers[30]	8	Yes
Remember familiar sounds ≥24 hours[29]	7.5	Yes
Recognize stress-based cues	7.5	Yes
Recognize co-occurrence of syllables[41,42]	8	Yes
Sensitive to allophonic cues for word segmentation [43,44]	9	No
	10.5	Yes
Segment verbs from fluent speech[55]	10.5	No
	13.5	Yes
Sensitive to prosody of clauses	2[56,57]	Yes
Sensitive to prosody of phrases	9[58,59]	Yes
Sensitive to "function" words	10.5[61]	Yes
	11[60]	Yes

During the time these declines in sensitivity to nonnative speech contrasts were noted, an increased awareness of native-language sound organization was also noted. Between 6 and 9 months, infants begin to show sensitivity to the kinds of sounds (phones) and sound sequences (phonotactics) that can or cannot appear in native-language words. For example, Dutch words differ from English words primarily in terms of which phonetic segments and phonotactic sequences are allowed. English-learning 6-month-olds listen to unfamiliar Dutch words as long as they do to unfamiliar English words. By 9 months, both English and Dutch learners listen significantly longer to words from their own native language, suggesting that they are sensitive to the phonetic and phonotactic properties of these words.[18] Similarly, between 6 and 9 months, English learners show increased sensitivity to the kinds of prosodic patterns that are most characteristic of words in their native language.[19] Specifically, English two-syllable words are much more likely to be stressed on their initial syllables (eg, "falter") than on their final syllables (eg, "default"). The stress patterns of the former are said to be "strong/weak," whereas the latter are referred to as "weak/strong." English-learning 6-month-olds display no preference for either stress pattern. By comparison, 9-month-olds show a clear listening preference for the words with the predominant strong/weak stress pattern.

These findings show that during the second half of their first year, infants are learning about the specific sound organization of their native language. This growing knowledge positions them to learn about the kinds of cues that might mark the boundaries of words in fluent speech. Indeed, some of the sound features noted above, such as phonotactic sequences and stress patterns, are among the most often cited potential word-boundary cues. Thus, it is perhaps not surprising that there is evidence that infants first begin to segment words from speech at this time.

To examine infants' word-segmentation abilities, my colleagues and I devised a procedure whereby we familiarized 7.5-month-olds with different repetitions of a pair of words (eg, "bike" and "feet") that were produced in isolation by a single talker.[20] Next, four different six-sentence passages were played for the infants, and, using the headturn-preference procedure,[21,22] the infants' listening times to these passages was measured. Two of the passages included one of the familiarized words in each sentence; the other two passages were similarly structured but included two unfamiliar words. The infants listened significantly longer to the passages that contained the familiarized words, suggesting that they detected these in the sentences. Thus, 7.5-month-olds displayed some rudimentary ability to segment these words from fluent speech contexts. A group of 6-month-olds tested on the same materials, however, did not display any significant preferences for the passages with the familiarized words. Hence, English learners' word-segmentation abilities appear to develop sometime between 6 and 7.5 months of age.

Although it is impressive that infants who first hear words produced in isolation can later detect the same words in sentential contexts, many words that infants learn will be unlikely to occur in isolation. Consequently, we decided to explore whether 7.5-month-olds who were familiarized with words occurring in passages would later show recognition of the same words when they were produced in isolation. We familiarized infants with a pair of six-sentence passages, each of which included a particular word that appeared in each sentence (eg, "cup" and "dog"). Then, in separate trials, we measured infants' listening times to each of four different repeated, isolated words, two of which had occurred in the passages. The infants listened significantly longer to the words that had occurred in the familiarization passages. These findings indicate that 7.5-month-olds have the capacity to segment words from longer utterances, even when their initial exposure is to the words embedded in sentences.[20]

How Extensive Are Early Word-Segmentation Abilities?

Given that word-segmentation abilities are first evident at around 7.5 months of age, many questions arise about the extent of these abilities. For example, are infants extracting the whole sound patterns of such words from sentences or only a few salient features of these words? In our investigation, the target words that infants were familiarized with ("cup" and "dog") had vowels that differed greatly from each other and from the ones in the novel test words ("bike" and "feet"). In principle, the infants could have distinguished these items simply by attending to their vowels and ignoring the rest of the words. To test this explicitly we familiarized 7.5-month-olds with a pair of nonsense words ("gike" and "zeet") that included the same vowels and final consonants as words in two of the test passages ("bike" and "feet"). Had the infants only been responding to the vowels of the familiarized items, they should have listened longer to the passages that included the words with the same vowels and final consonants than to ones that had words with dissimilar sound properties. In fact, they showed no significant listening preferences for any of the passages.[20] Thus, the infants did not respond to the sound patterns of words in passages that only partially matched those that they had heard during familiarization.

As a further check on whether 7.5-month-olds may only extract some of the salient sound properties of words from continuous speech contexts, R. Tincoff and I tried familiarizing infants with other types of words that shared sound properties with words in the passages.[23] In particular, we focused on the possibility that infants might find the beginnings of words to be more salient than the ends of words. Infants were familiarized with a pair of items, such as "cut" and "bawg," and then tested on passages that included words such as "cup" and "dog." Once again, the infants did not show any tendency to listen longer to the passages containing the words that partially matched the ones with which they had been familiarized. These findings suggest that even at the beginning phases of word segmentation, infants are working with an accurate and fairly detailed representation of the sound pattern of words.

Might 7.5-month-olds' representations of words actually be too detailed? As mentioned earlier, listeners need to ignore the kind of acoustic variability that is related to production of the same words by different talkers. When infants first begin extracting the sound patterns of particular words from continuous speech, are they able to generalize from one talker's productions of these words to another's? Note that the studies mentioned above indicate that infants have some capacity to ignore certain kinds of acoustic variability. Specifically, utterances of the same words produced in isolation and in sentential context differ considerably from each other in their acoustic characteristics.[24,25] Still, all the items used in each of these studies were ones always produced by a single talker. Coping with the variability in speech produced by several different talkers has been shown to affect the speech-processing and memory capacities of both adults and infants.[9,26-28]

Together with Houston and Tager, I explored the extent to which 7.5-month-olds can generalize from words produced by one talker to those of another.[29] We familiarized infants at this age with isolated repetitions of two target words produced by one talker, then tested them on passages produced by a different talker. Provided the two talkers were of the same gender, the infants successfully detected the target words in the passages. When the talkers were of different genders, the 7.5-month-olds failed to generalize from the familiarized target words to the ones in the passages produced by the different talker. Hence, at this earlier stage in the development of word-segmentation abilities, infants only show a limited ability to generalize across words produced by different talkers. We then tested a group of 10.5-month-old infants. These older infants *did* generalize across talkers from different genders, suggesting that the ability to deal with talker variability in segmenting words from continuous speech develops over the course of several months.

Word Segmentation and the Beginnings of a Lexicon

As discussed above, word-segmentation abilities are necessary for building up a lexicon of words in one's native language. Can we assume, then, that the lexicon begins to develop at the point at which infants first begin to segment the sound patterns of words from fluent speech? Alternatively, might the formation of the lexicon occur only when the learner begins to store information that links sound patterns with particular meanings? This is not an easy issue to resolve. If the lexicon does begin to form when infants start to segment words, we should expect to find some indication that infants show long-term retention of the sound patterns of words that they extract from fluent speech. Several recent investigations suggest that infants do engage in such long-term retention of sound patterns.

In one study English-learning 8-month-olds were visited in their homes 10 times during a 2-week period.[30] At each visit, the infants heard a 25-minute audiotape of three separate children's stories. On each occasion, the same stories were heard in a different order or in a different talker's voice. Two weeks after the last visit to their homes, the infants were brought into the laboratory and tested using the headturn preference procedure on two word lists. One list was made up of words that had appeared frequently in the stories. The other was composed of foil words that had not appeared in the stories but that had similar phonetic properties and were as likely to be familiar to the infants as the story words. The infants who had been exposed to the stories listened significantly longer to the lists of story words than to the lists of foil words. Another group of infants, who had not been exposed to the stories, did not show a significant preference for either type of list.[30] What these findings show is that the 8-month-olds did apparently segment the sound patterns of frequently occurring words from the stories and that they retained information about these patterns over a 2-week interval. Moreover, because many of the story words were not ones commonly used around infants (eg, "hornbill," "peccaries"), it appears that infants stored information about the sound patterns of these words, even though they did not know their meanings.

More recently, Houston and colleagues investigated the extent to which infants retain information about specific words with which they are familiarized in word-segmentation studies.[29] They familiarized 7.5-month-olds with repetitions of a pair of isolated words, then waited 24 hours to test them on passages with or without these words. They found that infants listened longer to the passages containing the familiarized target words. In fact, infants' performance after the 24-hour delay was about the same as that for infants who are tested on the passages immediately after the familiarization period.

These investigations demonstrate that the lexicon begins to form when infants start to segment words from speech. Thus, infants do remember some of the sound patterns of words that they segment from fluent speech. Moreover, they appear to retain such information even when they do not know the meanings of these words. One implication of these findings is that word learning appears to occur in two different ways: Sometimes infants learn meanings prior to learning the sound patterns that go with them. At other times, they learn sound patterns before attaching particular meanings to these patterns.

What Information Do Infants Use in Segmenting Words?

Words are rarely spoken as isolated utterances to infants,[31] even in situations in which mothers are explicitly asked to teach their children new words.[32] Also, words in conversational speech are usually not separated from each other by silence. As a result, any success that infants have in segmenting words from fluent speech depends on learning about potential markers of word boundaries that occur in the speech signal. Two such potential sources of information are stress patterns and phonotactic cues. Consider how each of these could be used in signaling word boundaries. For stress patterns, if a language has a very regular pattern of stressing a particular syllable, a listener could use the occurrence of stressed syllables as an indicator of word boundaries. For example, Czech is very regular in stressing the first syllable of words, whereas Polish typically stresses the penultimate syllable. Thus, when listening to conversational speech in these languages, listeners can use the location of stressed syllables as a rough guide to where words are likely to begin and end.

Phonotactic patterns can also be useful in locating potential word boundaries. For example, certain phonotactic sequences are impermissible at the beginnings and endings of words. English does not allow words to begin with sequences such as "kt," "db," or "gd." Hence, when such sequences occur in

English utterances, there is a high likelihood that there is a word boundary in between each of these sequences. While true for English sound organization, this does not necessarily hold for other languages. For instance, the sequences above can occur at the beginnings of words in Polish. Thus, to use such information for word segmentation, a listener must already know something about the phonotactic organization of the language.

Another type of information that has been suggested as a potential marker of word boundaries has to do with the variants (or allophones) of particular phonemes. That is, certain allophones are restricted to occurring in some positions of a word (eg, initially) but not in others (eg, finally). Listeners who are sensitive to the contexts in which these allophones typically appear could use this information in inferring potential word boundaries.[33-35] Listeners might also take advantage of their knowledge of certain co-occurrence relations between syllables to determine whether these are likely or unlikely to occur together within the same word.[36] Consider how this would work for a sequence such as "grumpy man." The transitional probability of "man" following "py" is low, given all the other words that could conceivably occur before "man" in the language. Thus, these two syllables likely belong to different words. By comparison, the transitional probabilities between "grum" and "py" are relatively high. Hence, these two syllables likely come from the same word.

Which of these potential sources do English learners use when they begin to segment words from fluent speech? It has been observed that a very high proportion of content words in English conversational speech begin with strong syllables.[37] Because of this regularity in stress patterns, Cutler and colleagues have proposed that as a first pass at word segmentation, listeners might assume that strong syllables mark the onsets of new words in fluent speech.[38-40] To test whether English-learning infants might use such a metrical segmentation strategy, my colleagues and I familiarized 7.5-month-olds with words that had either strong/weak (eg, "kingdom" and "hamlet") or weak/strong (eg, "surprise" and "guitar") stress patterns. Infants familiarized with strong/weak words correctly detected these words in fluent speech passages but did not detect familiarized weak/strong words when these appeared in such passages. Furthermore, 7.5-month-olds gave evidence of missegmenting weak/strong words. Specifically, infants familiarized with "prize" and "tar" responded when these items occurred in passages containing the words "surprise" and "guitar." Thus, English-learning 7.5-month-olds appear to identify word onsets with the occurrence of strong syllables in fluent speech.

In fact, English learners' reliance on stress-based cues at the initial phases of word segmentation is such that they appear to use this strategy even when listening to a foreign language such as Dutch, which has stress patterns similar to English. Houston et al (unpublished data) found that 9-month-old English learners who were familiarized with a pair of Dutch words were able to detect these targets in fluent speech passages about as well as Dutch 9-month-olds were. By 10.5 months, however, English learners begin to show less exclusive reliance on stress-based cues. For example, we found that infants at this age were now able to segment English weak/strong words from fluent speech. This clearly shows that the older infants are using other sources of information in addition to metrical stress cues in segmenting words.

In regard to co-occurrence relations between syllables, Saffran, Aslin, and Newport showed that 8-month-olds can use this kind of information to infer word boundaries in fluent speech.[41,42] After 2 minutes of familiarization with a continuous string of connected consonant-vowel syllables, infants responded differentially to three-syllable sequences that consistently co-occurred with each other during familiarization vs three-syllable sequences that only co-occurred together relatively infrequently. Similarly, in our investigation, we found that when a weak/strong word in a passage was consistently followed by the same weak syllable (eg, "guitar is"), 7.5-month-olds responded as though they detected a word with a strong/weak pattern ("taris"). This indicates that infants do attend to co-occurrence relations in extracting words from fluent speech.

Given that infants are sensitive to such co-occurrence patterns in fluent speech, might they simply respond to any consistently co-occurring sequence, regardless of whether it comes from the same word or from parts of different words? Suppose the word "ice" is always preceded in a passage by words that end in [d] (eg, "cold," "hard," "weird"). Will infants segment the word "dice" from such passages? My colleagues and I found that English-learning 7.5-month-olds did not missegment "dice" from such contexts, even though they correctly segmented "dice" when it really did appear as a lexical item in a passage. What seems to inhibit infants from incorrectly segmenting "dice" from "cold ice" is the presence of allophonic information that indicates that the final [d] in "cold" is not the onset of a new word. Indeed, evidence from other investigations suggests that between 7.5 and 10.5 months, infants develop sensitivity to allophonic and phonotactic cues.[43,44]

In summary, although infants may initially segment words by relying on one source of information, such as English learners' use of metrical stress, developing effective and efficient word-segmentation strategies depends on multiple sources of information. This is because none of the potential cues to word boundaries in English is completely foolproof. All of these cues can be shown to fail in one situation or another. Although English learners' initial reliance on metrical stress cues may sometimes lead to the missegmentation of some words, it also provides increased opportunities for discovering other potential cues to word boundaries. Specifically, the use of metrical stress cues to divide the input into smaller chunks may allow English learners to observe that certain kinds of allophones and phonotactic sequences are likely to occur at the beginnings of these chunks, but others are not. In this way, learners may gain knowledge of how allophones and phonotactic sequences are typically distributed within words.

There are other issues that must be addressed in this context. Why do English learners begin by using metrical stress cues in word segmentation? Furthermore, how can they learn the predominant stress patterns of English words without some prior ability to segment words from fluent speech? The answer seems to be that many of the words that are spoken in isolation to infants (eg, names, nicknames, and diminutive terms, such as "mommy," "daddy," "doggie," "kitty") are ones with the predominant stress pattern of English words. The occurrence of such patterns may serve to bias English learners to expect that words occurring in longer utterances are likely to have strong/weak stress.

Linking Sound Patterns With Meanings

A number of early investigations estimated the onset of word-comprehension abilities at about 9 months of age or even later.[45-49] These estimates of when infants begin to associate sounds with meanings were typically based on how infants responded to the names of familiar but relatively immobile objects. More recently, Tincoff and I explored whether infants might show some comprehension of names that refer to animate figures very socially salient to infants, namely their own parents.[50] To investigate this possibility, we showed 6-month-olds side-by-side videos of their parents and a voice on an audio track said the words "mommy" and "daddy." They found that the infants looked significantly more at the video of the mother when they heard "mommy" and more at the video of the father when they heard "daddy."[50]

A second experiment demonstrated that infants associated these labels with their particular parents and not with men and women in general. Thus, infants who were shown videos of unfamiliar adults did not adjust their looking patterns in response to the verbal labels "mommy" and "daddy." One interesting implication of these results is that infants may first learn the general principle that sound patterns can be used to symbolize meanings by first learning to attach names to specific individuals such as their parents. Of course, learners eventually must be able to go beyond attaching names to specific individuals and discover that such labels can apply to whole classes of objects. Indeed, other recent evidence suggests that 9-month-olds categorize groups of objects differently depending on whether a linguistic label is spoken when they are viewing the objects.[51] Thus, there is growing evidence that infants begin to link sound patterns and meanings relatively early in the second half of their first year.

How Word-Segmentation Abilities Help in Learning Grammatical Structure

An ability to segment words from fluent speech provides the learner with an opportunity to discover how certain words are typically positioned within utterances in the language. This is especially useful for infants learning languages such as English, in which word order is the principal means of specifying the syntactic relations among words. For example, the positioning of the nouns in a sentence such as "the dog chased the cat" is critical for understanding who chased whom. The word-segmentation studies discussed so far have all involved nouns. Although an ability to extract nouns from fluent speech is certainly useful, learners also need to be able to extract other kinds of words. Of course, if all parts of speech had exactly the same sound structure, an ability to extract nouns would naturally be indicative of an ability to segment other types of words. In English, although nouns typically have stress on their initial syllable, verbs are more likely to have stress on noninitial syllables.[52-54] For example, when the English word "discount" occurs as a noun, the accent falls on the initial syllable; when the same word occurs as a verb, the accent occurs on the second syllable.

My colleagues and I examined English learners' abilities to segment verbs with weak/strong stress patterns, such as "incites" and "discounts," from fluent speech.[55] We began by testing 10.5-month-olds, because previous findings indicated that English learners begin to segment nouns with weak/strong stress patterns at this age.[37] Surprisingly, we found that 10.5-month-olds did not segment the weak/strong verbs from fluent speech, although 13.5-month-olds did. To determine why English-learning 10.5-month-olds segment weak/strong nouns but not weak/strong verbs from fluent speech, we compared the materials used in the two studies. The target words occurred in almost exactly the same contexts in both types of passages; however, the nouns were more likely to be pitch accented in the sentences than were the verbs. For this reason, nouns may stand out more than verbs in these sentences.

Detecting the occurrence of nouns and verbs in fluent speech is important in building a vocabulary, but learning about the syntactic properties of such words requires that infants know how they are distributed within utterances. One possibility is that language learners discover how words are positioned with respect to other words that are marked in the prosody of speech. There is evidence that even 2-month-olds show some sensitivity to the prosodic marking of clauses,[56,57] and English-learning 9-month-olds display sensitivity to prosodic phrases.[58,59] Thus, infants may be able to track how the specific nouns and verbs they recognize in fluent speech line up with prosodic phrase boundaries. For example, is a particular word found more typically toward the beginning or end of a prosodic phrase?

Another possibility is that nouns and verbs are marked in relation to other words (function words and grammatical morphemes) that are likely to have a fixed position within phrasal units. For this possibility to be useful, infants first must be able to detect function words in fluent speech. In a study using an auditory evoked potential (AEP) measure, English-learning 11-month-olds reacted to the substitution of nonsense syllables for function words in sentences.[60] More recently, these findings were replicated and extended using the Headturn Preference Procedure in which we found that 10.5-month-olds listened significantly longer to passages with real function words than to ones with nonsense words substituted for the function words.[61] This pattern of responding held even when the nonsense words had very similar phonetic properties to those of real English function words. By comparison, when nonsense words were substituted for content words instead of function words, no significant differences in listening times to these two types of passages occurred. The latter findings indicate that infants in the earlier experiment were not simply reacting to the occurrence of nonsense words in the passages but had expectations about function words that should occur in English utterances.

Together with M. Shady, I examined whether 10.5-month-olds can segment particular function words from fluent speech. In one experiment, infants familiarized with either "this" or "that" listened significantly longer to passages containing these targets. A second experiment explored whether infants familiarized with "a" or "the" would detect these items in fluent speech. When "a" and "the" occur in fluent speech, they tend to be greatly reduced and phonetically altered from when they are produced in citation form. Nevertheless, the 10.5-month-olds did listen significantly longer to the passage that contained the appropriate target word.

Therefore, by 10.5 months, English learners are beginning to track certain function words in utterances. Evidence from other studies suggests that infants may not discover the actual positioning of these words in utterances until between 14 and 16 months of age.[61] The very fact that infants are sensitive to the occurrence of these words allows them to begin to learn about how these words are distributed within prosodic phrases. With respect to "a" and "the," they may discover that when these words occur near a prosodic phrase boundary, it will almost certainly always be at the beginning rather than at the end of such a phrase. Moreover, attending to the fact that "a" and "the" occur immediately before some known adjectives and nouns, but not before verbs, could help in identifying the likely syntactic category of some unknown words in an utterance. In this way, the ability to segment and identify certain function words can contribute to the infant's discovery of the syntactic organization of the native language.

Conclusions

During the second half of their first year, infants learn much about the structure and organization of sound patterns in their native language. This information apparently plays a key role in their developing abilities to segment words from fluent speech. Word-segmentation abilities develop considerably between 7 and 11 months of age. At the same time, infants appear to be developing an increased sensitivity to the marking of linguistically relevant units, such as prosodic phrases, in utterances. Together, the ability to segment words and the ability to divide utterances into coherent chunks may allow the infant to track the distributional properties of certain elements that recur frequently in speech, thus paving the way for learning about the syntactic organization of the native language.

References

1. Eimas PD, Siqueland ER, Jusczyk PW, Vigorito J. Speech perception in infants. *Science.* 1971;171:303-306.

2. Eimas PD. Auditory and linguistic processing of cues for place of articulation by infants. *Perception & Psychophysics.* 1974;16:513-521.

3. Eimas PD. Auditory and phonetic coding of the cues for speech: discrimination of the [r- l] distinction by young infants. *Perception & Psychophysics.* 1975;18:341-347.

4. Morse PA. The discrimination of speech and nonspeech stimuli in early infancy. *Journal of Experimental Child Psychology.* 1972;13:477-492.

5. Trehub SE. Infants' sensitivity to vowel and tonal contrasts. *Developmental Psychology.* 1973;9:91-96.

6. Lasky RE, Syrdal-Lasky A, Klein RE. VOT discrimination by four to six and a half month old infants from Spanish environments. *Journal of Experimental Child Psychology.* 1975;20:215-225.

7. Streeter LA. Language perception of 2-month old infants shows effects of both innate mechanisms and experience. *Nature.* 1976;259:39-41.

8. Trehub SE. The discrimination of foreign speech contrasts by infants and adults. *Child Development.* 1976;47:466-472.

9. Jusczyk PW, Pisoni DB, Mullennix J. Some consequences of stimulus variability on speech processing by 2-month old infants. *Cognition.* 1992;43:253-291.

10. Kuhl PK. Speech perception in early infancy: perceptual constancy for spectrally dissimilar vowel categories. *Journal of the Acoustical Society of America.* 1979;66:1668-1679.

11. Kuhl PK. Perception of auditory equivalence classes for speech in early infancy. *Infant Behavior and Development.* 1983;6:263-285.

12. Eimas PD, Miller JL. Contextual effects in infant speech perception. *Science.* 1980;209:1140-1141.

13. Miller JL, Eimas PD. Studies on the categorization of speech by infants. *Cognition.* 1983;13:135-165.

14. Werker JF, Tees RC. Cross-language speech perception: evidence for perceptual reorganization during the first year of life. *Infant Behavior and Development.* 1984;7:49-63.

15. Best CT, McRoberts GW, Sithole NM. Examination of the perceptual re-organization for speech contrasts: Zulu click discrimination by English-speaking adults and infants. *Journal of Experimental Psychology: Human Perception and Performance.* 1988;14:345-360.

16. Best CT, Lafleur R, McRoberts GW. Divergent developmental patterns for infants' perception of two non-native contrasts. *Infant Behavior and Development.* 1995;18:339-350.

17. Polka L, Bohn O-S. Cross-language comparison of vowel perception in English-learning and German-learning infants. *Journal of the Acoustical Society of America.* 1996;100:577-592.

18. Jusczyk PW, Friederici AD, Wessels J, Svenkerud VY, Jusczyk AM. Infants' sensitivity to the sound patterns of native language words. *Journal of Memory and Language.* 1993;32:402-420.

19. Jusczyk PW, Cutler A, Redanz N. Preference for the predominant stress patterns of English words. *Child Development.* 1993;64:675-687.

20. Jusczyk PW, Aslin RN. Infants' detection of sound patterns of words in fluent speech. *Cognitive Psychology.* 1995;29:1-23.

21. Jusczyk PW. Using the headturn preference procedure to study language acquisition. In: Bavin E, Burnham D, eds. *Advances in Infancy Research.* In press.

22. Kemler Nelson DG, Jusczyk PW, Mandel DR, Myers J, Turk A, Gerken LA. The Headturn Preference Procedure for testing auditory perception. *Infant Behavior & Development.* 1995;18:111-116.

23. Tincoff R, Jusczyk PW. Are word-final sounds perceptually salient for infants? Poster presented at the 5th Conference on Laboratory Phonology, Northwestern University, Evanston, Ill, 1996.

24. Lieberman P. *Intonation, Perception, and Language.* Cambridge, Mass: MIT Press; 1967.

25. Pollack I, Pickett JM. The intelligibility of excerpts from conversation. *Language and Speech.* 1964;6:161-171.

26. Martin CS, Mullennix JW, Pisoni DB, Summers WV. Effects of talker variability on recall of spoken

word lists. *Journal of Experimental Psychology: Learning, Memory, and Cognition.* 1989;15:676-684.

27. Mullennix JW, Pisoni DB, Martin CS. Some effects of talker variability on spoken word recognition. *Journal of the Acoustical Society of America.* 1989;85:365-378.

28. Mullennix JW, Pisoni DB. Stimulus variability and processing dependencies in speech perception. *Perception & Psychophysics.* 1990;47:379-390.

29. Houston D, Jusczyk PW, Tager J. Talker-specificity and the persistence of infants' word representations. In: Greenhill A, Hughes M, Littlefield H, Walsh H, eds. *Proceedings of the 22nd Annual Boston University Conference on Language Development.* Somerville, Mass: Cascadilla Press; 1998:385-396.

30. Jusczyk PW, Hohne EA. Infants' memory for spoken words. *Science.* 1997;277:1984-1986.

31. van de Weijer J. *Language Input for Word Discovery.* Nijmegen: University of Nijmegen; 1998. Dissertation.

32. Aslin RN, Woodward JZ, LaMendola NP, Bever TG. Models of word segmentation in fluent maternal speech to infants. In: Morgan JL, Demuth K, eds. *Signal to Syntax.* Hillsdale, NJ: Erlbaum; 1996: 117-134.

33. Church K. Phonological parsing and lexical retrieval. *Cognition.* 1987;25:53-69.

34. Hockett CF. *A Manual of Phonology.* Baltimore, Md: Waverly Press; 1955.

35. Lehiste I. *An Acoustic-Phonetic Study of Internal Open Juncture.* New York, NY: S. Karger; 1960.

36. Saffran JR, Newport EL, Aslin RN. Word segmentation: the role of distributional cues. *Journal of Memory and Language.* 1996;35:606-621.

37. Cutler A, Carter DM. The predominance of strong initial syllables in the English vocabulary. *Computer Speech and Language.* 1987;2:133-142.

38. Cutler A, Norris DG. The role of strong syllables in segmentation for lexical access. *Journal of Experimental Psychology: Human Perception and Performance.* 1988;14:113-121.

39. Cutler A. Exploiting prosodic probabilities in speech segmentation. In: Altmann GTM, ed. *Cognitive Models of Speech Processing: Psycholinguistic and Computational Perspectives.* Cambridge, Mass: MIT Press; 1990:105-121.

40. Cutler A, Butterfield S. Rhythmic cues to speech segmentation: evidence from juncture misperception. *Journal of Memory and Language.* 1992;31:218-236.

41. Saffran JR, Aslin RN, Newport EL. Statistical learning by 8-month-old infants. *Science.* 1996;274:1926-1928.

42. Aslin RN, Saffran JR, Newport EL. Computation of probability statistics by 8-month-old infants. *Psychological Science.* 1998;9:321-324.

43. Jusczyk PW, Hohne EA, Bauman A. Infants' sensitivity to allophonic cues for word segmentation. *Perception & Psychophysics.* In press.

44. Myers J, Jusczyk PW, Kemler Nelson DG, Charles Luce J, Woodward A, Hirsh-Pasek K. Infants' sensitivity to word boundaries in fluent speech. *Journal of Child Language.* 1996;23:1-30.

45. Benedict H. Early lexical development: comprehension and production. *Journal of Child Language.* 1979;6:183-201.

46. Huttenlocher J. The origins of language comprehension. In: Solso RL, ed. *Theories in Cognitive Psychology.* New York, NY: Wiley; 1974:331-368.

47. Oviatt SL. The emerging ability to comprehend language: an experimental approach. *Child Development.* 1980;51:97-106.

48. Thomas DG, Campos JJ, Shucard DW, Ramsay DS, Shucard J. Semantic comprehension in infancy: a signal detection analysis. *Child Development.* 1981;52:798-803.

49. Woodward AL, Markman EM, Fitzsimmons CM. Rapid word-learning in 13- and 18-month-olds. *Developmental Psychology.* 1994;30:553-566.

50. Tincoff R, Jusczyk PW. Some beginnings of word comprehension in 6-month-olds. *Psychological Science.* 1998;10:172-175.

51. Balaban MT, Waxman SR. Do words facilitate object categorization in 9-month-old infants? *Journal of Experimental Child Psychology.* 1997;64:3-26.

52. Cassidy KW, Kelly MH. Phonological information for grammatical category assignments. *Journal of Memory and Language.* 1991;30:348-369.

53. Kelly MH. Rhythmic alternation and lexical stress differences in English. *Cognition.* 1988;30:107-137.

54. Kelly MH. Using sound to solve syntactic problems: the role of phonology in grammatical category assignments. *Psychological Review.* 1992;99:349-364.

55. Nazzi T, Jusczyk PW, Bagarath K. Infants' segmentation of verbs from fluent speech. Presented at *Biennial Meeting of the Society for Research in Child Development,* Albuquerque, NM, 1999.

56. Mandel DR, Jusczyk PW, Kemler Nelson DG. Does sentential prosody help infants to organize and remember speech information? *Cognition.* 1994;53:155-180.

57. Mandel DR, Kemler Nelson DG, Jusczyk PW. Infants remember the order of words in a spoken sentence. *Cognitive Development.* 1996;11:181-196.

58. Gerken LA, Jusczyk PW, Mandel DR. When prosody fails to cue syntactic structure: nine-month-olds' sensitivity to phonological vs syntactic phrases. *Cognition.* 1994;51:237-265.

59. Jusczyk PW, Hirsh-Pasek K, Kemler Nelson DG, Kennedy L, Woodward A, Piwoz J. Perception of acoustic correlates of major phrasal units by young infants. *Cognitive Psychology.* 1992;24:252-293.

60. Shafer V, Gerken LA, Shucard J, Shucard D. "The" and the brain: an electrophysiological study of infants' sensitivity to English function morphemes. Presented at *Boston University Conference on Language Development,* Boston, Mass, 1992.

61. Shady M, Jusczyk PW, Gerken LA. Infants' sensitivity to function morphemes. Presented at *23rd Annual Boston University Conference on Language Development,* Boston, Mass, 1998.

Acknowledgments

Support for many of the research studies described in the present manuscript was facilitated by a Research Grant from NICHD (15795) and a Senior Scientist Award from NIMH (01490). In addition, the author wishes to thank Ann Marie Jusczyk for helpful comments that she made on an earlier version of this manuscript.

The Role of Experience in Early Language Development: Linguistic Experience Alters the Perception and Production of Speech

Patricia K. Kuhl, PhD

Introduction

How does an individual acquire a specific language? Is it appropriate to call it "learning" in the traditional sense?

Historically, two dramatically opposed views formed the cornerstones of the debate on language. In one view, a universal grammar and phonology are innately provided – input serves only to trigger the culturally appropriate version. In the other view, no innate knowledge is provided – language is acquired through a process of external feedback and reinforcement. Both theories are based on assumptions about the nature of language input to the child and the nature of the developmental change it induces. These theories may be revised in light of new data reviewed in this paper that demonstrate the effects of early language development in infants. For example, by 1 year of age, prior to the time infants begin to master higher levels of language, their perceptual and perceptual-motor systems have been altered by linguistic experience. Phonetic perception has changed dramatically to conform to the native-language pattern, and language-specific speech production has emerged. According to the model described here, this developmental change is caused by a complex "mapping" of linguistic input. This account is different in two respects from traditional views: (1) language input is not a trigger for innate options, and (2) the developmental change that occurs is not brought about through reinforcement contingencies.

What's New: The Historical Debate and a Modern View

At a recent conference, someone in the audience asked what the new data on language development had done for theory – essentially, the question was, "What's new?" After thinking for a moment I replied, "Everything."

The language debate was historically cast in terms of a confrontation between a strong nativist and a strong learning theorist. Chomsky's reply to Skinner's *Verbal Behavior*, published just over 40 years ago, ignited the debate.[1,2] In Chomsky's nativist view, language was innately specified as a set of universal rules, linguistic input served to "trigger" the appropriate subset of rules, and developmental change in language ability was viewed as biological growth akin to that of other bodily organs.[3,4] In the Skinnerian view, language was explicitly learned. Language was brought about in the child through a process of "shaping," explicit feedback, and the external control of reinforcement contingencies.[2]

Both views made assumptions about three critical parameters: the biological preparation infants bring to the task of language learning, the role of language input, and the nature of developmental change. Chomsky asserted, through the "poverty of the stimulus" argument, that language input to the child is greatly underspecified. Critical elements are missing; thus the necessity for innately specified information. Skinner viewed speech as simply another operant behavior, shaped through parental feedback and reinforcement as are all other behaviors.

In the decades that have passed since these positions were developed, new data have led to a revision of theory. This paper will primarily concentrate on the phonetic level of language, using the elementary components of sounds – the consonants and vowels that make up words – to structure an argument about what is given by nature and gained by experience in the acquisition of language. Studying the sound structure of language allows us to test the perception of language in infants just hours old, addressing the question of what language capacities are innate in infants. Then, by tracking the development of infants raised in various cultures listening to different languages, we can determine when infants begin to diverge based on experience with a particular language. This approach provides a strong test of the historically opposing views, and the results of the tests deliver dramatic evidence of the interaction between biology and culture.

New experiments address more than whether language is instinctual or learned; they teach us something about the actual steps involved in infants' acquisition of a particular language. The findings reveal how infants move from one level to another, acquiring novel information from exposure to language using strategies we had not predicted. The new data revise three aspects of theory: what we believe is innate, how we conceive of learning, and the role of language input in creating developmental change.

First, infants' innate abilities to perceptually separate the phonetic units of all languages are now considered to be shared by nonhuman animals, changing the view that infants' innate abilities are attributable to a specialized language module.[5,6] Second, our concept of learning is very different from the traditional form described by Skinner, wherein change is brought about through careful management of reinforcement contingencies and the "shaping" of responses. Instead, the kind of learning seen in language development is unconscious and requires no external reinforcement. Exposure to a particular language restructures infant perception early and in an interesting way – it resembles "mapping" rather than learning in the traditional sense.[6] What occurs during this "mapping," however, is not well captured by Chomsky's classic view that the growth of language is a maturational process in which experience sets innately determined parameters.[4] Last, the role of language input, particularly how we view what parents do when speaking to infants ("motherese" or "parentese"), is gaining in importance as we examine how the speech spoken to infants might assist them in the learning process.

Our understanding of infants' innate abilities, their early and avid mapping of language input, and the role played by caretakers in aiding the mapping, have led to an important shift in the theories of language development. Interestingly, the emerging view on language acquisition shares key elements with infants' acquisition of knowledge about people and objects.[7] The data and arguments produced in research on language have also had an impact in broader areas, including neuroscience,[8,9] neurobiology,[10] and computational modeling.[11]

Explaining Developmental Change in Speech

One of the puzzles in language development is the orderly transitions that all infants go through during development. Infants the world over achieve certain milestones in linguistic development at roughly the same time, regardless of the language to which they are exposed. Moreover, developmental change can include cases in which infants' early skills exceed their later ones. Explaining these transitions is one of the major goals of developmental linguistic theory.

One of these transitions occurs in speech perception. At birth, infants discern differences between all the phonetic units used in the world's languages regardless of the language environment in which they will be raised.[12] Indeed, where language is concerned, they are "citizens of the world" at birth. This capability is very advantageous – infants need not acquire the ability to hear the relevant distinctions between words, they hear them from the beginning. Data on nonhuman animals' perception of speech has demonstrated that nonhuman animals have the same skill.[13] The ability to partition the basic building blocks of speech was thus shown to be deeply rooted in our evolutionary history.[5]

If infants begin life as universal listeners, when do infants from different cultures begin to diverge? By the end of the first year, infants lose their ability to discriminate foreign-language sound contrasts[14]; they become more adultlike and have difficulty discriminating speech sounds not used in their native language. Adult native speakers of Japanese, for example, have great difficulty discriminating American English /r/ and /l/,[15,16] and American English listeners have great difficulty hearing the difference between Spanish /b/ and /p/.[17]

Studies show that infants rapidly make the transition from universal speech perception to one that is language specific. Our recent study in Japan demonstrated that 7-month-old Japanese infants responded to the American English /r-l/ distinction as accurately as American 7-month-olds. But by 10 months of age, Japanese infants no longer demonstrated this ability (Fig 1) while American infants had become even better at discriminating the two sounds.[18]

A similar transition occurs in speech production. Regardless of culture, all infants go through five distinct phases in the development of speech: *cooing* (1 to 4 months), in which infants produce sounds that resemble vowels; *canonical babbling* (5 to 10 months), during which infants produce strings of consonant-vowel syllables, such as "babababa" or "mamamama"; *first words* (10 to 15 months), wherein infants use a consistent phonetic form to refer to an object; *two-word utterances* (18 to 24 months), in which two words are combined in a meaningful way; and *meaningful speech* (15 months and beyond), in which infants produce both babbling and meaningful speech to

Fig 1. English /r-l/ discrimination by American and Japanese infants showing the effects of experience.

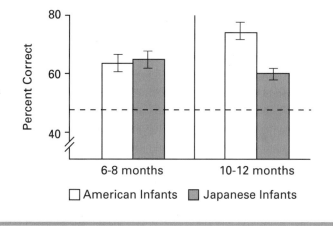

produce long, intonated utterances.[19] Interestingly, deaf infants exposed to a natural sign language, such as American Sign Language, are purported to follow the same progression using a visual-manual mode of communication.[20]

While infants begin life producing a universal set of utterances that cannot be distinguished, their utterances soon begin to diverge, reflecting the influence of the ambient language to which they are listening. By the end of the first year of life, the utterances of infants reared in different countries begin to be separable; infants show distinct patterns of speech production, both in the prosodic (intonational patterns) and phonetic aspects of language, that are unique to the culture in which they are being raised.[21] In adulthood, these distinctive speech patterns contribute to our "accents" when we attempt to speak another language.[22]

The transition in speech perception and production from a pattern that is initially universal to one that is highly specific presents one of the most intriguing problems in language acquisition. What causes the transition? We know that it is not simply maturational change. In the absence of natural language input, as in the case of socially isolated children, or abandoned children raised quite literally in the wild,[23-25] full-blown linguistic skills do not develop. Linguistic input and social interaction provided early in life appear to be necessary.

The thesis herein is that linguistic experience produces a special kind of developmental change. Language input alters the brain's processing of the signal, resulting in the creation of complex mental maps. The mapping *warps* underlying acoustic dimensions, altering perception in a way that highlights distinctive categories. This mapping is not like learning from the traditional psychological viewpoint. It depends on external information from the environment (language input), but it does not require explicit teaching or reinforcement contingencies. With exposure to language in a normal and socially interactive environment, language learning occurs, and the knowledge gained about a specific language is long-lasting and difficult to undo.

Language Experience Alters Perception

Hearing ambient language appears to produce a mapping that alters perception. A research finding that helps explain how this occurs is called the "perceptual magnet effect." It is observed when sound tokens perceived as exceptionally good representatives of a phonetic category ("prototypes") are used in tests of speech perception.[26]

Our results showed that what listeners considered a prototype of a phonetic category differed in speakers of different languages.[27-29] Moreover, they suggested that phonetic prototypes function like perceptual magnets for other sounds in the category.[26] For example, when listeners heard a phonetic prototype and attempted to discriminate it from sounds that surround it in acoustic space, the prototype displayed an attractor effect on the surrounding sounds. It perceptually pulled other members of the category toward it, making it difficult to hear differences between the prototype and surrounding stimuli. Nonprototypes did not have this magnet effect. A variety of experimental tasks produce this result with both consonants and vowels.[30-33]

Developmental tests revealed that the perceptual-magnet effect was exhibited by 6-month-old infants for the sounds of their native language.[26] In later studies, cross-language experiments showed that the magnet effect is the product of linguistic experience.[34] In the cross-language experiment, infants in the United States and Sweden were tested with two vowel prototypes, an American English vowel prototype, /i/ (as in "peep"), and a Swedish vowel prototype, /y/ (as in "fye"). The results demonstrated that the perceptual-magnet effect in 6-month-old infants was influenced by exposure to a particular language. American infants demonstrated the magnet effect only for the American English /i/; they treated the Swedish /y/ like a nonprototype.

Swedish infants showed the opposite pattern, demonstrating the magnet effect for the Swedish /y/ and treating the American English /i/ as a nonprototype. This is the youngest age at which language experience has been shown to affect phonetic perception.

The perceptual-magnet effect thus occurs prior to word learning. It appears that language input sculpts the brain to create a perceptual system that highlights the contrasts used in the language, while de-emphasizing those that do not, and this assists word learning.

"Warping" Perceptual Space

Tests on adults suggest that the magnet effect distorts perception to highlight sound contrasts in the native language. Studies conducted with adults from two cultures, America and Japan, on the perception of American English /r/ and /l/, illustrate this point. We used computer-synthesized syllables beginning with /r/ and /l/, spacing them at equal physical intervals in a two-dimensional acoustic grid (Fig 2). American and Japanese listeners identified the syllables, rated how well they sounded, and estimated how similar pairs of sounds were on a scale from 1 (very dissimilar) to 7 (very similar). Similarity ratings were scaled using multidimensional scaling techniques and provided a kind of map for each language group that indicated the perceived distance between the sounds in the grid.

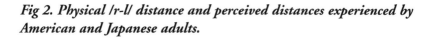

Fig 2. Physical /r-l/ distance and perceived distances experienced by American and Japanese adults.

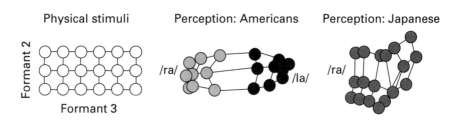

The resulting maps revealed that perception distorts physical space. The physical (acoustic) differences between pairs of stimuli were equal (Fig 2, left panel). However, perceived distance was "warped" (Fig 2, right panels). On the American map, perceptual space around the best /r/ and the best /l/ was greatly reduced for American listeners, as predicted by the perceptual-magnet effect, while the space near the boundary between the two categories was expanded.[31] In contrast, Japanese adults heard almost all the sounds as /r/; no /l/ sounds were identified, and there was a complete absence of magnet and boundary effects in the Japanese multidimensional scaling solution (Kuhl et al, unpublished data). The results suggest that linguistic experience results in the formation of perceptual maps specifying the perceived distances between speech stimuli and that the maps differ greatly across cultures.

The critical point is that neither group perceived physical reality, the actual physical differences between sounds. For each language group, experience altered perception to create a language-specific map of auditory similarities and differences. The map highlights sound contrasts of the speaker's native language by increasing internal category cohesion and maximizing the difference between categories. Moreover, the data suggest that American and Japanese people attend to different acoustic cues when listening to /r/ and /l/. Americans weight one dimension (Formant 3) more heavily than another (Formant 2), whereas Japanese adults do the opposite, weighting Formant 2 more heavily than Formant 3. (Formants are frequency regions in which the concentration of energy is very high. Formants are numbered [F1, F2, F3, etc] from low frequencies to high.)

Additional tests confirm this point across several languages for the exact same stimuli. Speakers of Mandarin,[35] German (Iverson et al, unpublished data), and Finnish[36] support the view that each language group develops a unique perceptual map for speech. The three languages are of interest because Mandarin speakers, like those of Japanese, perceive only one of the two sounds; but unlike the Japanese, Mandarins perceive /l/, not /r/. Both sounds are perceived by German and Finnish speakers, because /r/ and /l/ are used in both languages, but they are realized differently across languages (Finnish and German /r/s are trilled and the /l/s are darker).

The theoretical position supported by these data is that the development of these speech maps begins early in infancy. To use the example of our Japanese infants, their failure to discriminate American English /r/ from /l/ at 10 months of age, even though they did so perfectly well at 6 months of age, is assumed to be due to the mapping described here.[18] We predict, then, that Japanese infants will show the development of a magnet effect for Japanese /r/ between the ages of 7 and 10 months and that they would never show a magnet effect for American English /r/ and /l/. American infants should do the opposite, showing a magnet effect for American English /r/ and /l/ that develops between 7 and 10 months and never showing the effect for Japanese /r/.

There is also evidence to suggest that infants' "cue-weighting" is altered as they listen to speech. In a developmental study now in progress, 7-month-old American infants were tested with /r-l/ stimuli that neutralize either F2 or F3 while the other dimension is allowed to vary. The purpose of the test is to examine on which dimension infants rely more heavily when discriminating /r/ and /l/ and how this is changed by linguistic experience.[37] The data show that at 7 months (argued to be prior to magnet development for consonants), American infants discriminate the /r-l/ stimuli differing only in F2 better than they discriminate the /r-l/ stimuli differing only in F3. In other words, American 7-month-old infants weighted F2 more than F3 in discrimination, mimicking the pattern shown by Japanese adults. We are now examining infants at 11 to 12 months to see whether the F3 dimension becomes more important as infants are exposed to American English sounds. These studies suggest that in development, the entire phonetic space is being altered as the infant focuses on the sound patterns in his or her language and the acoustic information that distinguishes them.

These data on phonetic learning are consistent with those from other studies showing that older infants use information about phonetic units to recognize wordlike forms. Work by Jusczyk and colleagues shows that just prior to word learning, infants prefer word forms that are typical of the native language, ones in which the stress patterns and phonetic combinations conform to the native-language pattern.[38] At about this age, infants have also shown the capacity to learn the statistical probabilities of sound combinations contained in artificial words.[39] Infants' mapping at the phonetic level is thus seen as assisting them in breaking up the sound stream into higher-order units.

Forging the Link Between Speech Perception and Production

Infants also show dramatic change in speech production. Infants, who can only cry at birth, produce their first words at around 1 year using the phonetic units, vocal inflections, and stress and intonation patterns typical of the mother tongue. How do they learn to produce speech like a native speaker?

We know little of the process except that it critically depends on the ability to hear both oneself and others. Vocal learning – dependence on auditory input to acquire a vocal repertoire – is not common among mammals but is exhibited strikingly in human infants and in song birds.[40-42] A great deal of research suggests commonalities between the process in babies and birds.[43] Both groups show that hearing the vocalizations of others and hearing oneself produce sound are essential components in the development of vocalizations. Deaf infants do not babble normally,[44] nor do deafened birds.[45,46] Tracheotomy of infants at the time at which they would normally be babbling also produces abnormal patterns of development that persist.[47]

In the case of humans, speech patterns learned while young become difficult to alter later in life. Speakers who learn a second language after puberty, for example, produce it with an accent typical of their primary language.[48] Most speakers of a second language would like to speak like a native speaker, without a foreign accent, but this is difficult to do, even with long-term instruction.

Learning Our Native Accent

When do we adopt the indelible speech patterns that mark us as native speakers of a particular language for our entire lives? Developmental studies suggest that by 1 year of age, language-specific patterns of speech production appear in infants' spontaneous utterances.[21,49] The fundamental capacity to reproduce the sound patterns one hears, however, is in place much earlier. In a recent study, A.N. Meltzoff and I recorded infant utterances at 12, 16, and 20 weeks of age while the infants watched and listened to a video recording of a woman producing a vowel, either /a/, /i/, or /u/.[50] Infants watched the video for 5 minutes on each of 3 consecutive days. The results showed that there was developmental change in infants' vowel productions between 12 and 20 weeks of age. The areas of vowel space occupied by infants' /a/, /i/, and /u/ vowels became progressively more tightly clustered at each age, and by 20 weeks, a "vowel triangle" typical of that produced in every language of the world had emerged in infants' own region of the vowel space (Fig 3). This demonstrated that between 12 and 20 weeks of age, infants' sound productions were changing in a way that brought them closer to the adult pattern.

By 20 weeks, infants were also shown to imitate the vowels they heard. Infants exposed to /a/ were more likely to produce /a/ than they were either /i/ or /u/ when exposed to them; infants performed similarly when initially

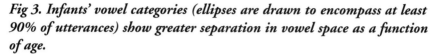

Fig 3. Infants' vowel categories (ellipses are drawn to encompass at least 90% of utterances) show greater separation in vowel space as a function of age.

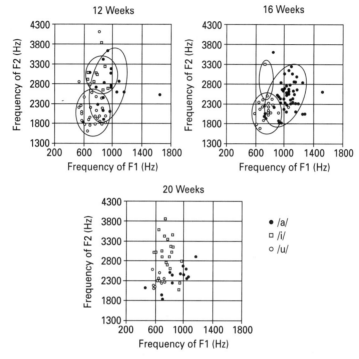

Reprinted with permission from Kuhl PK, Meltzoff AN. Infant vocalizations in response to speech: vocal imitation and developmental change. *Journal of the Acoustical Society of America.* 1996;100:2425-2438. Copyright 1996, Acoustical Society of America.

exposed to either /i/ or /u/. The total time of exposure to a specific vowel in the laboratory was only 15 minutes, yet this was sufficient to influence infants' productions. If 15 minutes of laboratory exposure to a vowel is sufficient to influence infants' vocalizations, then listening to ambient language for weeks would be expected to provide a powerful influence on infants' production of speech. These data suggest that infants' stored memories of speech not only alter their perception but alter production as well, serving as auditory patterns that guide vocal production. Stored representations of speech are thus viewed as the common cause for change in infants' perception and production during the first year.

Perception, Production, and Memory

This sequence of learning and self-organization, in which perceptual patterns stored in memory serve as guides for production, is strikingly similar in bird-song,[43] in visual-motor learning (in which nonspeech oral movements such as tongue protrusion and mouth opening are imitated),[51,52] and in language involving both sign and speech.[53,54] In each of these cases, perceptual experience establishes a representation that guides sensory-motor learning. In the case of infants and speech, perception affects production in the earliest stages of language learning, reinforcing the idea that the speech-motor patterns of a specific language are formed very early in life. Once learned, motor patterns may also further develop by altering the probability that infants will acquire words that contain items they are capable of producing.

Visual Cues

The link between perception and production can be seen in another experimental situation. Speech perception in adults is strongly affected by the sight of a talker's mouth movements, indicating that our brains recognize both auditory and visual information. One of the most compelling examples of this occurs when discrepant information is provided, for example, when auditory information for /b/ is combined with visual information for /g/.[55-58] The test subjects reported the phenomenal impression of an intermediate articulation (/da/ or /tha/) despite the fact that this information was not delivered by either sense modality. This is a very robust phenomenon and is readily obtained even when the information from the two senses comes from different speakers, such as when a male voice is combined with a female face.[56] In this case, the illusion is still unavoidable – our perceptual systems combine the multimodal information (auditory and visual) to give a unified percept.

Young infants are also affected by visual information. Infants just 18 to 20 weeks old recognize auditory-visual correspondences for speech, akin to what adults do when we lipread. In these studies, infants looked longer at a face pronouncing a vowel that matched the vowel sound they heard than at a mismatched face.[50] Additional demonstrations of auditory-visual speech perception in infants suggests that there is a left-hemisphere involvement in the process,[59] and more recent data suggest that the ability to match auditory and visual speech is present in newborns.[60,61]

The studies on vocal imitation and those on the role of visual information reinforce the views that knowledge of speech production is developing rapidly in the first year and that it is affected by listening to and watching the speech produced by caretakers.

Language Input to the Child

Given the profound effects of language environment on the infants' perception and production of speech, there is considerable interest in what infants are hearing. We estimate that by 6 months of age, infants have heard hundreds of thousands of instances of the vowel /i/ as in "mommy," "daddy," "baby," and "cookie." By 2 years of age, a typical listening day includes 20,000 to 40,000 words.[62] Moreover, we know that there is a novel speaking style (often called "motherese" or "parentese") used by caretakers around the world when they address infants and that infants prefer it over other complex acoustic signals.[63-65] This kind of speech is acoustically unique: it has a higher pitch, slower tempo, and exaggerated intonation contours, and it is syntactically and semantically simplified.

In new studies, we have uncovered another speech modification made by parents when addressing infants that may be important to learning. We examined natural language input at the phonetic level to infants in the United States, Russia, and Sweden and found that infant-directed speech exhibited a universal alteration of phonetic units compared with adult-directed speech.[66] Mothers' vowels in speech to infants were "hyperarticulated" and perceived by adults as better instances of vowel categories. This was seen in plots of the vowel's Formants. When the Formants of the vowels /a/ (as in "hop") /i/ (as in "heap") and /u/ (as in hoop) are connected, a vowel "triangle" emerges. The study demonstrated that mothers across these languages produced bigger vowel triangles when talking to their babies, meaning they used clearer speech (Fig 4).

As shown in Figure 4, mothers produced acoustically more extreme vowel sounds, resulting in a "stretching" of the vowel triangle. A stretched vowel triangle means that mothers are producing speech more carefully when talking to their babies. This not only makes speech more discriminable for infants, it highlights critical acoustic parameters that allow speech to be produced by the child. Parental speech thus contains more "prototypical" instances, and these are the very kinds of sounds that produce the perceptual magnet effect.

Fig 4. Infant-directed vowels (solid lines) are exaggerated, acoustically "stretching" the vowel triangle.

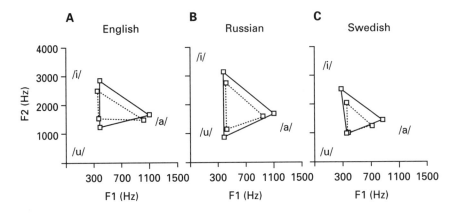

Language input to infants may therefore provide an ideal signal for constructing perceptual maps. The results suggest that at the phonetic level of language, linguistic input to infants provides exceptionally well-specified information about the units that form the building blocks for words.

A Theory of Speech Development

Given these findings, how might infants' innate language predispositions prepare them for experience? One view is a three-step model of speech development, the Native Language Magnet (NLM) model,[67] that includes the infants' innate abilities as well as changes brought about by experience with language (Fig 5).[67] The model demonstrates how infants' developing native-language speech representations might alter both perception and production of speech.

The following example of NLM is for vowels, although the same principles apply to both vowel and consonant perception.

Phase 1 describes infants' initial citizen-of-the-world abilities. At birth, they discriminate the phonetic distinctions of all languages. This is illustrated by a hypothetical vowel space partitioned into categories that separate the vowels

Fig 5. NLM posits initial boundaries (1), magnet development (2), and a restructuring of perception (3).

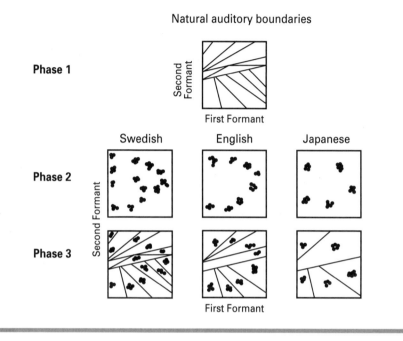

of all languages. According to NLM, infants' ability to hear all phonetic differences at this stage does not depend on specific language experience.

The divisions shown in Phase 1 initially structure perception in a phonetically relevant way but are not likely to be due to a "language module." This notion is buttressed by data on nonhuman animals that display abilities once thought to be exclusively human.[5,13,68-70] This has been interpreted as evidence that the evolution of speech capitalized on acoustical distinctions well separated by the mammalian auditory system.[5,41]

Phase 2 describes the vowel space at 6 months of age (this stage is presumed to be slightly later for consonants) for infants reared in three very different language environments, Swedish, English, and Japanese. At this stage, infants show evidence of language-specific magnet effects. The magnet effects stem from differences in the distributional properties of vowels heard by infants in the three countries.

Interesting but unanswered questions about Phase 2 magnet effects are how much language input it takes to show these effects, and whether all language heard by the child (including that from a radio or television) is effective in producing this kind of learning. At present we have no idea how much language infants must hear to produce this kind of learning. Moreover, it is unclear whether language from a disembodied source (television, radio) would be sufficient. Our estimates suggest that infants have heard thousands of instances of vowels in communication with their parents,[65] but that does not tell us what amount is necessary. Studies presently under way will provide some information regarding these issues.

Phase 3 shows how magnet effects recursively alter the initial state of speech perception and affect the processing of foreign-language stimuli. Magnet effects stretch and shrink the perceptual space, causing certain perceptual distinctions to be minimized while others are maximized. The consequence is that some of the boundaries that initially divided the space disappear as the perceptual space is reconfigured to incorporate a language's particular magnet placement. Magnet effects functionally erase certain boundaries – those relevant to foreign but not native languages. Listeners' auditory systems still process the acoustic differences that separate these categories, but their perceptual maps cause them to no longer pay attention.

In Phase 3, a perceptual space once characterized by basic "auditory cuts" – boundaries that divide all speech categories – has been replaced by a warped space that restructures perception. It is at this phase that infants begin to understand and produce their first words, but become unable to discriminate foreign-language contrasts. The mapping of incoming speech has altered the acoustic differences infants respond to, producing a language-specific listener and speaker.

What happens to infants exposed to two different languages? We are only beginning to study this issue, but the theory predicts that infants will develop magnet effects for the sound categories of both languages. Interestingly, preliminary data suggest that two sets of magnets are particularly likely to develop when the two languages are spoken by different speakers (mother speaks one language, father speaks another). As mentioned previously, we presume that mapping two languages, each spoken by a different speaker, is made easier when infants can perceptually separate the input from the two languages.

NLM theory offers an explanation for the developmental change observed in speech perception. A developing magnet pulls sounds that were once discriminable towards it, making them less discriminable. Magnet effects should therefore developmentally precede changes in infants' perception of foreign-language contrasts. The magnet effect also helps account for the results of studies on the perception of sounds from a foreign language by adults.[16,48] For example, NLM theory may help explain Japanese listeners' difficulty with American /r/ and /l/. The magnet effect for the Japanese /r/ category prototype (which is neither American /r/ nor /l/) will attract both /r/ and /l/, making the two sounds difficult for native-speaking Japanese people to discriminate (Kuhl et al, unpublished data). NLM theory argues that early experience established a complex perceptual network (a neural "filter") through which language passes. In this view, one's primary language and the map that results from early experience will determine how other languages are perceived. Speech production is similarly affected; the stored representations that altered speech perception serve as the guide to production, allowing infants' production of speech to become ever more precise as they focus on and imitate the patterns of spoken speech produced by adult speakers of the language.

Reinterpreting "Critical Periods"

The interaction between genetic programming and environmental stimulation is nowhere more evident than in the literature on critical periods in learning.[71,72] While critical periods were originally viewed as strictly timed developmental processes with rigid cutoff periods that restrict learning to a specific time frame, recent studies showing that learning can be stretched by a variety of factors has caused a shift in the terminology used to describe these periods. It is now understood that during "sensitive periods," exposure to specific kinds of information may be more effective than at other times but that a variety of factors can alter these periods of learning. Knudsen's work on the sound-localization system in the barn owl, for example, shows that the sensitive period for learning the auditory-visual map in the optic tectum can be altered by a variety of factors that either shorten or extend the learning period; the learning period closes much earlier, for instance, if experience occurs in a more natural environment.[73]

The idea that sensitive periods define "windows of opportunity" for learning, during which environmental stimulation is highly effective in producing developmental change, remains well supported both in the human and the animal literature. The ability to learn is not equivalent over time. The question is: What causes changes in the ability to learn over the lifespan?

The sensitive period denotes a process of learning that is constrained primarily by time or factors such as hormones that are outside the learning process itself. The work on speech, however, suggests an alternate possibility: Later learning may be limited by the fact that prior learning has itself altered the brain; the brain's altered structure may "interfere" with later learning. For instance, if NLM's argument that learning involves the creation of mental maps for speech turns out to be correct, it would suggest that learning "commits" neural structure in some way. Future speech processing would be affected by this neural structure. The mechanisms governing an organism's general ability to learn may not have changed. Rather, initial learning may result in a structure that reflects environmental input, and, once committed, this structure may interfere with the processing of information that does not conform to the learned pattern. On this account, initial learning alters future learning independently of a strictly timed period.

Regarding the relationship between neural structure and interference with future learning, the brain's "plasticity" could be governed from a statistical standpoint. When additional input does not cause the overall statistical distribution to change substantially, the organism becomes less sensitive to input. Hypothetically, for instance, the infant's representation of the vowel /a/ might not change when the millionth token of the vowel /a/ is heard. Plasticity might thus be independent of time but dependent on the amount and variability provided by experience. At some time in the lifetime of an organism, new input no longer substantially alters the underlying distribution, and this could, at least in theory, reduce the system's plasticity.

The interference theory may account for some aspects of second-language learning. When acquiring a second language, certain phonetic distinctions are notoriously difficult to master both in perception and production of speech. Take the case of the /r-l/ distinction for native speakers of Japanese. Hearing the distinction and producing it are very difficult for native speakers of Japanese.[74-76] According to NLM, this is because exposure to Japanese early in life altered the Japanese infant's perceptual system, resulting in magnet effects for the Japanese phoneme /r/ but not for American English /r/ or American English /l/. Once in place, Japanese magnet effects would not make it easy to process American English. American English /r/ and /l/ would be assimilated to Japanese /r/.

A second language learned later in life (after puberty) may require separation between the two systems to avoid interference. Data gathered using modern neuroimaging techniques indicate that adult bilinguals who learned both languages early in life activate closer regions of the brain when processing the two languages than do those who learned the second language later in life. In contrast, late bilinguals activated two very distinct regions of the brain for the two languages.[77] This is consistent with the idea that the brain's processing of a primary language can interfere with the second language.

The general thesis is that acquiring new phonetic categories as adults is difficult because the brain's mental maps for speech, formed on the basis of the primary language, are incompatible with those required for the new language; hence, interference results. Early in life, interference effects are minimal. Two new languages can be learned because two sets of maps develop. As mentioned earlier, limited evidence suggests that infants exposed to two languages do much better if each parent speaks one of the two languages, rather than both parents speaking both languages. This may be true because it is easier to map two different sets of phonetic categories (one for each of the two languages) if there is some way to keep them perceptually separate. Males and females produce speech in different frequency ranges, which could also make it easier to maintain the separation, if they each speak a different language.

These two factors – the temporal window governed by genetic factors and the neural commitment resulting from initial learning – could both be operating to produce constraints on learning a second language later in life. If a maturational process induces neural readiness at a particular time, input that misses this timing could reduce learning. At the same time, an interference produced by initial language learning might provide an independent mechanism that contributes to the difficulty in readily learning a second language in adulthood.

Future Directions

We are very interested in measurements of the brain that examine the effects of linguistic experience. Recently, we developed a procedure for measuring in young infants an event-related potential, MMN (mismatched negativity).

MMN is an auditory cortical evoked response that is triggered when a novel auditory stimulus is presented; it is especially sensitive to perceived acoustic changes. Recent studies have shown that MMN reflects experience-related changes. For example, MMN increases following training on speech stimuli and it mirrors improvements in behavioral performance.[78,79] Also, there are now a number of studies, in addition to ours,[80] that have successfully measured MMN in young awake infants.[81] Finally, the MMN response has been shown to be enhanced when a native-language phonetic prototype (as opposed to a foreign-language prototype) was used as the "mismatched" stimulus in studies of infants and adults.[28,82]

In a recently completed MMN study, we tested 6- to 12-month-old infants' responses to speech.[80] Thirty normally developing infants were tested at two ages (6 to 7 and 11 to 12 months). The auditory stimuli were computer-synthesized syllables (/ba/ and /wa/), which differ only in the critical acoustic information that distinguishes them. Stimuli were presented and electroencephalographic data acquired using Neuroscan hardware and software. Data were collected from electrode sites using an infant-sized Electrocap (Fig 6, left panel).

The MMN was obtained by subtracting the averaged waveforms for each subject under two conditions: the average of the standard and the average of the mismatches in the context of the standard. The difference wave, calculated by subtracting the two waveforms, reveals the MMN (Fig 6, right panel). The

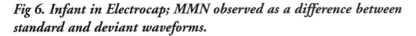

Fig 6. Infant in Electrocap; MMN observed as a difference between standard and deviant waveforms.

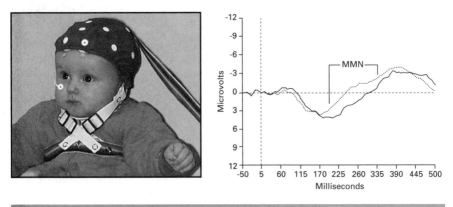

MMN was observed to be equally robust at the two ages for this native-language contrast and was shown to be stronger at electrode sites over the left than over the right hemisphere.

Conclusions

Research has shown that in the first year of life infants learn a great deal about the perceptual characteristics of their native language. According to the NLM model, perceptual learning early in life results in the formation of stored representations that capture native-language regularities. This theory emphasizes the role of linguistic input ("parentese") and the way in which it enhances speech contrasts. Infants map speech information, and the mapping creates a perceptual space in which distances near a sound category's most typical instances are shrunk and distances between categories are stretched. Perceptual maps differ in adults from different countries who have different native languages. The magnet effects and the mental maps they produce help explain how native-language speech develops, as well as our relative inability as adults to acquire a foreign language readily. In future studies, brain measures will be used to track the development of the infant brain's response to speech.

References

1. Chomsky N. A review of B.F. Skinner's Verbal Behavior. *Language.* 1957;35:26-58.

2. Skinner BF. *Verbal Behavior.* New York, NY: Appleton-Century-Crofts, Inc; 1957.

3. Chomsky N. *Aspects of the Theory of Syntax.* Cambridge, Mass: MIT Press; 1965.

4. Chomsky N. *Rules and Representations.* New York, NY: Columbia University Press; 1981.

5. Kuhl PK. Perception, cognition, and the ontogenetic and phylogenetic emergence of human speech. In: Brauth, SE, Hall, WS, Dooling, RJ, eds. *Plasticity of Development.* Cambridge, Mass: MIT Press; 1991:73-106.

6. Kuhl PK. The development of speech and language. In: Carew TJ, Menzel R, Shatz CJ, eds. *Mechanistic Relationships Between Development and Learning.* New York, NY: Wiley; 1998:53-73.

7. Gopnik A, Meltzoff AN, Kuhl PK. *The Scientist in the Crib: Minds, Brains, and How Children Learn.* New York, NY: William Morrow and Company, Inc; 1999.

8. Carew TJ, Menzel R, Shatz CJ. *Mechanistic Relationships Between Development and Learning.* New York, NY: Wiley; 1998.

9. Crair MC, Gillespie DC, Stryker MP. The role of visual experience in the development of columns in cat visual cortex. *Science.* 1998;279:566-570.

10. Brainard MS, Knudsen EI. Sensitive periods for visual calibration of the auditory space map in the barn owl optic tectum. *Journal of Neuroscience.* 1998;18:3929-3942.

11. Guenther FH, Gjaja MN. The perceptual magnet effect as an emergent property of neural map formation. *Journal of the Acoustical Society of America.* 1996;100:1111-1121.

12. Eimas PD, Miller JL, Jusczyk PW. On infant speech perception and the acquisition of language. In: Harnad S, ed. *Categorical Perception: The Groundwork of Cognition.* New York, NY: Cambridge University Press; 1987:161-195.

13. Kuhl PK, Miller JD. Speech perception by the chinchilla: voiced-voiceless distinction in alveolar plosive consonants. *Science.* 1975;190:69-72.

14. Werker JF, Tees RC. Cross-language speech perception: evidence for perceptual reorganization during the first year of life. *Infant Behavior and Development.* 1984;7:49-63.

15. Strange W, ed. *Speech Perception and Linguistic Experience: Issues in Cross-Language Research.* Timonium, Md: York; 1995

16. Best CT. Language-specific changes in non-native speech perception: a window on early phonological development. In: de Boysson-Bardies B, de Schonen S, Jusczyk P, McNeilage P, Morton J, eds. *Developmental Neurocognition: Speech and Face Processing in the First Year of Life.* Dordrecht, Netherlands: Kluwer Academic Publishers; 1993:289-304.

17. Abramson AS, Lisker L. Discriminability along the voicing continuum: cross-language tests. *Proceedings of the Sixth International Congress of Phonetic Sciences,* Prague, 1967. 1970:569-573.

18. Kuhl PK, Kiritani S, Deguchi T, Hayashi A, Stevens EB, Dugger CD, Iverson P. Effects of language experience on speech perception: American and Japanese infants' perception of /ra/ and /la/. *Journal of the Acoustical Society of America.* 1997;102:3135.

19. Ferguson CA, Menn L, Stoel-Gammon C, eds. *Phonological Development: Models, Research, Implications.* Timonium, Md: York; 1992.

20. Petitto LA. On the ontogenetic requirements for early language acquisition. In: de Boysson-Bardies B, de Schonen S, Jusczyk P, McNeilage P, Morton J, eds. *Developmental Neurocognition: Speech and Face Processing in the First Year of Life.* Dordrecht, Netherlands: Kluwer; 1993:365-383.

21. de Boysson-Bardies B. Ontogeny of language-specific syllabic productions. In: de Boysson-Bardies B, de Schonen S, Jusczyk P, McNeilage P, Morton J, eds. *Developmental Neurocognition: Speech and Face Processing in the First Year of Life.* Dordrecht, Netherlands: Kluwer Academic Publishers; 1993: 353-363.

22. Flege JE. Factors affecting degree of perceived foreign accent in English sentences. *Journal of the Acoustical Society of America.* 1988;84:70-79.

23. Fromkin V, Krashen S, Curtis S, Rigler D, Rigler M. The development of language in Genie: a case of language acquisition beyond the "critical period." *Brain & Language.* 1974;1:81-107.

24. Curtiss S. *Genie: A Psycholinguistic Study of a Modern Day "Wild Child."* New York, NY: Academic Press; 1977.

25. Lane HL. *The Wild Boy of Aveyron.* Cambridge, Mass: Harvard University Press; 1976.

26. Kuhl PK. Human adults and human infants show a "perceptual magnet effect" for the prototypes of speech categories, monkeys do not. *Perception & Psychophysics.* 1991;50:93-107.

27. Kuhl PK. Infants' perception and representation of speech: development of a new theory. In: Ohala JJ, Nearey TM, Derwing BL, Hodge MM, Wiebe GE, eds. *Proceedings of the International Conference on Spoken Language Processing.* Edmonton, Alberta: University of Alberta; 1992:449-456.

28. Näätänen R, Lehtokoski A, Lennes M, et al. Language-specific phoneme representations revealed by electric and magnetic brain responses. *Nature.* 1997;385:432-434.

29. Willerman R, Kuhl PK. Cross-language speech perception: Swedish, English, and Spanish speakers' perception of front rounded vowels. *Proceedings of the 1996 International Conference on Spoken Language Processing.* 1996;1:442-445.

30. Iverson P, Kuhl PK. Mapping the perceptual magnet effect for speech using signal detection theory and multidimensional scaling. *Journal of the Acoustical Society of America.* 1995;97:553-562.

31. Iverson P, Kuhl PK. Influences of phonetic identification and category goodness on American listeners' perception of /r/ and /l/. *Journal of the Acoustical Society of America.* 1996;99:1130-1140.

32. Sussman JE, Lauckner-Morano VJ. Further tests of the "perceptual magnet effect" in the perception of [i]: identification and change/no-change discrimination. *Journal of the Acoustical Society of America.* 1995;97:539-552.

33. Lotto AJ, Kluender KR. General contrast effects in speech perception: effect of preceding liquid on stop consonant identification. *Perception and Psychophysics.* 1988;60:602-619.

34. Kuhl PK, Williams KA, Lacerda F, Stevens KN, Lindblom B. Linguistic experience alters phonetic perception in infants by 6 months of age. *Science.* 1992;255:606-608.

35. Tsao FM, Hall M, Eyraud R, Kuhl PK. Perception of American English /r/ and /l/ by Mandarin speakers: influences of phonetic identification and category goodness. In: Kuhl PK, Crum L, eds. *Proceedings 16th International Congress on Acoustics and 135th Meeting of the Acoustical Society of America.* Woodbury, NY: Acoustical Society of America; 1998:2065-2066.

36. Eyraud R, Kuhl PK. Native and non-native phonetic speech perception of American and Finnish listeners. *Journal of the Acoustical Society of America.* 1996;100:2724.

37. Iverson P, Kuhl PK. Cue weighting for American English /r/ and /l/ by 7.5-month-old infants. *Journal of the Acoustical Society of America.* 1996;100:2725.

38. Jusczyk PW, Friederici AD, Wessels JMI, Svenkerud VY, Jusczyk AM. Infants' sensitivity to the sound patterns of native language words. *Journal of Memory and Language.* 1993;32:402-420.

39. Saffran JR, Aslin RN, Newport EL. Statistical learning by 8-month-old infants. *Science.* 1996;274: 1926-1928.

40. Marler P. Innate learning preferences: signals for communication. *Developmental Psychobiology.* 1990; 557:568.

41. Kuhl PK. On babies, birds, modules, and mechanisms: a comparative approach to the acquisition of vocal communication. In: Dooling RJ, Hulse SH, eds. *The Comparative Psychology of Audition: Perceiving Complex Sounds.* Hillsdale, NJ: Erlbaum; 1989:379-419.

42. Konishi M. Birdsong for neurobiologists. *Neuron.* 1989;3:541-549.

43. Doupe A, Kuhl PK. Birdsong and speech: common themes and mechanisms. *Annual Review of Neuroscience.* 1999. In press.

44. Oller DK, MacNeilage PF. Development of speech production: perspectives from natural and perturbed speech. In: MacNeilage PF, ed. *The Production of Speech.* New York, NY: Springer-Verlag; 1983:91-108.

45. Konishi M. Effects of deafening on song development in American robins and black-headed grosbeaks. *Zeitschrift für Tierpsychologie.* 1965;22:584-599.

46. Nottebohm F. The role of sensory feedback in the development of avian vocalizations. *Proceedings of the 14th International Ornithological Congress.* 1967:265-280.

47. Locke JL, Pearson DM. Linguistic significance of babbling: evidence from a tracheostomized infant. *Journal of Child Language.* 1990;17:1-16.

48. Flege JE. Production and perception of a novel, second-language phonetic contrast. *Journal of the Acoustical Society of America.* 1993;93:1589-1608.

49. Vihman MM, de Boysson-Bardies B. The nature and origins of ambient language influence on infant vocal production and early words. *Phonetica.* 1994;51:159-169.

50. Kuhl PK, Meltzoff AN. The bimodal perception of speech in infancy. *Science.* 1982;218:1138-1141.

51. Meltzoff AN, Moore MK. Imitation of facial and manual gestures by human neonates. *Science.* 1977;198:75-78.

52. Meltzoff AN, Moore MK. Imitation, memory, and the representation of persons. *Infant Behavior and Development.* 1994;17:83-99.

53. Petitto LA, Marentette PF. Babbling in the manual mode: evidence for the ontogeny of language. *Science.* 1991;251:1493-1496.

54. Kuhl PK, Meltzoff AN. Infant vocalizations in response to speech: vocal imitation and developmental change. *Journal of the Acoustical Society of America.* 1996;100:2425-2438.

55. McGurk H, MacDonald J. Hearing lips and seeing voices. *Nature.* 1976;264:746-748.

56. Green KP, Kuhl PK, Meltzoff AN, Stevens EB. Integrating speech information across talkers, gender, and sensory modality: female faces and male voices in the McGurk effect. *Perception & Psychophysics.* 1991;50:524-536.

57. Kuhl PK, Tsuzaki M, Tohkura Y, Meltzoff AN. Human processing of auditory-visual information in speech perception: potential for multimodal human-machine interfaces. In: *Proceedings of the International Conference on Spoken Language Processing.* Tokyo: Acoustical Society of Japan; 1994:539-542.

58. Massaro DW. *Speech Perception by Ear and Eye: A Paradigm for Psychological Inquiry.* Hillsdale, NJ: Erlbaum; 1987.

59. MacKain K, Studdert-Kennedy M, Spieker S, Stern D. Infant intermodal speech perception is a left-hemisphere function. *Science.* 1983;219:1347-1349.

60. Rosenblum LD, Schmuckler MA, Johnson JA. The McGurk effect in infants. *Perception & Psychophysics.* 1997;59:347-357.

61. Walton GE, Bower TGR. Newborns form "prototypes" is less than 1 minute. *Psychological Science.* 1993;4:203-205.

62. Chapman RS, Streim NW, Crais ER, Salmon D, Strand DEA, Negri NA. Child talk: assumptions of a developmental process model for early language learning. In: Chapman RA, ed. *Processes in Language Acquisition and Disorders.* St Louis, Mo: Mosby Year Book; 1992:3-19.

63. Fernald A. Four-month-old infants prefer to listen to motherese. *Infant Behavior and Development.* 1985;8:181-195.

64. Grieser DL, Kuhl PK. Maternal speech to infants in a tonal language: support for universal prosodic features in motherese. *Developmental Psychology.* 1988;24:14-20.

65. Fernald A, Kuhl P. Acoustic determinants of infant preference for motherese speech. *Infant Behavior and Development.* 1987;10:279-293.

66. Kuhl PK, Andruski JE, Chistovich IA, et al. Cross-language analysis of phonetic units in language addressed to infants. *Science.* 1997;277:684-686.

67. Kuhl PK. Learning and representation in speech and language. *Current Opinion in Neurobiology.* 1994;4:812-822.

68. Kuhl PK, Miller JD. Speech perception by the chinchilla: identification functions for synthetic VOT stimuli. *Journal of the Acoustical Society of America.* 1978;63:905-917.

69. Kluender KR, Diehl RL, Killeen PR. Japanese quail can learn phonetic categories. *Science.* 1987;237:1195-1197.

70. Dooling RJ, Best CT, Brown SD. Discrimination of synthetic full-formant and sinewave /ra-la/ continua by budgerigars (Melopsittacus undulatus) and zebra finches (Taeniopygia guttata). *Journal of the Acoustical Society of America.* 1995;97;1839-1846.

71. Thorpe WH. *Bird Song: The Biology of Vocal Communication and Expression in Birds.* New York, NY: Cambridge University Press; 1961.

72. Marler P. A comparative approach to vocal learning: song development in white-crowned sparrows. *Journal of Comparative and Physiological Psychology.* 1970;71:1-25.

73. Knudsen EI, Knudsen PF. Sensitive and critical periods for visual calibration of sound localization by barn owls. *Journal of Neuroscience.* 1990;10:222-232.

74. Goto H. Auditory perception by normal Japanese adults of the sounds "l" and "r." *Neuropsychologia.* 1971;9:317-323.

75. Miyawaki K, Strange W, Verbrugge R, Liberman AM, Jenkins JJ, Fujimura O. An effect of linguistic experience: the discrimination of [r] and [l] by native speakers of Japanese and English. *Perception & Psychophysics.* 1975;18:331-340.

76. Yamada RA, Tohkura Y. The effects of experimental variables on the perception of American English /r/ and /l/ by Japanese listeners. *Perception & Psychophysics.* 1992;52:376-392.

77. Kim KHS, Relkin NR, Lee KM, Hirsch J. Distinct cortical areas associated with native and second languages. *Nature.* 1997;388:172-174.

78. Kraus N, McGee T, Carrell T, Sharma A, Nicol T. Mismatch negativity to speech stimuli in school-age children. In: Karmos G, et al, eds. *Perspectives of Event-Related Potentials Research.* Dordrecht, Netherlands: Elsevier Science B.V.; 1995:211-217.

79. Tremblay KL, Kraus N, McGee T, Zecker S. The time course of learning: neurophysiologic changes during speech training. *Journal of the Acoustical Society of America.* 1998;103:2981.

80. Kuhl PK. Effects of language experience on speech perception. In: Kuhl PK, Crum L, eds. *Proceedings 16th International Congress on Acoustics and 135th Meeting of the Acoustical Society of America.* Woodbury, NY: Acoustical Society of America; 1998;3:1601-1602.

81. Pang EW, Edmonds GE, Desjardins R, Khan SC, Trainor LJ, Taylor MJ. Mismatch negativity to speech stimui in 8-month-old infants and adults. *International Journal of Psychophysiology.* 1998;29:227-236.

82. Cheour M, Ceponiene R, Lehtokoski A, et al. Development of language-specific phoneme representations in the infant brain. *Nature Neuroscience.* 1998;1:351-353.

Section 3:
Cognitive Development

Abstracts From Section 3. Cognitive Development

Development of Cognitive Functions Is Linked to the Prefrontal Cortex

Adele Diamond, PhD

The prefrontal cortex is involved in "executive functions" critical for higher-level problem solving, creative thought, and focused, sustained attention. Although full maturation is achieved by puberty or early adulthood, the prefrontal cortex makes possible important cognitive functions in infants as young as 9 months, and contributes to their ability to solve spatial problems and memory problems in creative ways. Cognitive deficits related to impaired or immature prefrontal cortex function may contribute to subtle learning and behavioral problems.

Born to Learn: What Infants Learn From Watching Us

Andrew N. Meltzoff, PhD

Imitation is a powerful form of learning commonly used by children, adults, and infants. A child's enthusiasm for imitative behavior prompts parental attention and interaction, and provides a mechanism for transmitting appropriate cultural and social behavior. Although simple imitative behavior is evident in the postnatal period, by around 14 months infants remember and repeat actions they observe in adults, other children, and on television. Imitation games provide early experience in mapping the similarities between self and other. Behavioral imitation, empathy, and moral sentiments may be part of the same developmental pathway.

Early Experience Matters for Spatial Development (But Different Kinds at Different Times)

Nora S. Newcombe, PhD

This paper reviews competing theories of cognitive/spatial development (as proposed by nativists, and followers of Piaget and Vygotsky) and discusses their salient features and shortcomings relative to each other and new research findings. Normal spatial development in the first year of life requires only a typical predictable environment in which children can explore and play. Beginning at 2 or 3 years of age, it is likely that children rely on cultural transmission to acquire understanding of symbols systems and mapping.

Development of Cognitive Functions Is Linked to the Prefrontal Cortex

Adele Diamond, PhD

Introduction: Babies Are Smarter Than People Thought

About a quarter of all cortex in the human brain is prefrontal cortex, located in the front of the brain, behind the forehead and in front of the motor areas. This is the region of the brain that has increased the most in size during the course of primate evolution and the region thought to be involved in "executive functions" critical for higher-level problem solving and creative thought. It is needed for focused, sustained attention, working memory, and inhibition of prepotent but inappropriate action tendencies. Not long ago, people thought that babies were not capable of these high-level abilities and that the prefrontal cortex did not function during the first few years of life. We now know, however, that even during the first year of life infants are capable of sophisticated cognitive operations, and there is a growing body of evidence that the prefrontal cortex makes possible important cognitive functions even during infancy (as early as 9 to 12 months of age).[1-4]

It is incorrect to assume that because the prefrontal cortex is not fully mature until puberty or early adulthood, it does not have any important cognitive functions during early life. Even though the prefrontal cortex will not be fully mature until years later, it is capable of performing cognitive operations before a child's first birthday. It would also be incorrect to assume that the prefrontal cortex is fully mature by 12 months of age in humans just because some of its functions begin to emerge by then. The prefrontal cortex continues to mature over the next 10, or even 20, years of a person's life, just as a person's cognitive development, while remarkable by 1 year, continues to unfold over the next 10 to 20 years.

Infants Are Creative Problem Solvers

Creativity and ingenuity are already evident before an infant's first birthday. For example, we all have a tendency to reach on a straight line for something we see that we want. If there is a barrier in the way, we have to detour around it. If a toy is placed in a transparent box open on one side, babies 6 to 8 months of age persist in trying to reach straight through the side of the box through which they are looking, instead of detouring around to the open side. By 8.5 to 9 months of age, infants start to get the idea of reaching through the open side. It is quite complicated, however, for an infant to plan a reach that goes off to the side and curves back around through an opening, and there is still the strong tendency to reach through the side through which they are looking.

Fig 1. Example of an "awkward reach" on both sides of box.

She leans down and looks into the right side.

Left side open, the young girl leans over and looks at the toy through opening.

She reaches awkwardly with far hand. (In this way, she can continue to look in opening and keep her hand in view.)

She reaches in awkwardly with her LEFT hand, keeping her eye on her hand and toy through opening.

To cope with these problems, infants of 8.5 to 9 months of age come up with a very clever and creative solution. They lean all the way over so they can look into the open side (Fig 1). This enables them to look along the line they will need to reach. Once down in that position, for instance if they are leaning to look into the right side of the box, their right arm is crumpled underneath them and is ready to help support them should they start to fall, so again they come up with a creative solution: They recruit their left hand to reach into the right side of the box and, similarly, their right hand to reach into the left side of the box. It looks very contorted and unusual (we call it the "awkward reach"), but it is a brilliant solution to their need at this age to be looking through the side into which they are reaching (AD, unpublished data).[1-3]

Infants Have Robust Memories

For years it was assumed that the memory support that is impaired when a person has amnesia matures late because children less than 2 years of age perform poorly on a test called the "delayed nonmatching to sample test,"which requires that memory system.[5,6] But that memory system functions quite well very early in infancy; it is another ability required for this test that matures late.

Earlier work with infants on the delayed matching to sample test – a classic test of the medial temporal lobe memory system that requires the ability to remember what you have just seen – revealed that toddlers cannot succeed on the test until they are almost 2 years old.[5,6] (See text box for details of the test.)

The delayed nonmatching to sample task

Here, a sample object is presented over a shallow "well" in the center of the testing table. The subject being tested displaces the sample to retrieve a reward from inside the well. A delay follows, then the familiar sample is presented to one side and a new object is presented to the other side, each over a well. The correct choice is to select the novel object, ie, the object that does not match the previously presented sample – hence the task's name (Fig 2). The well under the novel object contains a reward; the other well is empty. On each trial, new objects are used, and which side the novel one appears on is varied randomly over trials.

Fig 2. The delayed nonmatching sample test.

The test subject is expected to choose the novel stimulus object; that is, the stimulus that does not match the sample presented in 1. The smiley face indicates the location of the reward.

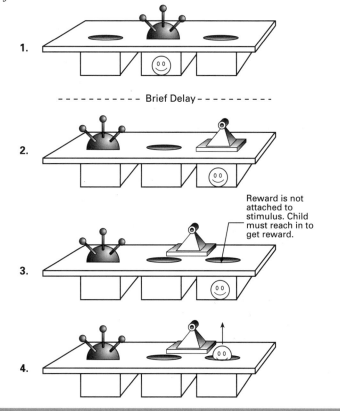

Given that success on this test appears so late in development and given that it has been shown convincingly and repeatedly that success requires proper functioning of the medial temporal lobe, it had been argued that the medial temporal lobe memory system must mature late.[7] The logic seemed reasonable: Here is a behavioral task that requires the functions the medial temporal lobe, but children cannot succeed on this task until quite late (21 months of age). Conclusion: This neural system must not be mature enough to subserve memory until about 21 months of age. That conclusion turns out to be incorrect, however. We now know that during the first year of life, infants can remember objects or actions they have seen for minutes, hours, days, and even weeks.[8-10]

But it is important to look at the *characteristics* of performance, not just success or failure rates, because a given test can be failed for many different reasons. Problems on a test can occur for various reasons, and different kinds of problems implicate different brain regions.

Similarly, developmental improvements on a task do not necessarily correspond to maturational changes in a particular neural region. In a broad sense, failure does not always mean a deficit in the single specific ability one was hoping to measure – success usually requires multiple abilities, not just the ability in which one is interested.

Consider the performance difference in human infants and in adult macaque monkeys with damage to the medial temporal lobe on the delayed nonmatching to sample test. Adult macaque monkeys with bilateral lesions of the medial temporal lobe (especially the rhinal cortical areas [perirhinal and entorhinal cortex]) do poorly on this task.[11-15] They appear to fail because they forget what the sample was. Consistent with this, their performance is better when there is a brief delay between sample and test (delays of 5, 10, or 15 seconds), and their performance progressively worsens as the delay increases to 60 seconds, 5 minutes, 10 minutes, and longer. Intact adult monkeys perform extremely well even after very long delays.

In contrast, human infants do not perform well, even with brief delays of 5 or 10 seconds.[5,6] Moreover, unlike adult macaques with medial temporal lobe lesions, whose performance progressively worsens with longer delays, when infants first succeed with the 5-second delay, they also succeed with delays of 30 and 60 seconds.[5]

If the developmental improvement on this test were measuring an improvement in memory, one would expect that young infants would succeed with brief delays and older, more mature children would succeed with longer delays. However, once children solve the task, they succeed after both long and short delays. Thus, one problem with making the leap from "performance on delayed nonmatching to sample is linked to the medial temporal lobe," to "therefore the developmental progression of performance on delayed nonmatching to sample must indicate the developmental progression of the medial temporal lobe" is that the performance characteristics of intact human infants are quite different from the performance characteristics of adult monkeys with damaged medial temporal lobes. Again, it is crucial to look at the characteristics of performance, and not just at success and failure rates.

A final argument against the theory of late medial temporal lobe memory system development is the large body of evidence of robust memory in very young infants. Indeed, if infants are not required to displace stimulus objects to receive the reward in the shallow well underneath but are allowed simply to explore the new stimulus objects themselves, infants as young as 6 months of age succeed on the task with delays as long as 3 minutes.[10]

Temporal vs Spatial Relationships

In being able to understand the relationship between one thing and another, a very small temporal separation can make a surprisingly large difference.

If infants have excellent memories even early in life, why then do they generally fail the delayed nonmatching to sample task until almost 2 years of age? The answer appears to be that infants do not understand the relationship between the reward in the shallow well and the stimulus object sitting on top of the well. For example, infants of only 9 to 12 months of age succeed on this test if the rewards are *attached* to the base of the sample (with Velcro®) instead of placed in wells *beneath* the sample (A. Diamond et al, In press, *Developmental Psychology*; see Fig 3). In the Velcro® condition, just as in the standard condition, the stimuli are placed atop wells, the rewards are in the wells below, and the rewards are separate objects from the stimuli; however, attaching the rewards to the stimuli with Velcro®, a seemingly minor variation in the procedure, appears to alter infants' understanding of the task dramatically.

Something very similar was observed in chimpanzees back in 1965 by Jarvik,[16] who asked why it takes a smart creature like a chimpanzee 100 to 200 trials to learn a simple color discrimination (eg, always choose red or always choose blue). Color discrimination is normally tested in primates by placing, for example, a red plaque over one shallow well and a blue plaque over another shallow well. The left-right placement of the two plaques is varied randomly over trials, but the reward is always under the plaque of a given color. Jarvik varied whether the reward was placed in the well under the plaque or taped to the underside of the plaque. When the reward was attached to the plaque, Jarvik found *one* trial learning.

In the Velcro® condition, the reward is physically closer to the stimulus than in the standard procedure. Is it that spatial proximity is that critical? Perhaps even a tiny spatial separation between stimulus and reward makes a task much more difficult than when there is no spatial separation at all.

Fig 3. Modified delayed nonmatching to sample.

In this test, the reward is affixed to the base of the novel object with Velcro®. The infant picks up the object and then pulls off the reward.

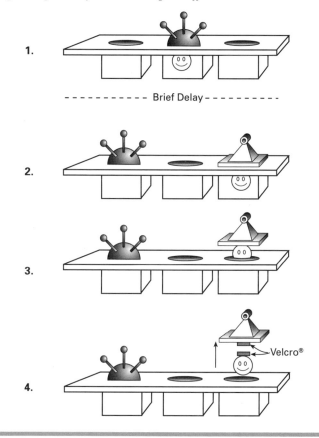

In the classic procedure, infants pick up the stimulus and then look into the well for the reward. There is thus a temporal gap between choosing a stimulus and seeing its reward. In the Velcro® procedure, when the rewards are attached to the base of stimuli, infants see the reward as soon as they lift and turn the stimulus. Instead of the reward remaining in the well, the reward moves with the stimulus. Could the critical factor be the close temporal proximity between displacing the stimulus and seeing the reward?

Is the Velcro® condition easy because of the close *spatial* proximity of the reward and stimulus or because of the close *temporal* proximity? To answer that question one needs to look at evidence from additional experiments.

We constructed an apparatus in which moving the correct stimulus triggered a jack-in-the-box to pop open behind it. The reward (the jack-in-the-box) was farther from the stimulus than in the classic procedure, but it was temporally closer, because it popped open immediately with the slightest movement of the stimulus.

Infants 9 and 12 months old perform every bit as well in the jack-in-the-box condition as they do in the Velcro® condition (Diamond & Lee, unpublished data). The tight temporal coupling of "reach-for-stimulus" and "jack-pops-up" almost makes it appear as if the stimulus is a trigger that causes the jack-in-the-box to pop open. This temporal proximity may enable infants to conceptualize the stimulus and the jack-in-the-box reward as connected, as two parts of a single unit. In both the Velcro® and jack-in-the-box conditions, the reward was temporally close to the stimulus. In the jack-in-the-box condition, however, the reward was spatially farther away from the stimulus than in even the standard condition. Thus, it appears that it is close temporal proximity between stimulus and reward that enables infants in the first year of life to begin to grasp the relationship between stimulus and reward.

Training, Experience, and Thresholds

Training and experience often have little effect until a child is at the threshold of acquiring a competence on his or her own. Thus, for example, Overman and colleagues tested infants every weekday, day after day, week after week, month after month, on the delayed nonmatching to sample test from 12 months of age onward.[6] Those infants succeeded at the same age (21 months on average) as the toddlers tested for the first time at 21 months by either Overman or Diamond, toddlers who had no prior experience with the task.[5,6]

On the task of reaching around a transparent barrier mentioned previously, I tried to see whether training experiences or cues would help infants succeed.[17] I found that cues or training helped only when infants were at the border of progressing to the next higher level of performance. Cues or training helped infants progress to the next level perhaps 2 weeks before they would have otherwise. When an infant was not near the border between one level and the next, however, nothing I tried made any difference. Infants could not profit from the cues or training until they were ready.

Measuring Function and Deficit

A global insult (such as lower or higher levels of a dietary amino acid) can have specific effects that do not show up on standard cognitive or behavioral tests.

Global measures, such as IQ tests, are poor indices of *specific* cognitive functions and poor indicators of what particular neural system might be affected if there is a problem. Developmental cognitive neuropsychologists now have precise measures of specific cognitive functions that are sensitive to the functions of particular neural subsystems. These measures can help in the study and treatment of diverse developmental disorders.

For example, cognitive deficits in children treated early and continuously for phenylketonuria (PKU) went officially unrecognized for many years because the children performed within the normal range on IQ tests, despite the protestations of parents and teachers that something was wrong. The global cognitive measures that were being used in the clinic were too imprecise.

The core problem in PKU is an inability to convert one amino acid, phenylalanine, into another amino acid, tyrosine. This is caused by a defect in the gene that codes for an enzyme, phenylalanine hydroxylase.[18,19] When a person who has PKU eats protein containing phenylalanine, it builds up in the bloodstream to levels that may be 20 to 30 times normal. Also, because phenylalanine is not converted to tyrosine, tyrosine levels are low (although not absent, because some tyrosine is also available in protein). Widespread brain damage and severe mental retardation result.[20,21] The treatment for PKU consists of limiting the amount of foods containing phenylalanine one eats. Eating a diet low in this amino acid succeeds in averting gross brain damage and produces children who have IQ scores in the normal range.[22,23] This is an example of an environmental, behavioral alteration that affects one's biochemistry and one's brain: Changing what children with PKU eat has a dramatic effect on the amino acid levels in their bloodstreams and, because of that, on the development of their brains.

Important cognitive problems are still evident, however.[24-26] The reason for this is that a diet low in phenylalanine rarely results in normal blood levels of this amino acid, because the diet must balance the need to minimize phenylalanine intake with the need for protein. The compromise diet reduces phenylalanine levels but not to normal concentrations, and does little to ameliorate the low blood levels of tyrosine. The consequence is that phenyl-alanine levels are mildly elevated and tyrosine levels are mildly reduced. Given that the levels of these amino acids in the bloodstream are not normal, it is perhaps not that surprising that there might be a problem. More surprising were the observations that the problems seemed to be *limited* to the cognitive functions dependent on the prefrontal cortex.[27] The clinical question became how could an amino acid imbalance affecting the entire body produce a specific effect limited to one region of the brain? The following model provides an explanation.

Because phenylalanine and tyrosine compete to cross into the brain, a moderate elevation in bloodstream phenylalanine results in a moderate reduction in the amount of tyrosine that reaches the brain.[28,29] Tyrosine is needed by the brain to make the neurotransmitter dopamine. Most dopamine systems in the brain can cope with modest changes in the level of tyrosine with no ill effects; however, the dopamine neurons that project to the prefrontal cortex are different from most other dopamine neurons – they fire faster and turn over dopamine faster.[30,31] This makes them sensitive to changes in the level of tyrosine that are too small to affect other regions of the brain.[32,33] Indeed, reductions in tyrosine too small to affect other dopamine systems in other neural regions profoundly reduce dopamine levels in the prefrontal cortex.[34] Reductions in dopamine in the prefrontal cortex have severe consequences on the cognitive functions that depend on this area of the brain.[35] In fact, drastically depleting the prefrontal cortex of dopamine produces cognitive deficits comparable to those caused by destroying the prefrontal cortex altogether.[36]

In a large, longitudinal study of children treated early and continuously for PKU, we found that children whose blood phenylalanine levels were 6 to 10 mg/dL (3 to 5 times normal), previously considered within the acceptable range, were impaired on tasks that required both holding information in mind (working memory) and inhibiting a dominant response (inhibitory control), tasks linked to dorsolateral prefrontal cortex.[4] The higher a child's current levels of phenylalanine, the worse that child's performance on these tests. These deficits were evident in all age groups (infants, toddlers, and young children) and remained significant even after we controlled for IQ, sex, health variables, and background characteristics. The deficits were clear whether the children were compared to other PKU children with lower phenylalanine levels, their own siblings, matched controls, or children from the general population. Children with PKU whose blood phenylalanine levels were 3 to 5 times normal were not impaired on any of the large battery of control tasks, which required functions dependent on other regions of the brain, such as the posterior parietal cortex or the medial temporal lobe. Because the functions of these areas were spared, the cognitive deficits appear to be selective.

How can children with serious deficits in their prefrontal cognitive abilities perform within the normal range on general IQ tests? It depends on how one defines "normal." "Within the normal range" means only IQs of 80 or better. Most children with PKU whose phenylalanine levels are 6 to 10 mg/dL have IQ scores in the 80s and 90s – as do most patients with damage to or destruction of the prefrontal cortex.[37] The prefrontal cortex is needed, for example, for problem solving, creativity, and manipulating several pieces of information at the same time. It is needed most when changed circumstances require some alteration of normal practice, or when new goals demand the modification of existing routines.[38] IQ tests, however, largely measure accumulated or stored knowledge. They test one's memory and past learning, and only in small measure, one's problem solving or creativity.

To investigate the biological mechanism more directly, my colleagues and I developed and characterized the first animal model of early- and continuously treated PKU.[39] This enabled us to study directly the effect of moderate, chronic phenylalanine elevations in the bloodstream on neurotransmitter levels in different brain regions. We found cognitive deficits (impaired performance on a behavioral task dependent on the prefrontal cortex) and reduced dopamine in the prefrontal cortex in the PKU animal model. In contrast, other neurotransmitters and other brain regions were much less affected.

Conclusion: The Prefrontal Cortex and Behavior

Young children can sometimes get stuck in a behavioral rut from which they cannot easily extricate themselves – despite their best intentions and despite knowing what correct performance entails. It is important to bear this in mind before mistakenly labeling a young child "bad," "intentionally difficult," or "willful."

It is not enough to know something or remember it; one must translate that knowledge into behavior. Infants and young children, in whom the prefrontal cortex is not yet mature, sometimes do the wrong thing even though they know what they should do and *are trying to do it*. For example, consider a child who has just been sorting a deck of cards by color and then is instructed to sort the cards by shape but continues sorting the cards by color – even though on each and every trial the child *correctly tells you what the new rule is and shows you where that means each card should be sorted.*[40] Because young children can sometimes have difficulty getting their actions to reflect their intentions, they may be labeled as "bad," "intentionally difficult," or "willful," when that is not the case.

The inhibitory ability dependent on the prefrontal cortex is important for many cognitive tasks. Consider that to sustain the focused concentration required for a difficult task, one needs to be able to resist distraction; to act in new ways, one needs to resist falling back into usual ways of acting or thinking; that is, one needs the inhibitory control ability that depends upon the prefrontal cortex. To relate several ideas and facts together, one must be able to resist focusing exclusively on just one idea or fact; to recombine ideas and facts in new, creative ways, one needs to be able to resist repeating old thought patterns; again, one needs the inhibitory control ability that comes from the prefrontal cortex.

It is easier for people to continue doing what they have been doing rather than to change, and it is easier to go on "automatic pilot" than to consider carefully what to do next. Sometimes, however, we need to change; sometimes we need to act differently than might have been our first inclination. The ability to exercise inhibitory control, which prefrontal cortex makes possible, frees us to act according to what *we choose to do* rather than being "unthinking" creatures of habit.

The ability to hold information in mind, which also depends on the prefrontal cortex, enables us to consider alternatives, to bring conceptual knowledge (and not just perceptual input) to bear on our decisions, and to consider our remembered past and our future hopes when planning our present actions. These two abilities, working memory and inhibitory control, make it possible for us to be creative problem solvers and to exercise free will and self-determination. Such capabilities are not needed all the time, but when they are needed, we would all like to be able to exercise them, and we would like the same for our children.

References

1. Diamond A. Differences between adult and infant cognition: is the crucial variable presence or absence of language? In: Weiskrantz L, ed. *Thought Without Language.* Oxford, England: Oxford University Press; 1988:337-370.

2. Diamond A. Neuropsychological insights into the meaning of object concept development. In: Carey S, Gelman R, eds. *The Epigenesis of Mind: Essays on Biology and Cognition.* Hillsdale, NJ: Lawrence Erlbaum Associates; 1991:67-110.

3. Diamond A. Frontal lobe involvement in cognitive changes during the first year of life. In: Gibson KR, Petersen AC, eds. *Brain Maturation and Cognitive Development: Comparative and Cross-Cultural Perspectives.* New York, NY: Aldine de Gruyter; 1991:127-180.

4. Diamond A, Prevor M, Callender G, Druin DP. Prefrontal cortex cognitive deficits in children treated early and continuously for PKU. *Monographs of the Society for Research in Child Development.* 1997;62(4):#252.

5. Diamond A, Towle C, Boyer K. Young children's performance on a task sensitive to the memory functions of the medial temporal lobe in adults – the delayed nonmatching-to-sample task – reveals problems that are due to non-memory-related task demands. *Behavioral Neuroscience.* 1994; 108:659-680.

6. Overman WH, Bachevalier J, Turner M, Peuster A. Object recognition versus object discrimination: comparison between human infants and infant monkeys. *Behavioral Neuroscience.* 1992;106:15-29.

7. Bachevalier J, Mishkin M. An early and a late developing system for learning and retention in infant monkeys. *Behavioral Neuroscience.* 1984;98:770-778.

8. Meltzoff AN. Towards a developmental cognitive science: the implications of cross-modal matching and imitation for the development of representation and memory in infancy. *Annals of the New York Academy of Sciences.* 1990;608:1-37.

9. Rovee-Collier C. Dissociations in infant memory: rethinking the development of implicit and explicit memory. *Psychological Review.* 1997;104:467-498.

10. Diamond A. Evidence of robust recognition memory early in life even when assessed by reaching behavior. *Journal of Experimental Child Psychology.* 1995;59(Special Issue):419-456.

11. Mishkin M. Memory in monkeys severely impaired by combined but not separate removal of amygdala and hippocampus. *Nature.* 1978;273:297-298.

12. Meunier M, Hadfield W, Bachevalier J, Murray EA. Effects of rhinal cortex lesions combined with hippocampectomy on visual recognition memory in rhesus monkeys. *Journal of Neurophysiology.* 1996;75:1190-1205.

13. Squire LR, Zola-Morgan S, Chen KS. Human amnesia and animal models of amnesia: performance of amnesic patients on tests designed for the monkey. *Behavioral Neuroscience.* 1988;102:210-221.

14. Zola-Morgan S, Squire LR, Amaral DG. Lesions of the hippocampal formation but not lesions of the fornix or mammillary nuclei produce long-lasting memory impairment in monkeys. *Journal of Neuroscience.* 1989;9:898-913.

15. Zola-Morgan S, Squire LR, Amaral DG. Lesions of the perirhinal and parahippocampal cortex that spare the amygdala and hippocampal formation produce severe memory impairment. *Journal of Neuroscience.* 1989;9:4355-4370.

16. Jarvik ME. Simple color discrimination in chimpanzees: effect of varying contiguity between cue and incentive. *Journal of Comparative and Physiological Psychology.* 1956;49:492-495.

17. Diamond A. Behavior changes between 6-12 months of age: what can they tell us about how the mind of the infant is changing? Cambridge, Mass: Harvard University; 1983. Dissertation.

18. Woo SLC, Lidsky AS, Güttler F, Chandra T, Robson KJH. Cloned human phenylalanine hydroxylase gene allows prenatal diagnosis and carrier detection of classical phenylketonuria. *Nature.* 1983;306:151-155.

19. DiLella AG, Marvit J, Lidsky AS, Güttler F, Woo SLC. Tight linkage between a splicing mutation and a specific DNA haplotype in phenylketonuria. *Nature.* 1986;322:799-803.

20. Hsia D Y-Y. Phenylketonuria and its variants. *Progress in Medical Genetics.* 1970;7:29-68.

21. Koch R, Azen C, Friedman EG, Williamson EL. Preliminary report on the effects of diet discontinuation in PKU. *Pediatrics.* 1982;100:870-875.

22. Bickel H, Hudson FP, Woolf LI, eds. *Phenylketonuria and Some Other Inborn Errors of Amino Acid Metabolism.* Stuttgart, Germany: Georg Thiese Verlag; 1971.

23. Holtzman NA, Kronmal RA, van Doornink W, Azen C, Koch R. Effect of age at loss of dietary control on intellectual performance and behavior of children with phenylketonuria. *New England Journal of Medicine.* 1986;314:593-598.

24. Dobson JC, Kushida E, Williamson ML, Friedman EG. Intellectual performance of 36 phenylketonuric patients and their non-affected siblings. *Pediatrics.* 1976;58:53-58.

25. Pennington BF, VanDoornick WJ, McCabe LL, McCabe ERB. Neuropsychological deficits in early treated phenylketonuric children. *American Journal of Mental Deficiency.* 1985;89:467-474.

26. Smith I, Beasley M. Intelligence and behaviour in children with early treated phenylketonuria. *European Journal of Clinical Nutrition.* 1989;43:1-5.

27. Welsh MC, Pennington BF, Ozonoff S, Rouse B, McCabe ERB. Neuropsychology of early-treated phenylketonuria: specific executive function deficits. *Child Development.* 1990;61:1697-1713.

28. Oldendorf WH. Stereospecificity of blood brain barrier permeability to amino acids. *American Journal of Physiology.* 1973;224:967-969.

29. Pardridge W. Regulation of amino acid availability to the brain. In: Wurtman RJ, Wurtman JJ, eds. *Nutrition and the Brain.* New York, NY: Raven Press; 1977:141-204.

30. Thierry AM, Tassin JP, Blanc A, Stinus L, Scatton B, Glowinski J. Discovery of the mesocortical dopaminergic system: some pharmacological and functional characteristics. *Advanced Biomedical Psychopharmacology.* 1977;16:5-12.

31. Bannon MJ, Bunney EB, Roth RH. Mesocortical dopamine neurons: rapid transmitter turnover compared to other brain catecholamine systems. *Brain Research.* 1981;218:376-382.

32. Wurtman RJ, Lorin F, Mostafapour S, Fernstrom JD. Brain catechol synthesis: control by brain tyrosine concentration. *Science.* 1974;185:183-184.

33. Tam S-Y, Elsworth JD, Bradberry CW, Roth RH. Mesocortical dopamine neurons: high basal firing frequency predicts tyrosine dependence of dopamine synthesis. *Journal of Neural Transmission.* 1990;81:97-110.

34. Bradberry CW, Karasic DH, Deutch AY, Roth RH. Regionally-specific alterations in mesotelencephalic dopamine synthesis in diabetic rats: association with precursor tyrosine. *Journal of Neural Transmission.* 1989;78:221-229.

35. Brozoski TJ, Brown RM, Rosvold HE, Goldman PS. Cognitive deficit caused by regional depletion of dopamine in prefrontal cortex of rhesus monkey. *Science.* 1979;205:929-932.

36. Sawaguchi T, Goldman-Rakic PS. D1 dopamine receptors in prefrontal cortex: involvement in working memory. *Science.* 1991;251:947-950.

37. Stuss DT, Benson DF. *The Frontal Lobes.* New York, NY: Raven Press; 1986.

38. Reason J, Mycielska K. *Absent-Minded? The Psychology of Mental Lapses and Everyday Errors.* Englewood Cliffs, NJ: Prentice-Hall; 1982.

39. Diamond A, Ciaramitaro V, Donner E, Djali S, Robinson M. An animal model of early-treated PKU. *Journal of Neuroscience.* 1994;14:3072-3082.

40. Zelazo PD, Frye D, Rapus T. An age-related dissociation between knowing rules and using them. *Cognitive Development.* 1996;11:37-63.

Born to Learn: What Infants Learn From Watching Us

Andrew N. Meltzoff, PhD

Introduction

Parents are being overwhelmed with information about their role in childrearing. Some headlines claim that "parents don't matter." Others lead parents to feel guilty because they matter too much – "early experience is destiny." Society is asking questions about the origins of thought, emotion, language, and personality. How should developmental scientists respond?

First, we should realize that our work is in the spotlight. From the White House to the state legislature, there is interest in research on early learning. Discoveries reported in *Science* and professional meetings are rapidly picked up by the media. Research about the mental life of babies no longer creeps quietly into the professional literature.

Second, basic researchers do not have to give up their day jobs to respond to society's call. Our studies of child development need not promise to cure teenage violence. There is plenty of room for those who want to stay close to the laboratory to study the basic mechanisms of learning and psychological development. Today's cutting-edge research turns into tomorrow's applications, and we can communicate that to policymakers.

Third, we can play a role in communicating the empirical discoveries to parents and healthcare professionals. This does not mean distorting the research. Rather, we should treat parents as intelligent consumers of information. Sharing the scientific discoveries can help them in two ways. Learning that babies and young children think, want, intend, and even perform their own mini-experiments, helps people see and enjoy babies in new ways. After all, such discoveries keep scientists going late at night, so why shouldn't it do the same for parents?[1] Also, communicating research and the scientific process can inoculate parents against the pseudoscience that surrounds them. We may not be able to stop the emergence of institutes that claim to build better babies but we can intrigue parents and policymakers in the value of genuine science. If astronomers can intelligently discuss the origins of the universe in newspapers carrying astrology, we can discuss the origins of the mind despite the pseudoscientific promises of those who claim to create super babies with pumped-up IQs and aesthetic tastes.

The goal of this paper is to organize a body of knowledge on early learning that should be useful for healthcare providers and policymakers. To show new research that infants are carefully watching our actions and committing them to memory. Babies naturally do as we do, not as we say, and what they see influences their behavior even after long intervals. Parents matter because babies are learning from us. Young children, even infants, look to us for guidance. This empiric research fascinates parents, and has policy implications.[2]

Born to Learn

Human beings are the most cognitively complex and behaviorally flexible of animals. Evolution has used an unlikely trick for achieving this state. Relative to most other animals, we are born "immature" and helpless.[3,4] Our extended period of infantile immaturity confers us with benefits. It allows us to learn and adapt to the specific physical environment into which we are born. Instead of relying on fixed reflexes adapted for a narrow ecological niche, our learning capacities allow us to colonize a wide range of ecological niches, from the Arctic to the Equator, modifying our dress and shelter accordingly. Also, it allows us to learn about the social environment. We organize ourselves into more different kinds of social groups, different cultures, than other species. Human cultures differ in terms of food, beliefs, and customs. Evolution's trick is that we are born to learn. Learning is to behavioral psychology what brain plasticity is to neuroscience.

Not surprisingly, we have evolved a special and very powerful form of learning. That form of learning is "imitation," the ability to learn behavior from observing the actions of others. Imitation is so commonplace among adults and children that it is often overlooked in infancy, but infants make good use of imitation. Understanding imitation in infancy changes the way we look at infants. In so doing, it changes the way we look at ourselves, because we begin to see ourselves reflected in the behavior of our youngest children.

The Value of Imitative Learning in Infancy

It is obvious that infants do not have the skills of adults, so what accounts for the developmental change? There are at least four sources of behavioral change in infancy: maturational changes in the sensory, motor, and cognitive systems; trial-and-error learning; independent invention and discovery; and imitative learning. The first three have been widely celebrated in the developmental literature, often at the expense of the fourth. A review of supporters of the first three reads like a *Who's Who* in psychology. Maturation was celebrated by Gesell in his famous studies on infancy at Yale. Trial-and-error learning was championed by Skinner. Independent invention and solitary discovery lay at the center of Piaget's theory. Missing from this list is a strong advocate for imitative learning. Bandura has emphasized the role of social learning in school-age children, but even he did not trace the origins of imitation back to infancy.

Imitative learning is useful for infants. It is more flexible and responsive to cultural norms than Gesell's maturation. It is safer than Skinnerian trial-and-error learning (who would want their own baby restricted to learning from dangerous errors?). It is faster than relying on Piagetian solitary discoveries. Our research program has been devoted to showing the importance, power, and functional significance of imitation to preverbal children.[5,6]

Learning to Use Novel Tools by Imitation

Human beings are consummate tool users, and some have argued that this played an important role in our evolutionary history. We use levers, wheels, and computers that enhance our natural powers. Evolutionary biologists used to think that tool use was unique to humans. Modern studies of animal behavior show that chimpanzees and other animals sometimes use simple tools to achieve their ends. Jane Goodall found that chimpanzees use sticks to fish for nutritious termites, for example.

Research has now shifted from simple documentation to finding out how animals learn to use tools. Mother chimpanzees do not deliberately instruct their young in the art of stick manufacture and use, and there is only scant evidence that the young learn by imitating their elders. Instead, the babies learn at first by picking up discarded sticks and enjoying a few remaining morsels. This gets them close to the termite nest while holding the tool, and trial-and-error learning and independent discovery cement the skill.[7]

In contrast, the human dyad is composed of parents who intentionally teach and babies who are prolific imitators. Our discussion here will focus on the babies, because they imitate even when we do not deliberately teach them. Consider the Western baby's favorite toy – the toy telephone.

There is nothing "natural" about holding objects to our ear while we speak to invisible people; however, our babies use toy telephones in this manner. They also pretend that other objects, like bananas, are telephones. Why do Western babies act this way? It is not due to maturation, trial-and-error learning, or independent discovery. It is attributable to imitative learning. Babies watch as we drop everything and dash to pick up the ringing telephone. Some of us carry telephones in our cars, on our belts, or in our purses. They must be important objects to command so much attention, so they are among the baby's favorite playthings.

We can conduct laboratory studies showing that very young infants observe and remember the way adults use objects. In one study, 14-month-old infants were shown how to perform particular actions on six novel objects. Each of the actions was demonstrated, but the experimenter never used the words, "do what I do" or "copy me." He simply performed the actions on the objects and then put the objects away. The infants were not allowed to touch the objects but were confined purely to watching what the adult did. This ensured that there was not any reinforcement or shaping by the adult. A 1-week memory delay was then interposed to assess whether the experience of watching the adult had an effect on the child's behavior.[8]

One of the actions was intentionally designed to be quite unusual. The object was a flat box with a yellow top panel. The adult looked at it, and then leaned forward and touched it with the top of his head, which made the top panel light up (Fig 1). The experimental question was whether the infants would imitate what they saw the adults do.

To make certain it was imitation, two other groups of infants were tested. Infants in Control-1 were not exposed to the adult model. They were simply given the toys to play with. This tested whether infants this age would produce the target actions spontaneously or by chance. Infants in the Control-2 group watched the same adult manipulate the same objects for the same length of time as in the imitation group – however, the adult did not demonstrate the target behaviors. This group controlled for the possibility that the infants would be "generally interested" in the toy because the adult was seen

Fig 1. A 14-month-old infant imitating the novel action of touching a panel with the forehead.

Infants often react with a smile, as shown in photo 6.

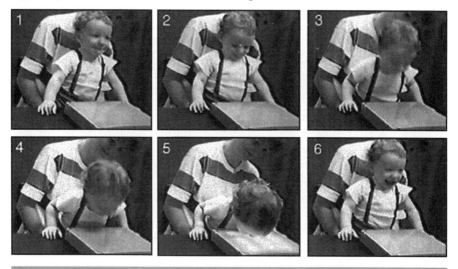

manipulating it, and that production of the target behavior resulted from trial and error.

The results demonstrated imitation after the 1-week delay. Infants in the imitation group produced significantly more of the target acts than did infants in either of the control groups. Moreover, infants even performed the novel action of head touching (Fig 1). Fully 67% of the infants in the imitation group leaned down and touched the panel with their foreheads when they were first presented with it after the 1-week delay. This is dramatic evidence for the power of imitative learning. None of the 24 control infants spontaneously leaned forward and touched the panel with their heads. This experiment illustrates that infants carefully watch what we do and repeat those actions when they are given a chance.

How Lasting Are the Effects of Early Social Experience?

What babies do, and how they behave with objects, often depends on what they have seen others do. Questions about how long their imitative learning lasts can be addressed by studies of what is called "deferred imitation." In one study, we demonstrated actions on objects for 14- or 18-month-old infants and then imposed a 2- or 4-month memory delay.[9] The infants remembered and imitated up to the 4-month delay, and they did so regardless of their age when they first acquired the information.

The results taught us something interesting about infant forgetting. Infants are not like (proverbial) elephants: They do forget. Fig 2 shows that with increasing delay, there was a decline in imitative performance (although performance after the 4-month delay was still above control-group levels). The results also reveal that the sharper drop-off was between the immediate and 2-month delay, rather than the 2- and 4-month delays. It thus seems that infant memory is like adult memory in that respect. Not all events make it into long-term memory (as shown by the large difference between the immediate and 2-month performance), but once an event is locked into long-term memory, it is long lasting and only gradually fades.

The mothers who accompanied the children were truly amazed at the duration of their children's memories. By their own report, they began to realize that what their babies saw them do made a long-lasting impression, and this altered their conceptions about what was going on in their babies' minds.

Fig 2. Mean number of target acts produced as a function of memory delay.

Infants remembered even after a 4-month delay, showing significantly higher performance than the controls at each delay.

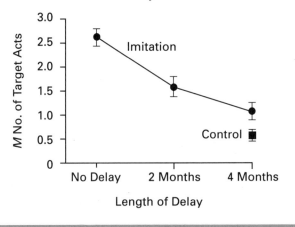

Early Memories Can Be Accessed in New Contexts

Another question concerns whether early memories are highly constrained or generalizable. An example makes this clear. In a series of studies, Rovee-Collier showed that 3- to 6-month-old babies can learn to kick their feet to make a mobile move.[10] She also discovered that if she inserted a delay of a few days, the babies would remember to kick when they saw the mobile again. These young babies looked pretty sophisticated. Further research, however, showed stunning limitations. The memory was highly context bound. Everything had to remain exactly the same for the infant to demonstrate memory. If infants were trained to kick in one crib and then moved to another crib where they saw the same mobile, their earlier experience had no effect. They had to learn all over again to kick to make it move. If the crib was moved to another room, they also failed to remember. The clinching experiment showed that even if babies were tested in the exact same crib in the same room but with a different pattern on the crib liner, their performance dropped to chance. They stared blankly at the mobile as if they had never seen it before just because they now saw it in a new context.

I wanted to test whether imitative memory was context bound. If it was, when infants learned something in the living room, they should not be able to remember and imitate it in the kitchen. Such context-bound learning could be interesting in the laboratory, but it would not have very far-reaching implications in everyday life.

In our study, infants watched an adult demonstrate actions on objects within an odd-looking tent.[11] The tent was constructed of orange and white polka dots and extended from floor to ceiling, filling the infants' entire field of view (Fig 3). Mothers were asked to wear blindfolds so that they did not see what the infants saw. A series of three studies were conducted with 12-month-old infants.

In Experiment 1, infants were randomly assigned to six independent groups. Infants in the two control groups did not see the target demonstrations so that the likelihood that they would produce the target acts by chance could be assessed. In the four experimental groups, length of delay (3-minute or 1-week) was crossed with context (no change or change). The context-change infants saw the initial demonstrations in the polka-dot tent and were subsequently tested in the plain laboratory room. The no-context-change infants saw the initial demonstration in the plain room and were subsequently tested for memory in that same room.

Fig 3. The polka-dot tent. Infants who learned in this context transferred their knowledge to more ordinary rooms.

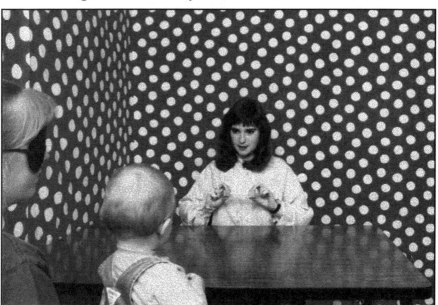

Reprinted with permission from Klein PJ, Meltzoff AN. Long-term memory, forgetting, and deferred imitation in 12-month old infants. *Developmental Science.* 1992;2:102-113. Copyright 1999 Blackwell Publishers.

The results were clear. Infants produced significantly more target acts after both the 3-minute and the 1-week delays, and they did so equally well, whether or not they changed context. Although there was a significant reduction in performance after the 1-week delay, showing forgetting, infants in the 1-week-delay group still produced significantly more target acts than the controls.

In the next experiment, we instituted a larger, more ecologically valid change in context by conducting the trials in the infants' homes. Infants in the imitation group saw the adult demonstrate target actions at the kitchen table, on the living room floor, or in other familiar play spaces. Infants in the control group were also visited at home by the experimenter but did not see demonstrations. After a 1-week delay, infants came into the laboratory and were tested by a different experimenter. Thus infants were tested in a novel context by a novel adult. The results showed that infants in the imitation group produced significantly more target acts than controls, again demonstrating long-term memory and generalization across a change in context.

Finally, we increased the length of the memory delay to 4 weeks. The results showed that 12-month-olds remembered the actions they saw for 4 weeks and easily generalized across the change in context. Taken together, this research established that imitative learning can be recovered in new settings. What infants see adults do affects their behavior even when we are not there to watch them. They carry the lessons they learn from us wherever they go.

Learning From Peers in Day-Care Centers

The ecology of child rearing is changing in the United States. With increasing numbers of women in the work force, infants are spending more time with peers in day-care settings. This raises the question – Do infants learn from and imitate their peers in day-care centers and other sites? In all previous experiments, adults were used as models. In the next series of studies we moved into the field, examining peer imitation in day-care centers and homes.[12]

The first study developed a controlled procedure for assessing peer imitation. Fourteen-month-old infants observed "tutor infants," 14-month-olds previously trained to play with the toys in novel ways. After observing the peers play with five objects, the "student infants" left the test room. They returned 5 minutes later and were presented with the test objects in the absence of the peers. The results showed imitation (see Fig 4). A second study used a day-care setting. The "tutor infant" was strapped into a car seat and driven to a variety of day-care sites. As the naive infants sat around a table, drinking juice, sucking their thumbs, and generally acting in a babylike manner, the tutor picked up and acted on novel toys in particular ways. The naive infants were not allowed to approach or touch the toys. After a 2-day delay, a new experimenter (not the one who had accompanied the tutor) brought a bag of objects to the infants' homes and laid them out on a convenient table or floor. Neither the parent nor this new experimenter had been present in the day-care center 2 days earlier. The only person who knew what actions had been demonstrated was the "student infant" him- or herself. The results showed significant imitation.

The fact that infants readily imitate actions they see performed by peers in day-care, and will bring those lessons home with them, indicates that

Fig 4. (A) A "tutor infant" demonstrates how to pull apart a novel toy. (B) After a delay, the "student infant" imitates the peer's action from memory.

imitation may play a role beyond the laboratory. Evidently, even prelinguistic infants are influenced by their peer groups at school.

Does It Matter That Infants Watch Television?

Of today's American homes, 99% have at least one TV set.[13] According to a Nielsen report, the average 2- to 5-year-old views about 28 hours per week of TV. There is evidence for purposive, selective, and systematic viewing by children between 2 and 3 years of age,[14] and research has revealed that by 3 years of age, 75% of American children can name their favorite TV program.[15] No wonder that the American Academy of Pediatrics issued new recommendations about children's TV viewing in the summer of 1999.

Although little work has been done concerning the amount of TV viewing by children under 2 years of age, home observations of infants reveal TV viewing interspersed throughout a typical day. Perhaps the most striking empiric evidence for the impact of TV on infants comes from work on TV exposure and early language. In one study, a 23-month-old listening to a commercial jingle suddenly began to croon, "Coke is it, Coke is it, Coke is it." Another repeated, "Diet Pepsi, one less calorie."[16]

This suggests that the audio track of TV may be picked up by infants, but it does not show that the visual images have a similar effect. There is little difference between "real" and "TV" speech, but this is not so with the visual modality. Television pictures present a miniaturized, two-dimensional depiction of three-dimensional space – Mae West did not want to appear on TV, because she despised being reduced to anything less than full size.

Can infants relate the activities they see on a miniature, 2D screen to the real, 3D world? To answer this it is not enough to know that infants are fascinated by TV. They may be attracted to the visually changing mosaic of colors. Visual attention does not mean that they "understand" or can "decode" what they see.

I used infants' tendency to reproduce events to get at this question.[17] I tested imitation from TV in a total of 120 infants at two ages, 14 and 24 months. In an immediate-imitation condition, infants watched an adult's action on TV and were allowed to copy with little delay. In the deferred-imitation condition, infants watched the action on TV but were not presented with the real toy until they returned to the lab after a 24-hour delay. The results showed significant imitation at both ages and that 14-month-olds imitated after the 1-day delay (see Fig 5).

The real objects were not in the infants' perceptual field during the televised display, so they did not have the opportunity of looking back and forth between the TV depiction and the real objects. Nonetheless, the results showed that infants used their memories of the TV action as a guide for how they should behave with the objects when they were exposed to them in the real world. In this sense, we can say that infants understood the actions they saw on TV and mapped them to the real 3D world.

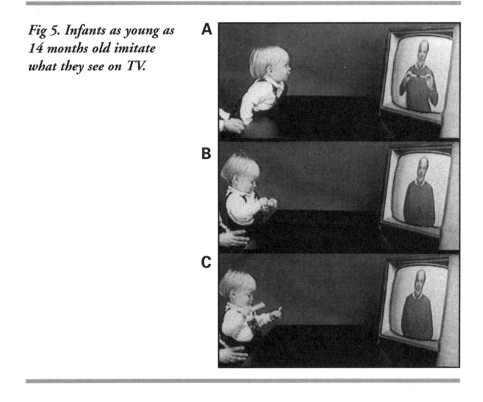

Fig 5. Infants as young as 14 months old imitate what they see on TV.

Admittedly, the test action was very simple and was purposely performed in a slow and deliberate manner, but knowing these results changes one's attitude. It is relevant to the debate of whether we should show young children television depicting violent use of knives, guns, or other weapons that may be around the house.[18,19] At least under ideal viewing conditions such as those used in the laboratory experiment, infants can learn from TV and will repeat what they see there. It is sobering.

Good-Enough Models: Infants Understand Our Intentions

In the studies discussed so far, the adult always demonstrated a well-formed act. The adult touched his head on a panel or pulled apart an object several times in plain view of the infant. In everyday interactions with children, however, adults are hurried and harried, and we do not behave perfectly. We often make mistakes and fail to complete our acts. The adult viewer "smooths over" this sloppiness. We hardly see the slips and mistakes but rather "see through" to what the adult was trying to do. Similarly, in language we often resort to, "You know what I mean," because we expect that from our interlocutor. The fact that we expect to see through meanings is apparent when we interact with computers. Computers take everything literally: "You stupid computer, don't you know what I mean?" The eerie literalness of computers makes them all the more inhuman.

At what age do babies begin to understand what we "mean to do" even if we don't successfully do it? When can they begin to understand the intentions lying behind our bumbling behavior? To address these questions, I traded on the infant's proclivity for imitation, but I used it in a new, more abstract way. I was not interested in whether the infants imitated the literal surface behavior shown to them, but rather in whether they read beyond the literal surface behavior to reenact something more abstract – the aim, intention, or goal of the act – even if it was not seen.

In this experiment, 18-month-old infants were shown a series of unsuccessful acts.[20] For example, the adult tried to perform a behavior, but his hand slipped. Thus the object was not transformed in any way, and the goal-state was not achieved. For other acts, the adult accidentally under- or overshot his target. To an adult, it was easy to read the actor's intentions. The experimental question was whether infants also could read through the surface behavior. The infants, who were too young to provide verbal reports, informed us how they interpreted the event by what they imitated. The results showed that infants could infer the goal of the act, even though it was never seen or achieved. Most infants reenacted what the adult meant to do, not what the adult actually did do.

This experiment indicates that infants can pick up information from the failed attempts of human actors. What if infants see the same movements produced by an inanimate device? A device was built that did not look human but nonetheless could mimic the movements of the actor (see Fig 6). The device had pincers that "grasped" a dumbbell on each end (just as the human hand did) and then pulled outward. These pincers then slipped off one end (just as the human hand did). The pattern of movements and the slipping motions were closely matched to human hand movements.

Fig 6. Human demonstrator (top panel) and inanimate device mimicking these movements (bottom).

Infants attributed goals to the person but not to the inanimate device.

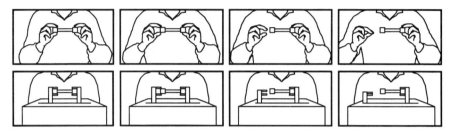

Reprinted with permission from Meltzoff AN. Understanding the intentions of others. Re-enactment of intended acts by 18-month old children. *Developmental Psychology.* 1995;31:838-850. Copyright 1995 American Psychological Association.

The infants were riveted by both displays (human and device); visual attention to the displays exceeded 98% for both. They were not more frightened by one display than by the other. The groups differed significantly, however, in their tendency to produce the target act. Infants who saw the human's failed attempt were six times more likely to produce the target behavior than infants in the other group. In fact, the infants who saw the movements of the inanimate device behaved virtually identically to infants in a baseline control group.

It appears that by 18 months of age, infants are already beginning to adopt an "intentional stance" toward their fellow human beings. They make an important differentiation between the acts of humans and the movements of inanimate devices. Human acts are not interpreted as mere movements in space, the transformations of an automaton with no deeper meaning. When they see an action they "read beyond" what was literally done and infer the goal or intention that lies behind it. This intention-reading skill we found in the laboratory also plays itself out in everyday life. It is probably why we feel that normally developing infants "get the gist" of what we are doing. Even though we may not act perfectly, toddlers respond to what we mean to do, rather than what we literally do. I have argued that this intention reading is an essential baby step toward the development of a "theory of mind," the idea that other humans do not just behave but have internal thoughts, emotions, and desires.[21-24] In my view, the development of understanding of another person's intentions may be a crucial first step along this developmental pathway.[25,26]

Infants Enjoy Being Imitated: The Nature of the Imitation Game

The social-developmental literature has reported that sensitive, middle-class parents play hours of imitation games with their babies. Infants shake a rattle and parents shake back; infants vocalize and parents do likewise. In the literature, the turn-taking aspect of these games is emphasized, the "rhythmic dance" between parent and child.[27-30] There is more to these games, however, than the timing. There is an additional value in the similarity of *form* in the participants' behavior. Reciprocal imitative games provide infants with special information about how they are like other people and how others are like them.

The salience of such behavior matching was tested in a series of studies with 14-month-olds.[31] In these studies, the infant sat across a table from two adults. One of the adults matched everything the infant did, and the other busily matched the behavior of a previous infant. Thus, both adults were acting like perfect babies, but only one adult was acting just like the subject being tested. The results showed that infants directed more visual attention and smiled more at the person who was imitating them. They preferred an adult who was playing a matching game.

Why did they prefer the adult playing the imitation game? At issue is whether infants prefer people who are acting "just *like* they act" (structural congruence) or "just *when* they act" (temporal contingency). To distinguish these alternatives I did another study in which both adults' actions were equally contingent on the infant's. Both experimenters sat passively until the infant performed one of the target actions on a predetermined list, and then both experimenters began to act in unison. One of the adults matched the infant, the other performed a mismatching response. The results again showed that the infant looked and smiled more at the matching adult. This proves that infants are sensitive to being imitated per se, not simply to the temporal contingencies.

This demonstration has several implications for clinical and applied work. In naturalistic interactions, parents speak in high-pitched, sing-song

"Motherese." Within the speech literature it is often remarked that the high fundamental frequency and pitch swoops may be alerting.[32] Given the current research, an additional reason that "Motherese" may be preferred by infants is that it is closer to the form of their own vocal productions. From a broader perspective, there may be deep psychological reasons that infants find mutual imitation games satisfying. It is interesting that therapists and marriage counselors often advise people to mirror back the thoughts and feelings of their partners. Patient: "I feel good about making that decision." Therapist: "You feel good?" Being imitated, having one's own behavior reflected by another, is a very salient experience for adults that facilitates communication. What we have discovered is that for the littlest humans, mirroring back behavior is also salient and affectively pleasing. It is no wonder that parents and children gleefully play mutual imitation games for long periods. If imitation is the sincerest form of flattery, infants and young children, like adults, apparently like to be flattered.

Innate Imitation

So far this review has discussed research in children in the second year of life – but imitation does not start there. Research in our laboratory has shown that there is a primitive capacity to mimic the actions of others starting from the neonatal period. In 1977, our research showed that 2- to 3-week-olds imitated tongue protrusion, mouth opening, lip protrusion, and simple finger movements (see Fig 7).[33] Because these findings did not fit with classic theory, they were initially the topic of much discussion in the field. The findings of early behavioral matching have now been replicated and extended in this country and cross-culturally in more than 24 different studies.[34] The effects are secure. The question is "how do infants do it?"

One possibility is that they learn to imitate very rapidly, during face-to-face interaction with their mothers in the first few weeks of life. To test this, we investigated newborns in a hospital setting. The average age of the infants tested was 32 hours, and the youngest infant was only 42 minutes old at the time of the test. The results again showed successful imitation.[35,36] Evidently, some primitive capacity for behavioral matching is present at birth.

Our hypothesis is that neonatal imitation is mediated by a process of "active intermodal mapping." The crux of this hypothesis is that imitation, even early imitation, is a matching-to-target process.[34,37] The goal or behavioral target is

Fig 7.
Imitation is
natural to
babies.

These
photographs
show imitative
responses in
2- to 3-week-
old infants.

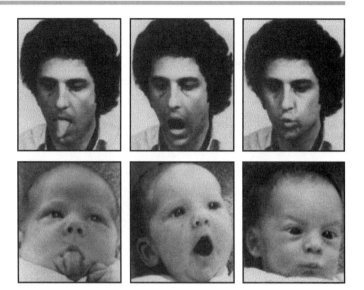

Reprinted with permission from Meltzoff AN, Moore MK. Imitation of facial and manual gestures in human neonates. *Science.* 1977;198:75-78. Copyright 1977 American Association for the Advancement of Science.

specified visually. Infants' self-produced movements provide proprioceptive feedback that can be compared with the visually specified target. Active intermodal mapping proposes that such comparison is possible because the perception and production of human movements are registered within a common "supramodal" representational system. Thus, although infants cannot see their own faces, their faces are not unperceived by them. They can monitor their lip and tongue movements through proprioception and compare this felt activity to what they see. Metaphorically, we can say that perception and production speak the same language; there is no need for "associating" the two through prolonged learning, because they are intimately bound at birth. In this view, infants may use imitation for subsequent learning, but they do not have to learn to imitate in the first place.

Conclusion: Some Developmental Speculations on the Role of Early Social Experiences

We are now in a position to examine the innate structure infants bring to their first encounters with other people and how this starting state is transformed through interpersonal interaction.

Let us start at the beginning. When a human act is shown to a newborn baby, it may provide a primordial "aha" experience. Human acts are especially relevant to infants because they look the way infants feel themselves to be and because they are things infants can intend. They may register: "Something interpretable: That seen event is like this felt event." On this view, it is not simply the features of the adults that are special for infants but the way the body moves and its relation to the self. Because human acts are seen in others and performed by the self, the infant can represent the other as "like me." Thus, the newborn is not a social isolate but is provided with a bridge connecting self and other. The imitation of bodily movements is a mechanism for making a primitive connection between self and other from the beginning of infancy.

Imitation is not only an initial toehold in self-other mapping but also provides a means for elaborating it. The same cognitive machinery that enables infants to imitate allows them to recognize when the social other is imitating them.

Human parents often act as good therapists, mirroring (and interpreting) infants' thoughts, feelings, and behaviors. When parents select certain behaviors to respond to in this way, it has significance not only because of the temporal contingencies involved but because infants can recognize the structural similarity between the adult's acts and their own. Imitative play thus offers a special channel for early communication, in which the timing and the form of the behavior give both partners an opportunity to share in the exchange. Mutual imitation produces a powerful impression in both the infant and the caretaker that they have psychologically "made contact," that they are in relationship.

Infants' ability to detect that something out there in the world is like them and can do what they do has cascading developmental effects. The reciprocal imitation games between parents and infants serve a didactic function, prompting infants to elaborate a sense of self and self-other correspondences beyond the neonatal level. The developmental progression would be from seeing a person as someone who behaves as they do, to seeing a person who shares deeper equivalences such as goals, desires, and intentions – and further along the developmental pathway, as someone eliciting feelings of empathy and demanding moral rights equivalent to one's own.

Imitation is thus thoroughly reciprocal for the baby, the parent, and the researcher. It is a channel through which we can learn about infants' minds and an avenue by which they come to understand ours. Infants are born to learn, and they learn at first by imitating us. This is why imitation is such an essential and far-reaching aspect of early development: It is not just a behavior but a means for learning who we are.

References

1. Gopnik A, Meltzoff AN. *Words, Thoughts, and Theories*. Cambridge, Mass: MIT Press; 1997.
2. Gopnik A, Meltzoff AN, Kuhl PK. *The Scientist in the Crib: Minds, Brains, and How Children Learn*. New York, NY: William Morrow & Co; 1999.
3. Bjorklund DF. The role of immaturity in human development. *Psychological Bulletin*. 1997;122: 153-169.
4. Bruner JS. Nature and uses of immaturity. *American Psychologist*. 1972;27:1-23.
5. Meltzoff AN, Moore MK. Object representation, identity, and the paradox of early permanence: steps toward a new framework. *Infant Behavior and Development*. 1998;21:201-235.
6. Meltzoff AN, Moore MK. Persons and representation: why infant imitation is important for theories of human development. In: Nadel J, Butterworth G, eds. *Imitation in Infancy*. New York, NY: Cambridge University Press; 1999:9-35.
7. Tomasello M, Call J. *Primate Cognition*. New York, NY: Oxford University Press; 1997.
8. Meltzoff AN. Infant imitation after a 1-week delay: long-term memory for novel acts and multiple stimuli. *Developmental Psychology*. 1988;24:470-476.
9. Meltzoff AN. What infant memory tells us about infantile amnesia: long-term recall and deferred imitation. *Journal of Experimental Child Psychology*. 1995;59:497-515.
10. Rovee-Collier C. The "memory system" of prelinguistic infants. In: Diamond A, ed. *Annals of the New York Academy of Sciences. The Development and Neural Bases of Higher Cognitive Functions*. New York, NY: New York Academy of Sciences; 1990:517-542.
11. Klein PJ, Meltzoff AN. Long-term memory, forgetting, and deferred imitation in 12-month-old infants. *Developmental Science*. 1999;2:102-113.
12. Hanna E, Meltzoff AN. Peer imitation by toddlers in laboratory, home, and day-care contexts: implications for social learning and memory. *Developmental Psychology*. 1993;29:701-710.
13. Singer JL, Singer DG. *Television, Imagination, and Aggression: A Study of Preschoolers*. Hillsdale, NJ: Erlbaum; 1981.
14. Anderson DR, Lorch EP. Looking at television: action or reaction? In: Bryant J, Anderson DR, eds. *Children's Understanding of Television: Research on Attention and Comprehension*. New York, NY: Academic Press; 1983:1-33.
15. Lyle J, Hoffman HR. Explorations in patterns of television viewing by preschool-age children. In: Rubinstein EA, Comstock GA, Murray JP, eds. *Television and Social Behavior. Vol 4. Television in Day-to-Day Life: Patterns of Use*. Washington, DC: US Government Printing Office; 1972:257-273.
16. Lemish D, Rice ML. Television as a talking picture book: a prop for language acquisition. *Journal of Child Language*. 1986;13:251-274.
17. Meltzoff AN. Imitation of televised models by infants. *Child Development*. 1988;59:1221-1229.
18. Centerwall BS. Television and violence: the scale of the problem and where to go from here. *Journal of the American Medical Association*. 1992;267:3059-3063.
19. Centerwall BS. Televison and the development of the superego: pathways to violence. In: Chiland C, Young JG, eds. *The Child and the Family*. Northvale, NJ: Jason Aronson; 1992:176-197.

20. Meltzoff AN. Understanding the intentions of others: re-enactment of intended acts by 18-month-old children. *Developmental Psychology.* 1995;31:838-850.

21. Flavell JH. Cognitive development: children's knowledge about the mind. *Annual Review of Psychology.* 1999;50:21-45.

22. Flavell JH, Miller PH. Social cognition. In: Kuhn D, Siegler R, eds. *Handbook of Child Psychology: Vol 2. Cognition, Perception, and Language.* New York, NY: John Wiley; 1998:851-898.

23. Taylor M. A theory of mind perspective on social cognitive development. In: Gelman R, Au T, eds. *Handbook of Perception and Cognition: Vol 13. Perceptual and Cognitive Development.* New York, NY: Academic Press; 1996:283-329.

24. Wellman HM. *The Child's Theory of Mind.* Cambridge, Mass: MIT Press; 1990.

25. Meltzoff AN, Gopnik A, Repacholi BM. Toddlers' understanding of intentions, desires, and emotions: explorations of the dark ages. In: Zelazo PD, Astington JW, Olson DR, eds. *Development of Intention and Intentional Understanding in Infancy and Early Childhood.* Mahwah, NJ: Erlbaum; 1999:17-41.

26. Meltzoff AN, Moore MK. Intersubjectivity: broadening the dialogue to include intention, identity, and imitation. In: Bråten S, ed. *Intersubjective Communication and Emotion in Early Ontogeny: A Sourcebook.* New York, NY: Cambridge University Press; 1999:47-62.

27. Brazelton TB, Koslowski B, Main M. The origins of reciprocity: the early mother-infant interaction. In: Lewis M, Rosenblum LA, eds. *The Effect of the Infant on its Caregiver,* New York, NY: Wiley; 1974:49-76.

28. Brazelton TB, Tronick E. Preverbal communication between mothers and infants. In: Olson DR, ed. *The Social Foundations of Language and Thought.* New York, NY: Norton; 1980:299-315.

29. Bruner JS. *Child's Talk: Learning to Use Language.* New York, NY: Norton; 1983.

30. Stern DN. *The Interpersonal World of the Infant: A View From Psychoanalysis and Developmental Psychology.* New York, NY: Basic Books; 1985.

31. Meltzoff AN. Foundations for developing a concept of self: the role of imitation in relating self to other and the value of social mirroring, social modeling, and self practice in infancy. In: Cicchetti D, Beeghly M, eds. *The Self in Transition: Infancy to Childhood.* Chicago, Ill: University of Chicago Press; 1990:139-164.

32. Fernald A, Kuhl PK. Acoustic determinants of infant preference for Motherese speech. *Infant Behavior and Development.* 1987;10:279-293.

33. Meltzoff AN, Moore MK. Imitation of facial and manual gestures by human neonates. *Science.* 1977;198:75-78.

34. Meltzoff AN, Moore MK. Explaining facial imitation: a theoretical model. *Early Development and Parenting.* 1997;6:179-192.

35. Meltzoff AN, Moore MK. Newborn infants imitate adult facial gestures. *Child Development.* 1983; 54:702-709.

36. Meltzoff AN, Moore MK. Imitation in newborn infants: exploring the range of gestures imitated and the underlying mechanisms. *Developmental Psychology.* 1989;25:954-962.

37. Meltzoff AN, Moore MK. Imitation, memory, and the representation of persons. *Infant Behavior and Development.* 1994;17:83-99.

Acknowlegment

Work on this chapter was supported by a grant from NIH (HD22514).

Early Experience Matters for Spatial Development (But Different Kinds at Different Times)

Nora S. Newcombe, PhD

Introduction

Everyone wants a bright, engaged, and happy child. How to achieve this end is, quite rightly, the focus of considerable professional interest and private advice giving, yet there is no consensus on what to do; indeed, various kinds of seemingly sage advice seem, on deeper examination, to conflict with one another. Consider the following two events, which might easily happen in any given day for a middle-class parent.

> On going to buy a present for a newly arrived nephew, the parent (call him Jack) spots a line of padded cloth toys and mobiles, made in patches of black and white with occasional splashes of red. The attached tags proclaim that "science has shown" that these toys speed infants' perceptual development. Babies focus on black-white contrast, the tag reads, so it is good to give them something to look at that will attract and guide their attention.

> After having acquired this development-promoting toy, Jack goes to a parents' meeting at his children's school. On the agenda are proposals to give minigrants to teacher-initiated curriculum ideas. One proposal is from a kindergarten teacher who wants to engage her children in reading and making maps of their community. "I don't really like this idea," says one parent, a former teacher. "I don't think children in kindergarten are developmentally ready to deal with maps."

Jack was puzzled by the contrast between these incidents. The positions seem to differ – the toy manufacturer has a model of development in which it can be accelerated and improved by stimulation, while the ex-teacher has a model of development in which stimulation is helpful only when children are ready for it. One model is "pushy," the other counsels restraint.

Strictly speaking, both the toy manufacturer and the ex-teacher could be right, because they considered different developmental periods. In fact, there is a middle ground between the toy manufacturer's and the teacher's positions, which can be called "critical-period conceptualization." In this view, *early* stimulation of infants is beneficial, indeed crucial, and careful attention should be paid to structuring and maximizing it. The impact of *later* stimulation is said (or implied) to be less dramatic (which means that formal education may work only when children are ready, as the teacher suggested). Critical-period conceptualization has lately attracted a good deal of attention, including coverage from the popular press, following the White House conference of 1997.

How can Jack decide which of these positions is scientifically supportable? A deep theoretical understanding of the nature of perceptual, cognitive, and emotional development should allow us to answer such questions. Unfortunately, more than a century of research and discussion has seemingly led to starkly contrasting viewpoints on the nature of early development, a daunting situation to those of us who claim that a good theory has applied value. Consider what we might conclude about early experience from three competing theories of cognitive development: nativism, Piagetian theory, and a Vygotskyan approach.

Nativism is the view that at birth all important ideas and abilities are innately specified and present, at least in some form, in the infant's nervous system. In terms of the role of early experience, this view teaches that any reasonable environment will lead to the inevitable unfolding of inborn potential. Nativism suggests that raising an intellectually competent child is simple, requiring nothing more than exposure to an environment that will trigger development. To use a cooking metaphor, the baby comes with a promise of "nothing to add but water."[1]

Piagetian theory is based on the work of Jean Piaget. This theory can be used in two very different ways in thinking about the role of early experience in development. On one hand, some aspects of Piagetian thought emphasize that interactions with almost any physical and social environment will allow the unfolding of normal cognitive development. This interpretation of Piaget comes close to agreeing with the nativists' "nothing to add but water" premise, although from a different theoretical perspective. (The Piagetian view places greater emphasis on the infant's activities leading to development, in contrast to the nativist view that important abilities are already specified at birth.) Theorists endorsing this style of Piagetian thinking tend to argue that children should be left alone to develop naturally rather than hurried along the path of development with enrichment programs.[2] This conclusion is similar to that reached by nativists even though based on a very different understanding of the nature of development.

On the other hand, some psychologists have argued for an interpretation of Piaget's theory that stresses the importance of a "match" between children's cognitive level and the experiences offered them.[3] This idea has led some early childhood education experts to propose curricula based on Piagetian principles. Such educators do not believe that there is "nothing to add but water" in children's development – instead they feel that caretakers make important contributions. (To pursue the cooking metaphor, development requires the correct ingredients, at the proper time.)

A third way to think about cognitive development comes from the writing of a Russian psychologist, *Lev Vygotsky*, who argued that the cultural transmission of language and tools for thought is essential to enriching the simple abilities present at birth.[4] Thus, he assigned a very high importance to early experience in determining the course of cognitive development. Vygotsky coined the phrase "zone of proximal development" to capture the idea that adults support early cognitive development by determining the areas into which a child's abilities can grow with support (or "scaffolding"), thereby allowing them to develop rapidly and easily. This idea is very similar to that of a "match" used in one style of Piagetian thought. More recently, Greenough has proposed that early spatial development is "experience-expectant" and, from the age of 3 years or so, spatial development is more "experience-dependent."[5]

Clearly, there are three divergent approaches to cognitive development that lead to divergent conceptualizations of the role of early experience, and each approach has its own body of supportive research. Consequently each approach has a corps of advocates who would advise "do nothing" or "buy clinically proven toys." Fortunately, an objective reality emerges for those willing to step back and broadly examine early infant development.

This paper will discuss three areas of research, each touching on one of the three different theoretical conceptualizations of development.

Nativism and its Shortcomings

Several investigators have suggested that the essential aspects of spatial understanding may be innately available to infants. This is based primarily on two kinds of evidence: First, it has been argued that very young children can perform spatial analysis based on metric coding (the coding of distance and direction), independent of visual input, based on one young blind child's performance on simple encoding and inference tasks.[6,7] Second, it has been argued that understanding space is a modular ability, based on evidence that young children rely on geometry, not landmarks, to reorient themselves following disorientation.[8-10] These observations have been widely accepted. For instance, Gallistel cited this work as evidence of the spatial competence of young children,[11] Geary used the work to justify the conclusion that certain aspects of sex differences in mathematics performance are built on innate foundations,[12] and Spelke and Newport regard the research as a foundation of a nativist approach to spatial understanding.[13] There are, however, many problems both with the data on these two points and with the conclusions drawn from them.

Early Appearance of Spatial Inference Without Visual Input

One of the cornerstones of nativism is a report by Landau and coworkers on research conducted with a 2½-year-old blind child named Kelli.[6,7] Kelli was tested in a room containing four objects, one at the midpoint of each of the four walls. She was taught the paths between some pairs of objects but not all (see Fig 1). Given this acquisition experience, she was reportedly able to infer the paths between novel pairs of objects. Such a performance, Landau and colleagues argued, indicated a Cartesian understanding of space, because only an encoding of distances and angles for the known objects would allow for the spatial inferences Kelli made. Furthermore, it was striking and surprising that Kelli was able to code information about distance and angle (and use it as a basis for inference) in the absence of vision, since her blindness prevented her from perceiving any two landmarks in the room simultaneously.

In critiquing this conclusion, it is useful to begin at the theoretical level and only then to consider the actual empirical work. The crux of the argument regarding Kelli's performance is that her ability to code spatial information

Fig 1. Layout for task used with Kelli.

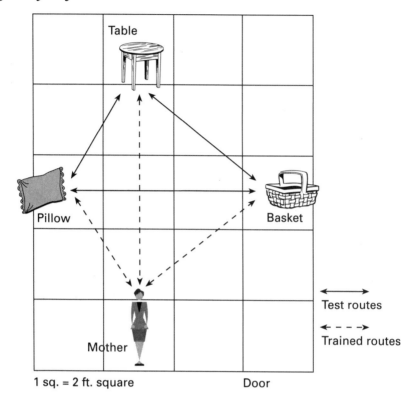

1 sq. = 2 ft. square

Adapted from Landau B, Spelke ES, Gleitman H. Spatial knowledge in a young blind child. *Cognition.* 1984;16:225-260.

and perform spatial inference, in the absence of visual input, indicates the presence of innate concepts of spatial metrics and Cartesian relationships. Unfortunately this argument is not clearly logical. Kelli lacks only vision; she is competent in her auditory, olfactory, and proprioceptive senses. It is very possible that these are sufficient for a 2-year-old to develop spatial coding and inference abilities. Perhaps such abilities can develop in the absence of the input clearly best suited to foster them.[14] That is a remarkable phenomenon, but it is hard to see how it is a proof of innateness.

Arguing about how to interpret Kelli's performance may be somewhat premature, however, because there are empiric problems with Landau's findings. First, the data from Kelli are not in good agreement with other research on the spatial abilities of blind individuals. Congenitally blind individuals generally have difficulties with spatial tasks, including quite basic spatial matters such as encoding distance and the angle subtended by objects, which varies as a function of distance.[15] They tend to represent routes in large-scale space as a progression of locations, rather than having an overall path representation, the formation of which may depend on being able to take in several distant locations in a single glance.[16] The degree of spatial impairment experienced by blind people is usually related to whether individuals had early vision.[17,18] Many comparisons of congenitally blind with sighted and visually impaired individuals indicate that some measure of visual experience, especially early in life, is necessary for the development of normal ability to gain spatial knowledge about the environment and construct accurate Euclidean relations,[19,20] although there may be some exceptions.[14] Thus, Kelli, blind since birth, would be exceptionally spatially talented if her performance was truly comparable with that of sighted children.

Was her performance comparable? Methodological critiques point out that the Landau procedure allowed for a good deal of inadvertent cuing from auditory and olfactory sources, as well as for self-correction by Kelli once she realized she had actually gone to the wrong goal.[18,21,22] Linked to these methodologic problems was the fact that the primary measure of Kelli's ability to make spatial inferences was her position when she stopped searching. Of course, prior to stopping, Kelli may have engaged in a good deal of exploration, self-correction, and on-line hypothesis testing. Indeed, an inspection of Kelli's published paths shows that they were far from direct (see Fig 2).

Although some of the methodologic flaws were corrected in later work with Kelli,[13] by the time these controls were used, Kelli was much older and may have learned to make simple spatial inferences because of her extensive experience with the situation and the task.[18] A recent attempt to replicate the Landau result yielded rather different findings. Even using the final-position measure that may allow for self-correction, Morrongiello and coworkers found that blind children were less accurate than age-matched sighted children.[23] Sighted children younger than 4 years of age, asked to wear blindfolds, were totally unwilling to perform task. Differences between blind and sighted children were thus found in children considerably older than Kelli, which further undermines the argument that spacial inference is early and easy.

It is noteworthy, however, that both the study with Kelli and the data gathered by Morrongiello suggest that blind children and blindfolded sighted

Fig 2. Paths taken by Kelli.

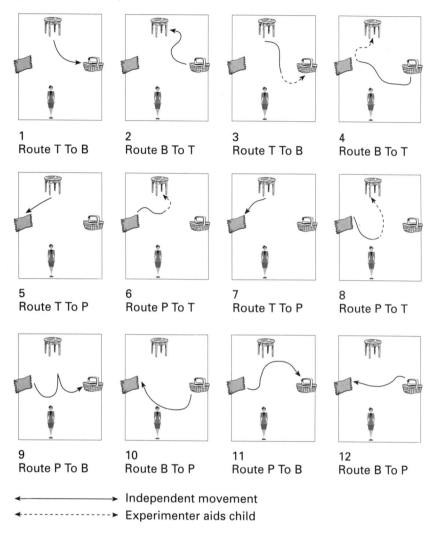

Adapted from Landau B, Spelke ES, Gleitman H. Spatial knowledge in a young blind child. *Cognition.* 1984;16:225-260.

children have a rough knowledge of location gained from inference in the absence of vision. For example, when blind children or sighted/blindfolded children are asked to *point* to a location that must be inferred, rather than go to it, both perform similarly – they do better than by random chance.

These findings are very important indicators of early competence, undermining claims by Piaget that early spatial coding is completely nonmetric or nonconfigural. The conclusion that young children can encode metric information is supported by other data as well. We have observed 16- to 24-month-olds searching for small toys buried in a 5-foot-long rectangular sandbox. The children did the task with impressive accuracy, showing that they were capable of remembering location in continuous space.[24]

The existing data on spatial inference in blind children suggest that their spatial development proceeds more slowly than in sighted children but that they eventually learn to construct spatial relationships on the basis of nonvisual experience. It appears that spatial abilities increase over time in response to perceptual and motoric feedback, rather than being mature early without relevant input. That is, rather than having innate access to Cartesian spatial understanding, children need perceptual and motoric interaction with the physical world to develop normal spatial skills.

Modularity

A second argument for innately based spatial understanding comes from recent data indicating that certain geometric principles constitute a "cognitive module" in the sense discussed by Fodor.[25] The basic idea of a module is that it consists of a set of operations that are self-contained and that operate without being affected by other potentially relevant sources of information. For example, we cannot force ourselves to see green instead of red using our will, because color perception is, in some sense, "encapsulated." Gallistel advanced a modular approach to spatial coding, relying heavily on a series of investigations of spatial coding in the rat conducted by Cheng.[11,26] In Cheng's work, rats were trained to dig for food in *one* of the corners of a rectangular enclosure. When they were disoriented, they were equally likely to dig in the correct corner or the diagonally opposite corner (diagonal angles are geometrically similar, with corresponding long and short sides). Most strikingly, the rats showed this pattern of search even when strong cues existed as to which of the two corners was actually correct, for instance, even when one of the sides of the enclosure was painted a bright color or when a distinctive odor marked the correct place. Gallistel argued that this imperviousness to cues showed the operation of an autonomous geometric module.

Hermer and Spelke, based on Gallistel's theory, argued for a modular view of early spatial coding in humans, suggesting that this module is penetrated by cognition relatively late in the course of development.[8,9] Basically, their studies with toddlers paralleled those conducted by Cheng with rats. They found, as had Cheng, that after disorientation, toddlers searched in areas defined geometrically, ignoring potentially helpful environmental cues (see Fig 3). Wang and Hermer replicated these findings with a child who had extensive experience in a room containing three white walls and one colored wall; despite this experience, the child never used the colored wall to help her decide in which corner a toy had been hidden after she had been disoriented.[27] Adults do, however, use the colored wall to find a hidden object, and Spelke suggested that they use linguistic coding to achieve this end.[10]

Fig 3. Search patterns of disoriented toddlers.

After being disoriented, toddlers searched for the toy using geometry (left side long – corner – right side short) rather than wall color. Note that they made almost the same frequency of errors whether or not they could cue off a blue colored wall, indicating that they ignored environmental clues.

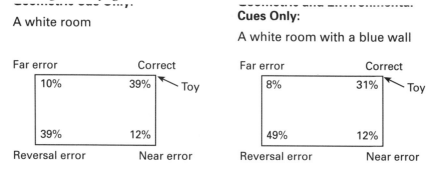

A white room

Cues Only:

A white room with a blue wall

Far error	Correct	Far error	Correct
10%	39% ↖ Toy	8%	31% ↖ Toy
39%	12%	49%	12%

Reversal error — Near error   Reversal error — Near error

Drawn from the data in Hermer and Spelke,[8,9] by permission.

The empiric phenomena reported by Hermer and Spelke are interesting and important. In particular, it is impressive that very young children not only code the length of walls (as they code distance in the sandbox in the Huttenlocher studies) but also use information about the relative length of the walls and left-right relationships to find objects (that is, they look for a hidden object based on whether the shorter wall is to the left or the right of the longer wall). But do these findings support a "geometry module"? Not using the blue wall as a landmark seems to support this claim, yet other findings in the literature place this conclusion in odd juxtaposition. For example, when place-learning and dead-reckoning systems conflict, the externally referenced system generally takes precedence, resetting both patterns of firing in hippocampal cells and actual spatial behavior.[28,29]

An alternative way to explain the lack of effect of landmarks in the Hermer-Spelke studies focuses on the kinds of landmarks they used. In some studies, the "landmarks" did not really qualify as landmarks, in that they were not stable (eg, toys such as trucks or dolls that the child had seen moved). In other studies, the "blue wall" was a piece of fabric with which the children played peekaboo. In some cases, the fabric was not always present in the room; children sometimes searched in an all-white room and sometimes in a room to which the fabric had been added. In any case, the color of a wall is not the kind of landmark typically studied in either the animal or the developmental literature. Using more typical (and truly permanent-looking) landmarks (a door and a bookcase), Learmonth, Newcombe, and Huttenlocher found that toddlers are able to use this information to find toys, even after effective disorientation.[30] This suggests that, while children do use geometric information, they do not possess an impenetrable geometric module, as proposed by nativist theorists.

Summary

The facts that support the nativist position are actually more consistent with an "interactional" model. In this view, the environment helps shape the nervous system (endowed at birth with considerable plasticity) rather than act as a mere trigger for preexisting behavioral modules. Blind children are able, albeit slowly, to learn to measure their spatial environment from nonvisual cues and to construct representations that allow them to infer distance and positions. Both blind and sighted children use a variety of spatial cues to learn location and navigate, including geometry (such as the relative length and orientation of walls), and stable permanent landmarks.

Considerable data support the idea that feedback from the environment is required to choose among systems when they conflict. For example, infants appear to begin spatial learning by paying attention to contiguous cues and their own motor actions, preferring the latter in situations of conflict. Later in the first year, in response both to the experiences afforded by crawling and to visual experience, this preference is adjusted to favor the role of cues.[31]

Nativists often respond to constructivists (or to environmentalists) by arguing that neonatal starting points are "fundamental" or "foundational," while environmental input, albeit required for normal development, is in some sense secondary. As Carey wrote, these theorists "conjecture that ordinary, intuitive cognitive development consists only of enrichment of innate structural principles."[32] Such claims are understandable as matters of emphasis or focus – one may be more interested in beginning points or in how environmental conditions change – but they are not statements about what would happen if the environment were radically changed. We tend to take a normal, expectable environment for granted, forgetting that development might be quite different in a science-fiction world in which there was no gravity or in which solid objects could pass through each other.[33] The fact that certain aspects of the environment do not normally vary widely does not mean that the environment does not play a crucial role in development.

Late "Natural" Development

Piaget's approach to spatial development was quite different from the nativist's. He held that spatial understanding was slowly constructed by the child from interactions with the physical world. While the environment played an important role in Piaget's thinking, he was famously hostile to the idea that manipulations of the environment could meaningfully hasten change, let alone enduringly optimize attained levels of competence.

One specific aspect of Piaget's approach to development was the idea that children take a decade to construct a mature system of spatial reference. This claim was based in large part on one of Piaget's most famous experiments. To examine whether young children can take the visual perspective of other observers, Piaget showed children of various ages a display consisting of three distinctive mountains (see Fig 4) and asked them to indicate what an observer located at another vantage point would see of the mountains. He found that children younger than 9 or 10 years old did not seem to be aware of what the other observer would see.[34] Piaget argued that these data showed a fundamental change in spatial representation: from an early "topological" form of spatial representation (in which only relations such as "closed or open" and "touching or separated" were encoded) to "projective" spatial representation (in which the orders of objects encountered along specific lines of projection were encoded).

Fig 4. Schematic representation of Piaget and Inhelder's experiment.[34]

Children were shown a model of three mountains and were unable to indicate what the scene would look like from other perspectives.

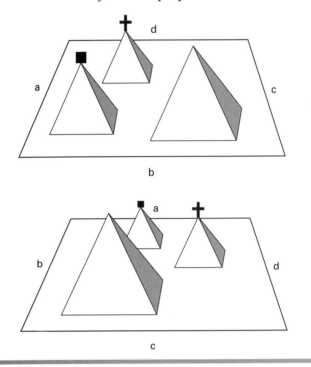

The idea that children have difficulty computing other observers' viewpoints is, however, questionable. Quite young children appear to have abilities in this area, and there is little evidence that their spatial representations are fundamentally different from those of older individuals. Instead, development may consist of the acquisition of strategies for dealing with intrinsically difficult task formats, strategies that can be taught to children through appropriate experience.

The key difficulty in Piaget's perspective-taking task seems to be that solving it requires picking from a set of alternative views, or making a model, both of which create a conflict between two frames of reference. Consider the classic perspective-taking situation, as shown in simplified form in Fig 5. A child sits facing a table, with a ball positioned on the left. The child, the table, and the ball are all, in turn, situated within a room that contains a desk, a cabinet, a

Fig 5. Example of room, array, and picture in a picture-selection task.

Diagram of original conditions

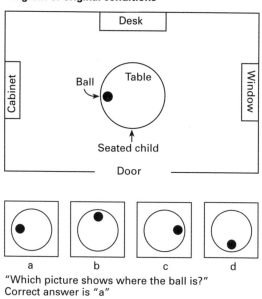

"Which picture shows where the ball is?"
Correct answer is "a"

Diagram with suggested new vantage point

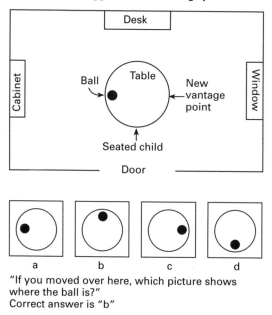

"If you moved over here, which picture shows
where the ball is?"
Correct answer is "b"

door, and a window. The most natural and powerful method of locating the ball, and one in place since the end of the second year of life, is to relate it to the external frame of reference, namely, the desk, cabinet, door, and window.

Suppose the child is asked to indicate what an observer at a new vantage point would see by pointing to a picture of that view. The correct picture shows the ball facing the child. But in this picture the ball is in the *wrong* position with respect to the existing frame of reference (ie, with the wrong relationship to landmarks such as desk, cabinet, etc). Picking this picture as the view from a new vantage point thus requires resolution of the conflict between the perceptually present frame of reference and the frame of reference the imagined observer would have.

The conflict between actual and imagined frames of reference in Piaget's task can be avoided by researchers when testing the ability to work out spatial relations from another point of view. Huttenlocher and Presson used what they called "item questions" instead of a selection task.[35] That is, they asked questions about what object would occupy a specified position with respect to another object, for example, "If you were over there, which toy would be closest to you?" They found that 9-year-old children had little difficulty answering item questions about other perspectives, even though they showed the usual problems with the classic task. Together with Janellen Huttenlocher, I demonstrated that children as young as 3 years old showed performance on item questions that was substantially above chance levels.[36] Preschool children seem to have relatively little difficulty with representing and reasoning about the location of objects if given specific reference points.

Given this analysis of perspective taking, it is natural and important to ask how *do* children eventually become able to solve the classic perspective-taking task. A likely possibility is that they learn to use a strategy that helps them overcome the conflict. Specifically, if one focuses on a single item in an array and asks oneself an item question about it ("If I were over there, what item would be in front?"), one can then use the answer to pick the correct picture or model. Bialystok found that 7-year-olds used such a strategy to a very limited extent but that it was consistently apparent by age 9 or 10.[37]

Although the present analysis highlights the nature of early competence in perspective taking, it does not deny that an important transition takes place in late childhood. The ability to deal with conflicting frames of reference using strategies is apparently not present until toward the end of elementary school. This ability is not to be dismissed; it is central to performing important spatial-cognitive tasks in the real world, as when an architect imagines how a building will look from a variety of perspectives and draws pictures of these views. From a functional point of view, adults and young children are quite different, because adults, unlike young children, are able to cope with such situations. Although adults take longer to answer classic perspective-taking questions than to answer item questions,[38] they can deal with conflicting frames of reference. Architects are happy to be able to use computer-assisted design to ensure swift and accurate visualization, but they did design buildings before such aids were available.

Summary

What develops with age on the perspective-taking task is not a fundamentally different form of spatial representation, as Piaget thought. Instead it is a strategy or set of strategies for dealing with a cognitive situation challenging to individuals of all ages: the situation in which two or more frames of reference must be maintained at once yet distinguished from each other and interrelated. The advent of success on such tasks in late childhood is a functionally significant transformation of cognitive ability. It is possible, however, to discuss perspectives with quite young children if one uses appropriate question formats. It is likely, although as yet undemonstrated, that exercises engaging perspective-taking skill and teaching appropriate transformation strategies could allow children in preschool or early elementary school to perform challenging spatial activities and accelerate the growth and eventual level of their spatial competence. At the least, there is no real basis for the ex-teacher's pessimism regarding the possibility of engaging kindergarten children in a meaningful spatial curriculum.

Spatial Symbolization

As sophisticated as human infants and toddlers are in many regards, they cannot be considered to have mature spatial competence until they can interpret spatial symbol systems. This is a uniquely human ability and one that allows us to learn from other people's experience as well as our own. Vygotsky believed that the transmission of such cultural inventions lay at the heart of cognitive development.[4] From this theoretical framework, one might think that appropriate teaching could lead to early development of mapping skills. However, Piaget and his adherents would say that preschool and elementary school children do not understand the concepts of proportionality and scaling necessary to interpret maps; this formal operational ability does not develop until early adolescence.

In truth, children are actually fairly inaccurate when they interpret maps to give distance and direction information. When asked to reproduce configurations of objects learned from a map, 4- and 5-year-olds reconstruct angular relations correctly, but they are not very accurate on scale, showing both shrinkage and expansion relative to a correct layout.[39] Preschoolers were better at scale translation when the configurations of objects were symmetric, but, of course, symmetry is uncommon on real maps. Preschoolers also have difficulty with metric placement of items, one at a time, in familiar classrooms.[40] Children of 6 and 7 years of age do better on reproduction tasks than preschoolers, although not as well as adults – who were, nevertheless, not perfect translators of scale.[39] Children as old as 7 years of age make substantial errors, usually of underestimation, when asked to use a map to place objects in a real space, and children through the age of 10 years perform worse than children of 11 to 13 years old.[41]

Piaget would see these findings as a vindication of his position, but Vygotsky would point out that children typically receive very little instruction in the use of maps and that there is no real way of knowing what abilities they might show in a supportive environment.

Our recent work has examined whether young children have some of the basic abilities that might put them in the "zone of proximal development" for building map understanding. Children's problems with the mapping tasks reviewed above may not derive from a fundamental inability to comprehend scale but rather from the complexity of the situations in which they have been tested. We recently studied 3- and 4-year-old children's use of a map of a 5-foot-long sandbox to acquire information about the location of a toy hidden in the sandbox.[42] This situation focuses the child's attention on only one object, whose location needs to be coded along only one dimension. The children were shown a dot in a small rectangle drawn on a piece of paper and asked to use this information to find a disc that had been hidden in the sandbox. To do this successfully, the children had to be able to encode proportional distance. The 4-year-olds, and even a good number of the 3-year-olds (15 of the 25 tested), were able to perform very well on this task, showing errors that averaged only 4 inches. This performance indicates an ability to scale observed distances in a simple situation – one in which only one object had to be considered at a time, in which only one dimension had to be considered, and in which the map was physically available to guide the search.

Interestingly, some of the 3-year-olds (10 of the 25 tested) were unable to use the map at all, with 6 of these 10 children simply pointing repeatedly to the same place, indicating a lack of understanding of the task. The fact that the 3-year-old group could be dichotomized easily into those who essentially did not understand the use of the map to give distance information and those who did as well as the 4-year-olds suggests that what we may be seeing here is insight. Similar changes, called "representational insight" by DeLoache,[43] have been found in children's understanding that an object or pictorial element can stand for something in the world.

Why do different studies show that scaling is difficult for older children but relatively easy for younger children? The answer may lie in a combination of changes in task understanding, increased ability to deal with task demands, and suppression of irrelevant task strategies. *First,* children in some of the studies may have been hindered by irrelevant response preferences (such as placing items in what look like "empty spaces" on maps).[40] *Second,* children may show difficulty where there are many spatial relationships to consider, thereby placing weighty demands on their working memory. Our study deliberately used a very simple scaling situation involving only one object and one dimension. *Third,* preschool children's scaling ability may depend on relative or proportional coding (eg, "a third of the way across") rather than on mathematical ratios. Relative coding allows an item to be located without measurement units, because perceptually present distances from edges can be compared directly (for example, the distance from one side is twice the distance from the other side). Use of measurement units and calculation of mathematical ratios using absolute distances based on such units may be a much later achievement.

Summary

The ability of 3- and 4-year-olds to deal with scaling shows evidence of initial early insight, which is followed by steady and progressive quantitative improvement in the ability to use maps. During the next 5 or 10 years, map- and model-reading skills greatly improve and the interpretation of scale becomes more precise. In addition, the ability to align the printed map and the real world becomes easier (but never simple) as children develop strategies for alignment, improve their ability to mentally rotate objects, become better planners, and develop comparison skills. All of these emerging talents eventually allow them to use maps in multistep navigation tasks. The building of these map skills likely requires cultural support – sequenced and guided instruction in the various components of map use.

Further understanding about the limits and possibilities of map instruction will come from greater systematic manipulation of inputs, as well as from observing whether children can learn from various types of exposure. For instance, one might explore how teaching measurement techniques relates to improvement in scaling on maps or, more directly, how teaching the principles of scaling improves scaling. Precise scaling requires mastery of multiplication and division, so one might also examine the reciprocal relationship between development of these mathematical skills and refinement of scale control in maps. The fact that spatial practice and input lead to spatial growth makes one optimistic that education can improve map skills, even for people who think of themselves as having difficulty with map tasks.[42,44,45]

The ability to acquire spatial information from symbolic representations such as maps (arguably what most radically distinguishes our cognitive abilities from those of other species) may not depend as completely on tutelage as Vygotsky imagined. Nevertheless, real map competence is culturally transmitted. Thus, external input is crucial to cognitive development, which does not proceed optimally without teaching.

Conclusion

This analysis of the literature reveals there is scant support for the idea that there is "nothing to add but water," and early experience *does* play an important role. Critical-period conceptualization, however, may be exactly backward, at least for spatial development.

The stimulation needed for early spatial development is adequately obtained from normal environments, without the addition of tailor-made toys. All normal environments contain contour, objects, locations, and so on, and normally developing infants perceive this environment, begin to move through it as motor development progresses, and observe the consequences of various actions within it. In Greenough's terms, early spatial development is "experience-expectant."[5] This view agrees with both nativists and Elkind-type Piagetians that the environment is rarely variable in ways that will affect development but that the environment and the infant's activity in it are regarded as crucial in development, and hence there is more agreement with Piaget than with nativism.

Variations in experience become more apparent after a few years of life. From the age of about 3 years, cultural interventions and carefully engineered input (also known as good teaching) are important for optimal growth in the spatial domain. Later spatial development is, in Greenough's terms, more experience dependent than experience expectant, likely because recently acquired and invented systems of spatial symbolization come into play. Stimulation of the growth of spatial competence needs to be done in a way that respects children's initial states, but we can also usefully push the envelope of children's current abilities and understandings, contrary to the observation of the former teacher at Jack's parent meeting.

Our best current guess about the role of experience in spatial development is as follows: Development in the first few years of life merely requires a normal predictable environment in which children can explore and play both perceptually and motorically. The kind of spatial competence infants acquire in the first 2 years is very basic to survival and is evident in our primate relatives and, in some species-relevant form, in every mobile organism.[11] It would be surprising if the development of these abilities were not deeply canalized, whereas other kinds of spatial development may be less canalized. Symbol systems seem to be species specific and to have originated in humans within the relatively recent evolutionary past. In addition, their attainment is very variable among individuals. All of these characteristics suggest that the degree of canalization might be smaller and the impact of varying environment within normal limits greater. Beginning at 2 or 3 years of age, it is likely that children depend on cultural transmission to acquire spatial symbol systems, including language, mapping, and other symbolic forms, and they will benefit from enriched experience in the use of these systems.

Future research will be needed to substantiate this judgment and to settle two issues. First, there are variations across environments in how much children explore independently. Are the more restrictive of these environments (within the limits of normal) adequate for spatial development to proceed, or are there degrees of restriction that impede development? Delineating the limits of what is a normal, predictable environment and when does it change into an abnormal, restrictive environment is a theoretically and politically crucial task, currently the subject of heated debate.[46-49] Second, calling for enriched experience with maps and graphic displays does not solve the problem of "what to do when." Creating curricula to maximize spatial development in the symbolic domain will require close collaboration between developmental and educational researchers and practitioners.

The outlook for answering such questions and rising to the challenge posed at the beginning of this paper is bright. For some time, researchers have been gathering extensive knowledge on particular domains of knowledge development. Domain-specific analysis is key to answering fundamental questions such as "What is the role of experience in infant development?" because answers may differ across domains. If a single domain is not focused on at a time, then we cannot ask specific questions about starting points and change. There are vital differences between domains that make it difficult to involve behavioral analysis with a discussion of neurologic substrates. Another example of "domain specificity" can be seen when comparing language development with spatial development. In language development much has been made of the lack of feedback to children regarding their syntactic errors. What is true of language development, however, is almost surely not true of spatial development. Children either find a lost object or fail to find it; they either get lost or they do not. Thus, the mechanisms as well as the substance of development may differ across domains.

Additionally, a view of cognitive development has been formulated in recent years that may transcend the schisms between the existing classic theories. We have been involved for quite a few decades in fruitless debates regarding nature vs nurture and regarding models of development in which change is qualitative vs ones in which it is quantitative. We have begun to see how nature and nurture are inextricably intertwined and how development can be simultaneously quantitative and qualitative.[50] Seeing human competence as an emergent property of relationships of the organism to the environment is the theoretical context in which we can comfortably do the hard scientific work of untangling exactly how particular lines of development proceed.[33]

References

1. Elman JL, Bates EA, Johnson MH, Karniloff-Smith A, Parisi D, Plunket K. *Rethinking Innateness.* Cambridge, Mass: MIT Press; 1996.

2. Elkind D. *The Hurried Child: Growing Up Too Fast Too Soon.* Perseus Press; 1989.

3. Hunt J. *Intelligence and Experience.* New York, NY: Ronald Press; 1961.

4. Vygotsky L. *Thought and Language.* Cambridge, Mass: MIT Press; 1986.

5. Greenough W, Black J, Wallace C. Experience and brain development. *Child Development.* 1988;58:539-559.

6. Landau B, Gleitman H, Spelke ES. Spatial knowledge and geometric representation in a child blind from birth. *Science.* 1981;213:1275-1278.

7. Landau B, Spelke ES, Gleitman H. Spatial knowledge in a young blind child. *Cognition.* 1984;16: 225-260.

8. Hermer L, Spelke ES. A geometric process for spatial reorientation in young children. *Nature.* 1994; 370:57-59.

9. Hermer L, Spelke ES. Modularity and development. *Cognition.* 1996;61:195-232.

10. Spelke ES. Nativism, empiricism, and the origins of knowledge. *Infant Behavior and Development.* 1998;21:181-200.

11. Gallistel CR. *The Organization of Learning.* Cambridge, Mass: MIT Press; 1990.

12. Geary DC. Reflections of evolution and culture in children's cognition: implications for mathematical development and instruction. *American Psychologist.* 1995;50:24-37.

13. Spelke EL, Newport EL. Nativism, empiricism, and the development of knowledge. In: Lerner RM, ed. *Handbook of Child Psychology. Vol 1: Theoretical Models of Human Development.* New York, NY: John Wiley and Sons, Inc; 1998:275-340.

14. Thinus-Blanc C, Gaunet F. Representation of space in blind persons: vision as a spatial sense? *Psychological Bulletin.* 1997;121:20-42.

15. Arditi A, Holtzman JD, Kosslyn SM. Mental imagery and sensory experience in congenital blindness. *Neuropsychologia.* 1988;26:1-12.

16. Iverson JM, Goldin-Meadow S. What's communication got to do with it? Gesture in children blind from birth. *Developmental Psychology.* 1997;33:453-467.

17. Warren DH. *Blindness and Children: An Individual Difference Approach.* New York, NY: Cambridge University Press; 1994.

18. Millar S. *Understanding and Representing Space: Theory and Evidence From Studies With Blind and Sighted Children.* Oxford, UK: Clarendon Press; 1994.

19. Bigelow AE. Blind and sighted children's spatial knowledge of their home environments. *International Journal of Behavioral Development.* 1996;19:797-816.

20. Rieser JJ, Hill EW, Talor CR, Bradfield A, Rosen S. Visual experience, visual field size, and the development of nonvisual sensitivity to the spatial structure of outdoor neighborhoods explored by walking. *Journal of Experimental Psychology: General.* 1992;121:210-221.

21. Liben LS. Conceptual issues in the development of spatial cognition. In: Stiles-Davis J, Kritchevsky M, Bellugi U, eds. *Spatial Cognition: Brain Basis and Development.* Hillsdale, NJ: Erlbaum; 1988:167-194.

22. Millar S. Models of sensory deprivation: the nature/nurture dichotomy and spatial representation in the blind. *International Journal of Behavioral Development.* 1988;11:69-87.

23. Morrongiello BA, Timmey B, Humphrey GK. Spatial knowledge in blind and sighted children. *Journal of Experimental Child Psychology.* 1995;59:211-233.

24. Huttenlocher J, Newcombe N, Sandberg EH. The coding of spatial location in young children. *Cognitive Psychology.* 1994;27:115-148.

25. Fodor JA. *Modularity of Mind: An Essay on Faculty Psychology.* Cambridge, Mass: MIT Press; 1983.

26. Cheng K. A purely geometric module in the rat's spatial representation. *Cognition.* 1986;23:149-178.

27. Wang RF, Hermer L. Children do not reorient using a nongeometric cue even with extensive training in the cue's stability. Poster presented at the *Biennial Meeting for the Society for Research on Child Development,* 1997.

28. Etienne AS, Teroni E, Maurer R, Portenier V, Saucy F. Short-distance homing in a small mammal: the role of exteroceptive cues and path integration. *Experientia.* 1985;4:122-125.

29. Goodridge JP, Taube JS. Preferential use of the landmark navigational system by head direction cells in rats. *Behavioral Neuroscience.* 1995;109:49-61.

30. Learmonth AE, Newcombe NS, Huttenlocher J. Disoriented children use landmarks as well as geometry to reorient. Poster presented at the *Annual Meeting for the Psychonomic Society,* 1998.

31. Newcombe NS, Huttenlocher J. *Making Space: Taking Cognitive Development One Domain at a Time.* Cambridge, Mass: MIT Press. In press.

32. Carey S. Knowledge acquisition: enrichment or conceptual change? In: Carey S, Gelman R, eds. *The Epigenesis of Mind: Essays on Biology and Cognition.* Hillsdale, NJ: LEA; 1991:257-291.

33. Newcombe NS. Defining the 'radical middle': essay review of *Rethinking Innateness: A Connectionist Perspective on Development. Human Development.* 1998;41:210-214.

34. Piaget J, Inhelder B. *The Child's Conception of Space.* New York, NY: Norton; 1967. (Original work published in 1948)

35. Huttenlocher J, Presson CC. The coding and transformation of spatial information. *Cognitive Psychology.* 1979;11:375-394.

36. Newcombe N, Huttenlocher J. Children's early ability to solve perspective-taking problems. *Developmental Psychology.* 1992;28:635-643.

37. Bialystok E. Children's mental rotations of abstract displays. *Journal of Experimental Child Psychology.* 1989;47:47-71.

38. Presson CC. Strategies in spatial reasoning. *Journal of Experimental Psychology: Learning, Memory & Cognition.* 1982;8:243-251.

39. Uttal DH. Angles and distances: children's and adult's reconstruction and scaling of spatial configurations. *Child Development.* 1996;67:2763-2779.

40. Liben LS, Yekel CA. Preschoolers' understanding of plan and oblique maps: the role of geometric and representational correspondence. *Child Development.* 1996;67:2780-2796.

41. Wallace JR, Veek AL. Children's use of maps for direction and distance estimation. Poster presented at the *Biennial Meeting of the Society for Research in Child Development,* 1995.

42. Huttenlocher J, Newcombe N, Vasilyeva M. Spatial scaling in young children. *Psychological Science.* In press.

43. DeLoache JS. Young children's understanding of models. In: Fivush R, Hudson J, eds. *Knowing and Remembering in Young Children.* New York, NY: Cambridge University Press; 1991:94-126.

44. Baenninger M, Newcombe N. The role of experience in spatial test performance: a meta-analysis. *Sex Roles.* 1989;20:327-344.

45. Baenninger M, Newcombe N. Environmental input to the development of sex-related differences in spatial and mathematical ability. *Learning and Individual Differences.* 1995;7:363-379.

46. Baumrind D. The average expectable environment is not good enough: a response to Scarr. *Child Development.* 1993;64:1299-1317.

47. Jackson JF. Human behavioral genetics, Scarr's theory and her views on interventions: a critical review and commentary on their implications for African American children. *Child Development.* 1993;64:1318-1332.

48. Scarr S. Developmental theories for the 1990s: development and individual differences. *Child Development.* 1992;63:1-19.

49. Scarr S. Biological and cultural diversity: the legacy of Darwin for development. *Child Development.* 1993;64:1333-1353.

50. Elman J, Bates E, Johnson M, Karmiloff-Smith A, Parisi D, Plunkett K. *Rethinking Innateness: A Connectionist Perspective on Development.* Cambridge, Mass: MIT Press; 1996.

Section 4:
Perceptual Development

Abstracts From Section 4. Perceptual Development

About Functional Brain Specialization: The Development of Face Recognition

Scania de Schonen, PhD

Faces convey information about social and cognitive activities that are important for developing infants and their parents. The processing of information conveyed by faces is believed to be achieved in adults by a dedicated cortical neural system. An extensive review of the development of the face recognition system in the cortex is provided herein.

The Development of Representations for Perception and Action

Rick O. Gilmore, PhD

Perception of spatial relations requires the capacity to process information from sources that include vision, proprioception, audition, and olfaction. Available evidence in adults suggests that the systematic combination of visual and proprioceptive information occurs in specialized areas of the occipital, parietal, and frontal cortex. However, the relative immaturity of an infant's nervous system implies spatial information is processed using a different set of neural subsystems than adults.

The Emergence of Future-Oriented Thinking in the Early Years

Marshall M. Haith, PhD

Future events play an important role in the life of a young child; even in the first months of life, infants are aware of "what comes next" and they organize their behavior around predictable events. The development of children's ability to think about the future is supported by a cluster of behaviors referred to as future-oriented processes (FOPs). These FOPs have been characterized by laboratory studies of infant reaction times, parental questionnaires of future-oriented thinking, and observation of future-oriented speech.

About Functional Brain Specialization: The Development of Face Recognition

Scania de Schonen, PhD

Introduction

Studying the relationship among changes in the brain during its maturation, interactions with the environment, and the emergence (or decline) of specific cognitive abilities is a useful way to approach the neural basis of competencies and behavior. How does the brain sort its surroundings into relevant categories of objects, events, and rules? And how does it build up appropriate representations so that children living in different environments all seem to sort out the same categories of objects and events at approximately the same stage of infancy? What constraints in the brain and the environment interact so consistently that they shape the learning processes of all members of the species in a similar fashion so that the competencies that eventually emerge are all organized in a similar way? How far can the developmental trajectories differ between children and groups?

This debate has been going on for a long time, but there is still relatively little empirical data on brain maturation, differential timing of cortical network development, the selectivity of the connections resulting from the maturational patterns, and the filtering of inputs and outputs during pre- and postnatal life. It is possible that organizational constraints (and other factors) that shape the patterns of neuronal connectivity during maturation might be sufficiently strong to bias some groups of networks toward one kind of processing function and determine what their function will be. This idea is compatible with distributed processing, if one takes this *a priori* network specialization to be a rough process, and the information will be distributed just onto some small parts of the cortex.

In this context, some interindividual differences may be due to timing discrepancies between biological signals within the brain or to systemic factors (such as sex hormones) during the maturation process. This model of development does not exclude the role of factors such as environmental events and personal history. There is obviously no simple, straightforward answer to the question of whether there exists a system specializing in one specific competence, such as face processing. The data on cortical network localization, on the dissociations between postlesion deficits, and on postlesion neuronal and functional plasticity are all in favor of a complex interaction between genetic determinants and environmental factors. Here, "environment" refers to the molecular environment, the cellular environment, and the neuronal network environment, as well as the child's environment.

One approach to this question is to examine how competencies develop in children, looking for functionally specific building blocks along the way. This paper will focus on the beginning of postnatal life, the relationships that may exist between postnatal maturation of neuronal networks involved in a given adult competence, and the development of the behavior corresponding to this competence. When and how is a group of networks allotted to a particular function, and when do they become irreversibly committed to that function? We have been asking these kinds of questions about the development of face recognition in human infants. Face processing is an interesting subject, because the ability to see shapes begins at birth and because faces carry information on social and cognitive activities that are very important for child-rearing. Also, a large body of data is available on the processing of faces and their recognition in adults.

Arguments in Favor of a Specific Face Processing System in the Adult Brain

From several studies in adults, it has been concluded that face processing relies on a specific neural system. This means that faces cannot be processed by another system and that this neural system processes only faces. The first argument for this is the so-called "inversion effect." When presented upside down, faces are very difficult to identify, whereas this is not the case for other objects.[1] It has been demonstrated that the inversion effect results from an expertise effect. People with an expert knowledge of dogs exhibit an inversion effect in dog recognition, whereas nonexperts show no inversion effect. The inversion effect is greater for human faces than for dogs. The existence of an inversion effect suggests that faces are processed in a different way than are other objects. The inversion effect on face processing might be a *result* of experience rather than *independent* of experience. It is possible, however, that whereas the inversion effect for dogs or other animals or objects results from expertise, the inversion effect for faces results from a specific process independent of experience.

The second argument in favor of a neural system committed specifically to face processing is the existence of prosopagnosia. Prosopagnosic patients are suddenly unable to recognize individual faces, even very familiar faces such as those of their families. These patients remain able to recognize objects and people on the basis of other nonphysiognomic information: gait, hairline, voice, etc. Some of these patients also remain able to identify facial emotional expressions, as well as to read lips.

A patient described by Moscovitch et al[2] showed the converse dissociation: The patient was agnosic for objects but could recognize faces, as long as the task involved configural information and not local information. It has been agreed that fast face recognition is based normally on configural information. It was also suggested that the inversion effect stems from a configural processing, whereas if a pattern or face is processed locally element by element, there is no inversion effect.[3] In this patient, configural processing was preserved, which might explain why face recognition was preserved, whereas local processing was not preserved, and, as a consequence, object processing was destroyed.

On one hand a cortical lesion associated with a deficit in face recognition, and on the other hand a lesion associated with a deficit in object recognition, strongly suggests that in adults face processing involves neural networks that are different from those involved in object processing. Configural processing seems to play a crucial role in this dissociation. Several studies with normal subjects have also shown that fast face recognition most often relies on configural information. The relationships between the inversion effect, the dissociation between face and object, and the processing of configural information suggest functional specificity.

The third argument supporting a specific face-processing system in adults comes from localization of the neural systems involved. Yin showed that the inversion effect with faces occurs only if the right hemisphere is intact.[4] This was confirmed by studies showing that in normal subjects, the inversion effect was more frequent when face stimuli were projected to the right than to the left hemisphere.[5-7] Other studies have shown a right hemisphere advantage in face recognition in normal subjects. The way we process faces relies on right hemisphere specificity, and the right hemisphere advantage in face recognition seems to be based on configural processing.

In prosopagnosic patients, observed brain damage is either bilateral or right ventrotemporal, but not unilateral left.[8,9] It cannot be ruled out, however, that the so-called right lesions are in fact bilateral, with a left damage not visible on magnetic resonance imaging.

Greater and more frequent involvement of the right hemisphere than of the left in face processing is confirmed by functional brain imaging. Within the right hemisphere, the fusiform gyrus seems to play a crucial role, as shown by several studies relying on different brain-imaging techniques: magnetoencephalography, functional magnetic resonance imaging, positron emission tomography, and event-related potential recording.[10-14] In a recent study, when faces were presented among either objects or flowers or nonobjects, the right fusiform gyrus (but not the left) was activated to a greater extent than when those items were presented without faces.[15] This does not mean that only the fusiform gyrus is involved in face processing. It means that among all the networks involved, there are some in the fusiform gyrus that are not involved in object processing. It also means that the networks involved in face processing can be found in the same cortical region in the majority of people tested so far.

Quite naturally, these findings lead to a plethora of questions. How does this specialization develop? Does face processing start in infancy? Is configural processing involved in face processing from the beginning, or does it result from experience? Is face processing localized from the beginning in the same region as in adults? How plastic is the system, and what happens in case of a early cortical damage? Does face processing develop in other regions with different or similar characteristics as in normal brains? Is there only one possible developmental trajectory, or are there several?

Attention to Facedness and Individual Face Processing in Neonates

Newborn infants' visual attention is spontaneously attracted toward faces.[16-18] The mechanism for this, called CONSPEC by Morton & Johnson (for the conspecific recognition of our own species),[18] underlies the particular automatic attention for a facelike structure. It constitutes one of the earliest constraints on visual attention that might shape the perceptual processes. An infant's gaze is attracted by faces for slightly longer periods than it is by other objects, as long as the spatial arrangement can be detected by the infant.[19,20] Since infants' vision is limited, faces can play an important role only under some conditions. They must, for instance, be quite near the subject (within a range of about 20 cm). People looking after infants tend to be about this distance away when they turn their faces towards an infant and speak to him or her, which presumably reinforces the attraction exerted by the target face. In addition, infants at birth are known to react by turning their visual attention toward any source of noise. The conditions are therefore highly favorable for infants to acquire representations of individual faces.

Whether subcortical or cortical, it is plausible that CONSPEC guides the cortical activity toward face acquisition because it orients visual fixation. Acquiring representations of individual faces, however, requires cortical participation. Three-day-old infants were said to recognize their mothers' faces on the basis of purely visual information[21]: they looked longer at their mothers' than at strangers' heads and faces. It was also shown that neonates, like 3-month-old infants, preferred a new face to a familiar face even when a 2-minute interval is interposed between the end of the familiarization period and the preference test.[22] In amnesic patients (with damage to their hippocampal and perihippocampal systems), the preference for a new face is not preserved after even a few seconds.[23] The study of newborns' memories therefore was interpreted as showing that some of the relationships between the cortex and the hippocampal and perihippocampal systems are functional at birth. Neonates are able to build, within about 1 to 2 minutes (a familiarization period), representations of complex stimuli such as a face that can last at least 2 minutes and then help orient attention to new faces.

These studies[21,22] could lead to the conclusion that the neonatal cortex is the site in which infants learn faces and that face processing might develop throughout this learning period. Things are not so simple, however. Other data suggest that between the sixth and the ninth weeks of life, some cortical reorganization occurs that impacts on face processing.

First, it was shown that 3-day-olds recognize their mothers' faces on the basis of the outer contour of the head and hairline rather than on the basis of facial configuration.[24] When a scarf is put on a woman's head (hiding the

Fig 1. Durations of visual fixation on mothers' and strangers' faces by 3-day-old infants according to whether the outer contour of the head and hairline are masked.

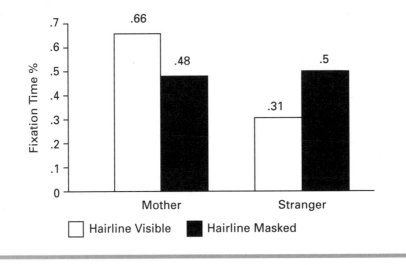

hair, hairline, and hair/forehead) a newborn does not show a preference for either its mother or a stranger (Fig 1). At about age 6 to 10 weeks infants begin to look longer at their mothers when the hairline is masked by a scarf.[25] Some prosopagnosic patients say they use the shape of the hairline to identify people.[26] It has also been established in several studies on healthy adults that the internal configuration (eyes, nose, mouth, etc.) is necessary for a person to be able to recognize familiar faces, whereas with new faces, the head contour can be used as a cue.[27-29]

Second, the preference for a simple right-side-up face-like model (over its inverted version) vanishes at the age of 6 weeks, and other kinds of face models that involve cortical activity become preferred.[18-20,30-33]

Third, the recognition memory and preference for a new face after a delay of 2 minutes observed in neonates seems to be absent at the age of 9 to 10 weeks (Pascalis, Fourreau, de Schonen, unpublished data) but is present again at the age of 3 months.[22,34]

The fact that neonates process the outer contour of the head during the first few weeks of life, the existence of a change in the representation of facedness, and the disappearance of the recognition memory capacity around the age of 6 to 9 weeks suggest a reorganization of cortical activity during this period. This is not to say that from the age of 9 weeks onwards face processing is adultlike. It has been shown, for instance, that infants do not become able to recognize a face from a point of view they have not yet experienced before the age of 3 to 4 months.[34] Nevertheless, it can be assumed that at about the end of the second month, a cortical system able to process and learn how to differentiate and recognize individual faces starts to develop.

Where in the Infant Cortex Are Faces Processed?

Is face processing localized from the beginning in the same region as it is in adults? In general, this question is answered from data on the long-term effects of neonatal brain lesions. For instance, it was observed that right and left hemisphere damage at birth slows the development of language in a similar manner.[35] From this observation, it was concluded that language develops in both hemispheres. The part played by the right hemisphere, however, is not clear. Damage in one hemisphere might affect the contralateral hemisphere by inducing some neural reorganization that (depending on the state of maturation) might or might not be functional.

Functional brain imaging, rather than long-term effects of brain damage, can provide better information on where in the cortex the networks involved in a given competence are. We performed a positron emission tomography study using $H_2^{15}O$ as marker on 2-month-old infants born at risk. Our goal was to develop a system of diagnosis and prognosis that would make it possible to apply suitable aid and rehabilitation procedures at an early age, before the onset of a behavioral deficit.[36] These infants were not under medication at the time of the study, and their neurological signs were mild. The regional patterns of brain activation were compared in two situations. In the first, the control situation, a visual stimulus was presented, consisting of a small circular set of red and green light-emitting diodes that blinked at a speed that varied every 4 seconds. In the second situation, color slides of women's faces under the same lighting conditions, with neutral expressions and wearing scarves, were presented for 4 seconds each.

At the age of 2 months, the density of the synapses in the human cortex is increasing rapidly,[37-41] but dendritic arborizations are still poorly developed.[42] Therefore, the presentation of blinking lights or a human face might seem unlikely to cause regional differences in cortical metabolic activity. Similarly, a visual stimulus such as a face may seem likely to trigger only a diffuse increase in the overall synaptic activity. Indeed, the results showed that cortical activity was relatively poor, but subcortical activity was high. Nevertheless, a significant level of activation in the right fusiform gyrus was revealed when the activity associated with the blinking lights was subtracted from the activity associated with the face.

In other words, when infants are just beginning to process and represent individual faces but still show poor face-recognition competence (for instance, recognition of a face from different viewpoints does not occur until the age of 3 to 4 months), the right fusiform gyrus is activated by the presentation of faces as it is in adults. Given that we do not know which structures would be activated by complex nonface stimuli, we cannot conclude that there exists a specific cortical system that processes faces in 2-month-olds. We *do* know that some constraints on the anatomical functional cortical organization are present at the age of 2 months that can explain that face processing is allotted to some particular region of the cortex and will develop there.

At an age when facial information processing is undergoing changes in infants, local patterns of activity occur that involve the same associative cortical areas as adults. This suggests that the cortical maturation process does not encompass one large cortical region after another, but rather groups of networks after others, according to a scheme where the emphasis is a more functional one, as if cortical maturation proceeds by successive waves in the whole cortex. Future research will show what kind of constraints can act to bias the development of a given competence in a given set of associative regions.

Some cortical regional activations were observed in infants that are not observed with face stimuli in adults. The additional regional activities in infants might be due to a weak control situation (the blinking circle of lights), but more likely to the existence of neural connections between regions that have a functional role (for instance, active relationships between faces, objects, and speech might be necessary for the development of speech). These relationships might be progressively inhibited or partially lost during development (for instance, the relationship between speech and the visual world might change once representation of the visual world by speech is achieved). Therefore, the architecture of the connections between networks involved in face or object processing and speech in adults might be different from those existing during the beginning of life when speech is to be developed.

Postlesional Functional Plasticity

A right hemisphere advantage in face processing was observed during the first year of life. Infants recognize their mothers' faces faster with their right hemisphere than with their left; and they discriminate between two faces better with their right hemisphere, even with presentation as short as 300 to 350 msec.[43,44] The right hemisphere advantage is not because the left hemisphere cannot recognize what is a face and what is not (both hemispheres are able to discriminate between facelike patterns and non-facelike patterns).[45] The right hemisphere advantage is also not due to a general advantage in pattern processing. Rather, it is likely due to the two hemispheres' processing different visual information.

Like adults, infants process configural visual information with their right hemisphere and more local information with their left hemisphere.[46,47] This is also true with faces; configural information within faces is processed by the right hemisphere.[48] The fact that the right hemisphere has a face-processing advantage might be because the right hemisphere is particularly suited for representing and recognizing patterns and objects as complex as individual human faces. The information processed by the left hemisphere may be invariant throughout smaller numbers or different kinds of transformations, but may be more adequate for efficiently detecting small local changes in patterns, such as the changes in the shape of the mouth that occur when a person is speaking.[49] What can be said quite definitely is that the two hemispheres do not extract the same information from the environment, or rather that they do not aggregate in the same way the lower-level pieces of information extracted from the environment. These early hemispheric characteristics are obviously not imposed by the external environment. They take shape because of the way in which the neuronal networks are organized. We do not know yet what cortical neuronal pathways may be responsible for these differences.

The right hemisphere advantage is all the more noteworthy in that it seems to be impossible for facial coding information to be transferred from the right hemisphere to the left. It was observed that a categorial learning rule that discriminates between facelike and non-facelike patterns can be transmitted from one hemisphere to the other in 19- to 26-week-old infants.[45] But no visual information about individual faces or patterns, however, seems to be transmitted between hemispheres during the first year of life.[44,46] It seems that it is only around the age of 24 months that visual information on patterns can be transferred from one hemisphere to the other.[11,50,51]

From at least their fourth or fifth month of life, infants process the configural information within faces with their right hemispheres, and the right hemisphere has an advantage in face recognition over the left hemisphere. In infants, as in adults, the left hemisphere is capable of encoding information that can be used to distinguish and recognize faces. The information processed by the left hemisphere is, however, not the same as that processed by the right, and the information processed by the left seems to be relevant to face recognition only under some conditions. Also, 2-month-olds show activation of the right fusiform gyrus when presented with faces. As soon as the ability develops to process the truly physiognomical information provided by faces, a functional anatomic feature of the adult brain (the right hemisphere advantage with involvement of the right fusiform gyrus) can be said to exist in infants.

Given these data, it is interesting to investigate whether early right posterior damage would preclude normal development of face processing or whether functional plasticity is the rule. Can face processing develop in the left hemisphere alone, and does it develop on the basis of local or configural information?

We studied face-processing competencies in six children aged between 6 and 14 years who had congenital right (n=3) or left (n=3) hemispheric damage.[52] Some patients had huge deficits in some of the competencies studied relative to control subjects. The patients did not show deficit in all the face tasks, indicating that some tasks involve a kind of processing that is preserved or that can be rescued by a different kind of processing. Also, the level of face-processing competency was independent of IQ level. In other words, years of daily exposure to faces is not sufficient to develop normal face-processing competencies. Similarly, Stiles and colleagues showed that postlesional plasticity seems to be poorer in the domain of visuospatial competence than that of language.[35,53-55]

In another study we investigated whether children with deficits in face processing also have deficits in other object processing and in configural processing. Patients with unilateral ischemic damage at birth (six with left hemisphere damage, five with right hemisphere damage) were divided into two groups: those whose performance on face-processing tasks was significantly lower than that of matched controls and those who did not differ from matched controls.

First we observed that posterior but not anterior brain damage was associated with a face-processing deficit. We confirmed the fact that damage to either hemisphere can be associated with a long-term deficit in face processing, despite the fact that the right has an advantage over the left in the first year of life. Next, we observed that patients who had a deficit in face processing also had a deficit in other object processing (no deficit specific to face processing was observed), and some patients had no deficit in face processing but a deficit in other object processing. More significant was the finding concerning configural processing. Children who had a face-processing deficit were more inclined to use local processing to recognize geometric patterns than were their matched controls, whereas patients without a face-processing deficit did not differ from their matched controls. This association between a deficit in face processing and configural processing implies that a deficit in configural processing can generate a deficit in face processing and that the face competencies developed by these patients rely on local processing. We have thus far observed that children can develop face processing with local processing; however, their level of performance is not as high as that of normal children. In summary, despite early cortical localization of the neural networks involved in face processing, a certain level of competence can develop in other cortical regions that uses different kinds of information than normal.

Given the very early right hemisphere localization observed in other studies, it is surprising that left hemisphere damage can cause deficits in face-processing and configural-processing. There are two possible explanations. First, the existence of a right hemisphere advantage does not rule out the possibility that processing by both hemispheres is necessary to develop a normal level of competence, even though only the right is necessary for face processing in adults. We have seen that in 2-month-olds, different cortical regions are activated than in adults; as suggested earlier, it might be that during development relationships between the activities of several regions are necessary for one or another competence to develop and for them to communicate later on.[56]

The second possible explanation is that early left hemisphere damage has effects on right cortical development. The corpus callosum does not seem able to coordinate perceptual information, but insult to its neurons can result in some contralateral reorganization that might not always be functional. This reorganization could result in a deficit in some perceptual competencies depending on the region affected. Currently, both theories seem to have equal support in the literature.

Functional Plasticity After Early Deprivation

Another way to investigate how much cortical localization and characteristics of face processing depend on the interaction between a given state of organization of the cortex and early visual experience is to study the effect of early visual deprivation. Maurer and collaborators studied patients deprived of patterned input during early infancy caused by bilateral congenital opaque cataracts. These patients were treated, at age 2 to 22 months, by surgical removal of cataracts and fitting of contact lenses. All patients were tested after age 10 and compared with 6- and 10-year-old normal children and adults. Compared with normal controls, the patients made more errors on tasks involving identity despite changes in head orientation, but they performed normally on other tasks (matching identity despite change in expression, matching expression, lipreading, gaze direction).[57] The results of tasks investigating whether the patients were using local, global (outer contour), or configural information suggest that they use global but not configural information regardless of how long they were visually deprived. It might be possible that recognizing a face across different orientations requires more configural information than recognizing faces across different expressions or recognizing different expressions. The results show that visual deprivation during the first 2 years of life modifies the characteristics of face processing without damaging it severely.

Conclusions

Some years ago, we proposed a scenario by which some neural networks become specialized for face processing by the convergence of several factors.[58,59] These factors are summarized below.

1. The associative cortical regions (those located in the temporal cortex), which receive the information about faces, objects, and patterns, might become functional at an earlier age in the right hemisphere than in the left.[59-63]

2. When functional networks become sufficiently large or numerous in this region (at about 6 to 9 weeks of age), they receive visual information that is conveyed mainly by the low-spatial-frequency channels.[64-67]

3. The networks capable of dealing with face processing, which can process differences between two individual faces ("capable" means that these networks receive the information required for face processing from the low-level visual-processing systems; these networks can be "capable" of without "specializing" in it) and perform other kinds of processing (such as voice), may first start doing so in the right hemisphere, mainly on the basis of low-spatial-visual-frequency information.

4. The advantage of this early processing system is not due only to the fact that the right temporal cortex matures earlier than the left. It is also due to the advantage of a configural encoding of faces. When a face is characterized and encoded through the configural information it carries, it might more frequently offer an opportunity for the same encoding despite changes in lighting or points of view, and therefore provide more opportunities for recognition. This might be one of the reasons the system persists even after a local processing system has developed and even after some left neural networks have become functional.

This scenario, and the data collected under its assumptions, underscore several points. *First,* early cortical maturation proceeds by waves, with different networks maturing before others and becoming progressively more specialized. *Second,* early cortical functional localization of a competence related to an adult competence does not mean that the infant's activated region contains a reduced model of the adult competence. The existence in infants of a localized cortical set of neural networks involved in face processing coincides with a very poor face processing competence that does not yet have all the characteristics of adult face processing. Some change in the processing and in the structure of the neural networks has to occur before a child's face processing becomes similar to an adult's. The relevant changes might occur through environmental effects (stimulation and learning), but some neural changes that are independent of environmental stimulation may also be involved.

Third, early cortical functional localization does not exclude the possibility of other developmental trajectories, if some constraints are not present at the proper time (in the case of early deprivation as well as of early brain lesion, some constraints normally present are lacking). Early localized cortical activity does not imply that only one region has the required characteristics to perform a given kind of computation. On the other hand, the existence of other possible developmental trajectories (and functional plasticity) does not exclude the existence of constraints on cortical localization and functional specialization. The development of competence probably results from the activity of several networks in several regions (for example, PET studies show that several cortical regions are activated by face presentations in 2-month-old infants, whereas these regions are not all activated in adults). If one region is damaged, the functioning of the other networks will differ from normal, but the preservation of these networks will probably constrain and bias the functioning of other preserved networks so that competence not totally similar to normal will develop. This would result in functional plasticity: Children who had early unilateral posterior damage have a deficit in face processing but are not prosopagnosic. We have also seen that the rescuing systems do not perform exactly the same kind of processing as the normal (most common) one: Children with early unilateral posterior damage develop face-processing competency based more on local processing than it is in normal children. As predicted by the scenario, timing of the input seems to be crucial: Children deprived of vision for a relatively short period after birth develop some face processing, but they use more local processing than do normal children.

All this suggests that there exists one most-efficient developmental pathway, and, in case some constraints normally present are lacking at the proper time, some variations around the normal pathway can preserve the general capacity (recognizing faces, expressions, etc) as long as a different kind of information processing can be used (local instead of configural information, for instance). If the preserved constraints are not strong enough, however, the outcome might be a severe deficit. The scope of the deficit might be very important if neural reorganization takes place that has no way to be functional.

References

1. Yin RK. Looking at upside-down faces. *Journal of Experimental Psychology*. 1969;81:141-145.

2. Moscovitch M, Winocur G, Behrmann M. What is special about face recognition? Nineteen experiments on a person with visual object agnosia and dyslexia but normal face recognition. *Journal of Cognitive Neuroscience*. 1997;9:555-604.

3. Farah MJ, Tanaka JW, Drain HM. What causes the face inversion effect. *Journal of Experimental Psychology: Human Perception and Performance*. 1995;21:628-634.

4. Yin RK. Face recognition by brain-injured patients: a dissociable ability. *Neuropsychologia*. 1970;8: 395-402.

5. Valentine T. Upside-down faces: a review of the effect of inversion upon face recognition. *British Journal of Psychology*. 1988;79:471-491.

6. Leehey SC, Carey S, Diamond R, Cahn A. Upright and inverted faces: the right hemisphere knows the difference. *Cortex*. 1978;14:411-419.

7. Hillger LA, Koenig O. Separable mechanisms in face processing: evidence from hemispheric specialization. *Journal of Cognitive Neuroscience*. 1991;3:42-58.

8. De Renzi E. Current issues in prosopagnosia. In: Ellis HD, Jeeves MA, Newcombe F, Young A, eds. *Aspects of Face Processing.* Dordrecht, NL, Boston, Mass, London, UK: Kluwer; 1986:199-210; 243-252.

9. De Renzi E, Prabi D, Carlesimo GA, Siveri MC, Fazio F. Prosopagnosia can be associated with damage confined to the right hemisphere – an MRI and PET study and a review of the literature. *Neuropsychologia.* 1994;32:893-902.

10. Lu ST, Hämäläinen MS, Hari R, Ilmoniemi RJ, Lounasamaa OV, Sams M, Vilkman V. Seeing faces activates three separate areas outside the occipital visual cortex in man. *Neuroscience.* 1991;43:287-290.

11. Sergent J, Ohta S, MacDonald B. Functional neuroanatomy of face and object processing. A positron emission tomography study. *Brain.* 1992;115:15-36.

12. Haxby JV, Grady CL, Horwitz B, et al. Dissociation of object and spatial visual processing pathways in human extrastriate cortex. *Proceedings of the National Academy of Sciences USA.* 1991;88:1621-1625.

13. Haxby JV, Horwitz B, Ungerleider LG, Maisog A, Pietrini O, Grady CL. The functional organization of human extrastriate cortex: a PET-rCBF study of selective attention to faces and locations. *Journal of Neuroscience.* 1994;14:6336-6353.

14. Kanwisher N, McDermott J, Chun MM. A module for the visual representation of faces? *Neuroimage.* 1996;3:S361.

15. McCarthy G, Puce A, Gore JC, Allison T. Face specific processing in the human fusiform gyrus. *Journal of Cognitive Neuroscience.* 1997;9:605-610.

16. Goren CC, Sarty M, Wu PYK. Visual following and pattern discrimination of face-like stimuli by newborn infants. *Pediatrics.* 1975;56:544-549.

17. Johnson MH, Dziurawiec S, Ellis HD, Morton J. Newborns' preferential tracking of face-like stimuli and its subsequent decline. *Cognition.* 1991;40:1-19.

18. Johnson M, Morton J. *Biology and Cognitive Development: The Case of Face Recognition.* Oxford, England: Blackwells; 1991.

19. Mondloch C, Lewis TL, Budreau DR, et al. Face perception during early infancy. *Psychological Science.* In press.

20. Kleiner KA. Specific versus non-specific face recognition device? In: de Boysson-Bardies B, de Schonen S, Jusczyk P, MacNeilage P, Morton J, eds. *Developmental Neurocognition: Speech and Face Processing in the First Year of Life.* Dordrecht, NL, Boston, Mass, London, UK: Kluwer; 1993:125-134.

21. Bushnell IWR, Sai F, Mullin JT. Neonatal recognition of the mother's face. *British Journal of Developmental Psychology.* 1989;7:3-15.

22. Pascalis O, de Schonen S. Recognition memory in 3-4 day-old human infants. *NeuroReport.* 1995;5:1721-1724.

23. McKee RD, Squire LR. On the development of declarative memory. *Journal of Experimental Psychology: Learning, Memory and Cognition.* 1993;19:397-404.

24. Pascalis O, de Schonen S, Morton J, Deruelle C, Fabre-Grenet M. Mother's face recognition by neonates: a replication and an extension. *Infant Behavior and Development.* 1995;18:79-85.

25. Bartrip J, de Schonen S, Morton J. Infant responses to the mother's face. *British Journal of Developmental Psychology.* In press.

26. Davidoff J, Matthews WB, Newcombe F. Observations on a case of prosopagnosia. In: Ellis HD, Jeeves MA, Newcombe F, Young A, eds. *Aspects of Face Processing.* Dordrecht, NL, Boston, Mass, Lancaster, UK: Martinus Nijhoff Publishers; 1986:279-290.

27. Ellis HD, Sheperd JW, Davies JM. Identification of familiar and unfamiliar faces from internal and external features: some implications for theories of face recognition. *Perception.* 1979;8:431-439.

28. Endo M, Takahashi K, Maruyama K. The effects of observer's attitude on the familiarity of faces: using the difference in cue value between central and peripheral facial elements as an index of familiarity. *Tohoku Psychologica Folia.* 1984;43:23-24.

29. de Haan EHF, Hay DC. The matching of famous faces, given either the internal or the external features: a study on patients with unilateral brain lesions. In: Ellis HD, Jeeves MA, Newcombe F, Young A, eds. *Aspects of Face Processing*. Dordrecht, NL, Boston, Mass, Lancaster, UK: Martinus Nijhoff Publishers; 1986:302-309.

30. Dannemiller JL, Stephens BR. A critical test of infant preference models. *Child Development*. 1988;59: 210-216.

31. Kleiner KA, Banks M. Stimulus energy does not account for two-month-old infants face preferences. *Journal of Experimental Psychology: Human Perception and Performance*. 1987;13:594-600.

32. Maurer D. Infant's perceptions of facedness. In: Filed TF, Fox N, eds. *Social Perception in Infants*. Norwood, USA: Ablex Publishing Corp; 1985:73-100.

33. Morton J, Johnson MH, Maurer D. On the reasons for newborns' responses to faces. *Infant Behavior and Development*. 1990;13:99-103.

34. Pascalis O, de Haan M, Nelson C, de Schonen S. Long term recognition memory for faces assessed by visual paired comparison in 3- and 6-month-old infants. *Journal of Experimental Psychology: Learning Memory and Cognition*. 1998;24:249-260.

35. Bates E, Thal D, Trauner D, Fenson J, Aram D, Eisele J, Nass R. From first words to grammar in children with focal brain injury. *Developmental Neurospsychology*. 1997;13:275-344.

36. Tzourio N, de Schonen S, Mazoyer B, et al. Regional cerebral blood flow in two-month-old alert infants. *Society for Neuroscience Abstracts*. 1992;18(2):1121.

37. Huttenlocher PR. Synaptic density in human frontal cortex – developmental changes and effects of aging. *Brain Research*. 1979;163:195-205.

38. Huttenlocher PR. Morphometric study of human cerebral cortex development. *Neuropsychologia*. 1990;28:517-527.

39. Huttenlocher PR. Synaptogenesis, synapse elimination and neural plasticity in human cerebral cortex. In: Nelson CA, ed. *Threats to Optimal Development: Integrating Biological, Psychological, and Social Risk Factors*. Minnesota Symposium on Child Psychology, vol 27. Hillsdale, NJ: Lawrence Erlbaum Associates; 1994:35-54.

40. Huttenlocher PR, de Courten C. The development of synapses in striate cortex of man. *Human Neurobiology*. 1987;6:1-19.

41. Huttenlocher PR, de Courten C, Garey L, van der Loos H. Synaptogenesis in human visual cortex: evidence for synapse elimination during normal development. *Neuroscience Letters*. 1982;33:247-252.

42. Scheibel A. Dendritic structure and language development. In: de Boysson-Bardies B, de Schonen S, Jusczyk P, MacNeilage P, Morton J, eds. *Developmental Neurocognition: Speech and Face Processing in the First Year of Life*. Dordrecht, NL, Boston, Mass, London, UK: Kluwer; 1993:51-62.

43. de Schonen S, Gil de Diaz M, Mathivet E. Hemispheric asymmetry in face processing in infancy. In: Ellis HD, Jeeves MA, Newcombe F, Young A, eds. *Aspects of Face Processing*. Dordrecht, NL, Boston, Mass, London, UK: Martinus Nijhoff; 1986:199- 210.

44. de Schonen S, Mathivet E. Hemispheric asymmetry in a face discrimination task in infants. *Child Development*. 1990;61:1192-1205.

45. de Schonen S, Bry I. Interhemispheric communication of visual learning: a developmental study in 3-6-month-old infants. *Neuropsychologia*. 1987;25:601-612.

46. Deruelle C, de Schonen, S. Hemispheric asymmetries in visual pattern processing in infancy. *Brain and Cognition*. 1991;16:151-179.

47. Deruelle C, de Schonen S. Pattern processing in infancy: shape and location of components are not processed by the same hemisphere. *Infant Behavior and Development*. 1995;18:123-132.

48. Deruelle C, de Schonen S. Do the right and the left hemispheres attend to the same visuo-spatial information within a face in infancy? *Developmental Neuropsychology*. 1998;14:535-554.

49. Campbell R, Landis T, Regard M. Face recognition and lipreading: a neurological dissociation. *Brain*. 1986;109:509-521.

50. Liegeois F, de Schonen S. Simultaneous attention in the two visual hemifields and inter-hemispheric integration: a developmental study on 20- to 26-month-old infants. *Neuropsychologia*. 1997;35: 381-385.

51. Liegeois F, Bentejac L, de Schonen S. Interhemispheric integration of visual events: a developmental study on 19-28 month-old infants. Data on file.

52. Mancini J, de Schonen S, Deruelle C, Massoulier A. Face recognition in children with early right or left brain damage. *Developmental Medicine and Child Neurology.* 1994;36:156-166.

53. Stiles J, Nass R. Spatial grouping ability in young children with congenital right or left hemisphere injury. *Brain and Cognition.* 1991;15:201-222.

54. Stiles-Davis J. Developmental change in young children's spatial grouping activity. *Developmental Psychology.* 1988;24(4):522-531.

55. Stiles-Davis J, Janowski J, Engel M, Nass R. Drawing ability in four young children with congenital unilateral brain lesions. *Neuropsychologia.* 1988;26:359-371.

56. de Schonen S. Comments on "Developmental Cognitive Neuroscience. An Introduction" by MH Johnson. *Early Development and Parenting.* 1998;7:133-139.

57. Mondloch C, Geldart S, Maurer D, de Schonen S, Lewis L, Brent HP. The importance of early visual experience for the development of face processing. Poster presented at the European Research Conference: *"Brain Development and Cognition in Human Infants."* San Feliu de Guixols, France, September 1998.

58. de Schonen S. Some reflections on brain specialisation in facedness and physiognomy processing. In: Young A, Ellis HD, eds. *Handbook of Research on Face Processing.* Amsterdam, The Netherlands: North-Holland; 1989:379-389.

59. de Schonen S, Mathivet E. First come first serve: a scenario about the development of hemispheric specialization in face processing in infancy. *European Bulletin of Cognitive Psychology* (CPC). 1989;9: 3-44.

60. Turkewitz G. Face processing as a fundamental feature of development. In: Young A, Ellis HD, eds. *Handbook of Research on Face Processing.* Amsterdam, The Netherlands: North-Holland; 1989: 401-404.

61. Turkewitz G. The origin of differential hemispheric strategies for information processing in the relationships between voice and face perception. In: de Boysson-Bardies B, de Schonen S, Jusczyk P, MacNeilage P, Morton J, eds. *Developmental Neurocognition: Speech and Face Processing in the First Year of Life.* Dordrecht, NL, Boston, Mass, London, UK: Kluwer; 1993:165-170.

62. de Schonen S, Deruelle C, Mancini J, Pascalis O. Hemispheric differences in face processing and brain maturation. In: de Boysson-Bardies B, de Schonen S, Jusczyk P, MacNeilage P, Morton J, eds. *Developmental Neurocognition: Speech and Face Processing in the First Year of Life.* Dordrecht, NL, Boston, Mass, London, UK: Kluwer; 1993:149-163.

63. Atkinson J, Braddick O. Development of basic visual functions. In: Slater A, Bremner G, eds. *Infant Development.* London, England: Lawrence Erlbaum; 1989.

64. de Schonen S, Liegeois F, Mancini J. About functional cortical specialization: the development of face recognition. In: Simion F, Butterworth G. *The Development of Sensory, Motor and Cognitive Capacities in Early Infancy: From Perception to Cognition.* Sussex, England: Erlbaum; 1998:99-115.

65. Banks MS, Stephens BR, Hartmann EE. The development of basic mechanisms of pattern vision. Spatial frequency channels. *Journal of Experimental Child Psychology.* 1985;40:501-527.

66. Banks MS, Dannemiller JL. Infant visual psychophysics. In: Salapatek P, Cohen L, eds. *Handbook of Infant Perception,* vol 1. Orlando, Fla: Academic Press; 1987:115-184.

67. Slater AM. Visual perceptual abilities at birth: implications for face perception. In de Boysson-Bardies B, de Schonen S, Jusczyk P, MacNeilage P, Morton J, eds. *Developmental Neurocognition: Speech and Face Processing in the First Year of Life.* Dordrecht, NL, Boston, Mass, London, UK; 1993:125-134.

Acknowledgements

This paper was supported by Grant RG-33/95B from the Human Frontier Science and Grant BMH4-CT97-2032 from the Biomedical Program of the European Community.

The Development of Representations for Perception and Action

Rick O. Gilmore, PhD

Introduction

How do babies know where things are? This is a central question in developmental psychology for which we do not yet have a complete and satisfying answer. Indeed, perceiving directions and distances of objects in the environment poses a fundamental problem for all animals, not just human infants. The perception of spatial relations demands the capacity to detect and represent information derived from many perceptual sources including vision, proprioception, audition, and olfaction. Moreover, this information must ultimately be made available in a form that can be used to guide a variety of different actions including looking, reaching, and locomotion.

Several lines of research have been brought to bear on the question of how infants perceive the world and plan to act within it. Recordings from neurons in the cerebral cortex have suggested that the nervous system uses a number of different representations of location, each centered on different parts of the body, such as the retina, head, trunk, and arm.[1-3] Behavioral studies of brain-injured adults have revealed how normal and injured brains process spatial information.[4,5] Computational models have suggested how spatial processing might occur in the brain.[6-9] Finally, developmental evidence has suggested that the numerous flexible ways in which adults represent space emerge gradually from much simpler forms.[10-13]

The work described herein attempts to incorporate evidence from all of these perspectives by exploring the development of spatial perception and action in terms of the neural systems and computational processes that support them. The motivation for the approach is straightforward. The human central nervous system develops in a rapid and dramatic fashion at a time early in life when there are equally rapid and dramatic changes in perception, cognition, and behavior. Consequently, patterns of change in the nervous system and its information-processing capabilities may provide fundamental constraints on infants' abilities to perceive, represent, and act on spatial information. Moreover, understanding the development of perception and action systems early in life may be essential to comprehension of how these mechanisms operate in adults.

The focus of my current research is on the joint role of visual and proprioceptive information in the perception of spatial relations and action planning. Perceptual and motor limitations over the first several months of life severely constrain the range and accuracy of spatial information available to young infants from vision and visually related motor behavior. As a consequence, infants' immature visual systems do not represent spatial relations in the flexible ways as those of older children and adults do. Rather the ability to detect and integrate spatial information from visual and proprioceptive sources improves significantly during the first year of life. The result is that mature representations for action emerge from simpler, more primitive forms and that spatial processing engages a different set of functional systems in the infant nervous system than in that of the adult.

Representations for Perception and Action in Adults

A simple model of action planning, perhaps the simplest possible model, has two components. The first involves determining the location or trajectory of a target in space. The second involves planning an action (or series of actions) that moves some part of the body into a position that will intercept the target. The first component, specifically the determination of direction, is reviewed below.

Typically, our abilities to perceive location proceed so effortlessly that we are often unaware of the complexity of the neural machinery that underlies our apparent skill. In fact, both perception and action planning involve representations of location that are coded in multiple frames of reference or coordinate frames (see Fig 1) that are defined relative to multiple points on the body or even features of the environment, depending on the desired behavioral goal.[1,14] Consider the predicament of a soccer player who sees a ball approach. The player may require an eye-based representation – in which the ball is located relative to the current line of gaze to move the eyes to fixate the ball. In addition, the player may require a hand-based representation (to catch the ball), a head-based representation (to deflect the ball), or even a foot-based representation (to kick the ball).

Fig 1. *Two types of coordinate frames useful in perception and action planning: body-relative frames anchored to different sense organs or effectors and environment-relative frames anchored to objects or physical features of the landscape.*

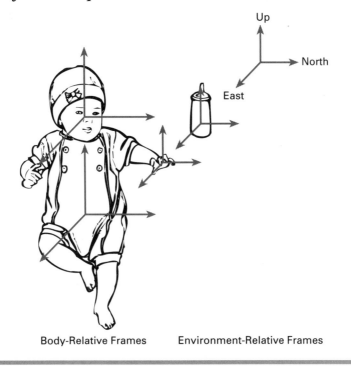

Body-Relative Frames   Environment-Relative Frames

These representations, or frames, seem to follow a logical hierarchy, one building upon another. The simplest possible representation of location, an eye-centered, or retinocentric, representation, could be derived from the topographic, point-to-point projection of the visual image onto the retina. At first glance, this would appear to be all the information needed to move the eyes toward a target in the periphery, but this is not strictly the case. Moving on, we see that a head-based representation would combine visual information (retinal position) and eye position relative to the head; a hand-based representation would combine retinal position, eye position relative to the head, head position relative to the trunk, and hand position relative to the trunk. Other frames of reference for actions involving other parts of the body can be derived in a similar fashion. What should be apparent is that specifying a target location in coordinates relative to any body part other than the retina requires the systematic integration of visual information, a target's position on the retina, and proprioceptive information, such as eye, head, or arm position. Consequently, for most practical purposes, determining the location of a visible object is not strictly a visual task.

von Helmholtz observed more than a century ago that the visual system must combine visual and nonvisual signals to maintain visual stability despite rapid changes of eye and head position.[15] More recent perceptual and neurological evidence supports von Helmholtz's insight that perceiving locations and planning actions engages representations in the brain that combine both visual and nonvisual sources of information. For example, information about eye position and eye movement influences the perception of the relative directions of visual targets, eye-movement planning, and the localization of coincident lights and sounds.[16-20] Neurophysiological studies have revealed the existence of neurons in the occipital, parietal, and frontal lobes of the primate cerebral cortex that appear to code visual target locations in retina-, head-, trunk-, and arm-based coordinates.[1,2] Evidence from patients who have sustained brain injuries suggests that damage to the parietal cortex causes a variety of deficits in spatial-orientation, cognition, and action-planning. These deficits appear to reflect the separate influence of multiple body-centered and even object-based spatial frames of reference.[4,5,21] The challenge for a developmental researcher is to determine how these representations emerge and from what initial form.

Constraints on the Development of Representations for Perception and Action

There are several reasons to believe that young infants are guided by far simpler representations of location than adults. Three interrelated factors constrain the capacity of the developing visual system to integrate visual and proprioceptive information into elaborate, flexible representations of space:

Poor visual acuity and contrast sensitivity. Young infants see poorly. At 1 month of age, infants' visual acuity and contrast sensitivity are an order of magnitude worse than adults'.[22] Infants' visual acuity and contrast sensitivity improve rapidly in the first several months of life,[22] but diminished visual capacities have potentially widespread impact on spatial perception and action planning early in life. Poor visual acuity limits the spatial resolution of retinal information about the position and velocity of visual targets.

Poor eye and head control. Because accurate information about eye and head position is essential for the head- and body-based representations of locations that characterize adult action planning, the ability to make accurate, precise eye and head movements appears crucial for mature spatial processing. The available data suggest, however, that accurate eye and head control does not emerge until several months after birth.

Patterns of development in infants' saccade, pursuit, and vergence behavior provide evidence that infants have poor control over eye position.[23,24] For example, newborns make saccades in the general direction (left/right, up/down) of peripheral stimuli, but they make large errors in amplitude compared with adults,[25] and their saccades are less sensitive to visual feedback than those of adults.[26] Studies of infant smooth pursuit suggest that intermittent smooth pursuit of moving visual targets appears between 6 and 8 weeks of age,[25,27] but eye position often lags target movement, and corrective saccades are common.[28] By 12 weeks, however, many infants anticipate the future location of a moving stimulus by making tracking responses that exceed the velocity of the moving object.[28] Similarly, changes in the magnitude and direction of eye convergence suggest that information regarding relative angular deviation of the eyes is unreliable until 3 to 5 months of age,[23] a period in which stereopsis commonly emerges.[29,30]

Head-position control develops along similar lines. Newborns do not reliably hold their heads erect without support until several weeks after birth; however, some eye movements related to gaze stabilization suggest that sensitivity to head movement may emerge early. Head rotation helps compensate for immature vestibulo-ocular responses by 1 month of age.[31] This behavior closely approximates adult head rotation by approximately 4 months of age.[32] Similarly, without head support "help," infants from 11 to 28 weeks of age showed steady improvements in matching the velocity of their heads to the motions of a visual target but much slower improvement in matching eye velocity to target velocity.[33]

In summary, young infants appear to have initially poor control of their eyes and heads. Eye- and head-movement control improves rapidly, but in the interim, eye- and head-position signals almost certainly provide less reliable sources of spatial information. This would further constrain the accuracy of head- or body-centered representations for actions that depend on this information. If visual and motor commands require a period of postnatal calibration to compensate for growth in the eye and migration of retinal photoreceptors,[34] then neonates' eye-position signals may not provide reliable information until the fine-tuning process is complete. The duration of the calibration period is unknown. Consequently, the first several months of life appear to consist of rapid improvements in infants' capacities to sense where the eyes and head are positioned.

Development of visual cortex. Extensive behavioral and neurological evidence suggests that much of the cortical circuitry related to high-level vision, including those regions thought to be crucial for spatial processing and action planning, is immature at birth.[24,35-38] For example, Huttenlocher showed that total synaptic densities in the neonate visual cortex are initially two to three times smaller than adult levels.[37] The number and density of synapses begin to rise rapidly between 2 and 6 months of age before peaking at twice the adult average in the second year of life. Synaptic numbers and densities subsequently decline, slowly reaching adult levels by approximately age 10 years. Similarly, Chugani and colleagues showed that resting glucose metabolic rates in the infant brain do not reach adult levels (or even approximate the adult distribution of activity) until the end of the first year.[38] These levels of activity eventually reach twice the adult average, by approximately age 9 years, before declining slowly to adult levels.

While the evidence is limited, other regions of the brain implicated in spatial processing appear to mature later and more slowly than primary visual cortex. For example, only minimal changes in metabolic activity in the parietal cortex were observed at 2 months of age compared with marked changes at 3 months.[38] Part of the limitation on early parietal activity may be due to incoherent or insufficiently strong inputs from primary visual cortex to other visual regions.[24] Also, several behavioral measures suggest that parietal circuitry does not strongly influence human-infant visual behavior until 2 to 4 months of age.[24,39]

Based on these data and others concerning patterns of relative immaturity of the infant brain, several authors have argued that visual perception in the first several postnatal months involves a gradual shift from subcortical to cortical control.[24,35,36] This implies that young infants' representations of location are limited by subcortical visual circuitry that develops early. Furthermore, until several months after birth, gradual postnatal development of the cortex limits the availability of flexible representations for perception and action. The available evidence is not conclusive, but it suggests that the subcortical circuits involved in visual perception do not combine visual and nonvisual signals in the same way that cortical circuits do.

Implications of Early Visual Perception

Neonates' limited visual acuity diminishes the resolution and accuracy of spatial information derived from vision. Changes in the accuracy of eye and head control suggest that young infants do not have precise information about the positions of their eyes and heads. Neurological evidence suggests that circuitry in the neonatal cortex devoted to spatial perception and action planning is initially synaptically sparse and metabolically inactive, but shows rapid synaptic proliferation and metabolic increases in the first several months after birth. Adult visual perception and oculomotor behavior involve the systematic integration of visual and proprioceptive sources of spatial information that permit head- or body-based frames of reference to guide behavior. Consequently, the months following birth may involve fundamental changes in the representations that govern visual perception and action planning because of changes in visual acuity, eye- and head-movement control, and cortical circuitry that combine visual and proprioceptive sources of information about spatial location. That intriguing possibility motivated the studies discussed below.

How Do Spatial Representations Change During Development?

Based largely on improvements in infants' capacities to reach for and retrieve hidden objects, Piaget suggested that during the first several years of life infants' representations of spatial relations necessary for problem solving are initially egocentric (body centered), then shift to being essentially allocentric (environment centered) several years after birth.[12,13] This account has been criticized for relying too heavily on infants' behavior toward hidden objects and for overlooking their early competence in using other measures to gain knowledge about object and spatial properties.[37] Nonetheless, several related lines of research have confirmed that infants do shift from egocentric to allocentric representations gradually and at an earlier age than Piaget predicted. In fact, both egocentric and allocentric information influence behavior throughout the first year of life.[10,11] The transition from one representation scheme to the other appears to mark infants' enhanced abilities to integrate mental representations of spatial location with perceptual information that specifies movement within the environment.

Recently, Mark Johnson and I sought to explore how body-centered representations of location develop prior to 6 months of age.[39,40] We adapted a double-step eye-movement paradigm that had been used successfully with adults to explore similar questions. This paradigm was specifically designed to determine whether retinal position alone or some combination with eye- or head-position signals was used in controlling saccades.[16-18] In adult versions of the task, subjects were instructed or trained to make saccades to two visual cues flashed briefly in a dark visual field; the second stimulus appeared and disappeared shortly before or during the first saccade. Retinal-position information alone did not permit observers to plan a saccade to the second target accurately, since the saccade to the first target shifted the center of gaze and with it the second target's position relative to the retina. Accordingly, to make accurate saccades to the locations of both stimuli, viewers would have had to plan the direction and magnitude of their saccades based on target positions defined relative to the head or body. In fact, adults made accurate saccades directly toward the second target without delay or significant error in most circumstances. This provided further support for the notion that adults typically code the location of saccade targets in head- or body-centered coordinates.

Fig 2. Design of double-step saccade experiments.
Stimulus sequences are in the first column, retinal position vectors in the second column, and response types in the third column.

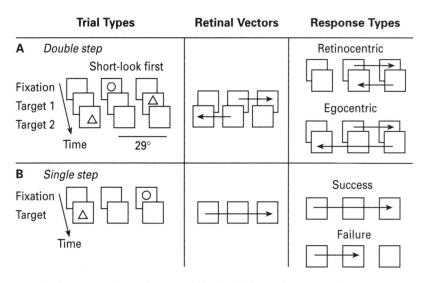

Our adaptation of the double-step paradigm for infants sought to determine what spatial representations guide behavior from the earliest months of life using a behavior that babies could perform from birth: saccadic eye movements (Fig 2). We hypothesized that young infants would be more likely than older infants to code the locations of the visual targets in strictly eye-centered coordinates. Our prediction was based on the presumption that coding the targets' locations in head- or body-centered coordinates would not be possible because it would require accurate integration of visual and proprioceptive information that depend on immature circuitry in the cerebral cortex. Specifically, we predicted that visually based representations of location would dominate saccade planning initially; later, during the first several months of life body-centered representations would gradually strengthen in influence.

In our first set of experiments, 4- to 6-month-old infants viewed a display on a central computer monitor that was followed by a sequence of two visual cues flashed to the left or right of the center of fixation one after the other, in a randomly selected left-right or right-left pattern (see Fig 3 top).[39] In both experiments, the targets elicited sequences of eye movements that were recorded on videotape and subsequently coded for direction and latency. Sequences were classified as *retinocentric* if the second saccade of the sequence ended at the midpoint of the center screen, or *egocentric* if the sequence ended at the midpoint of the screen where the second target had appeared (see Fig 3A top). Single-target trials (Fig 3 bottom) were presented to control for the possibility that 4- and 6-month-olds could differ in their capacity to make long eye movements independent of the specific form of spatial representation.

Fig 3 summarizes the results of the two studies. In both experiments, the ratio of egocentric to retinocentric sequences was significantly smaller in younger infants. A marginally significant difference in the ratio of long looks to short ones was found in the first study but not in the second. The smaller proportion of egocentric saccades to the target location in the younger group suggested that younger infants more often relied on retinocentric coding of visual-target position in planning their saccade sequences. The fact that the mean proportion of successful long saccades in the control trials did not differ significantly argues against an alternative explanation in terms of differences in the ability to make long saccades, but we conducted a second experiment to address this possibility directly.

Fig 3. Results of two double-step saccade experiments.
The mean relative ratio of egocentric to retinocentric saccades is plotted for the experimental trials in the first experiment, and the ratio of total egocentric to retinocentric sequences is plotted for the second experiment. The mean relative ratio of successful long looks to failures is plotted for the control trials.

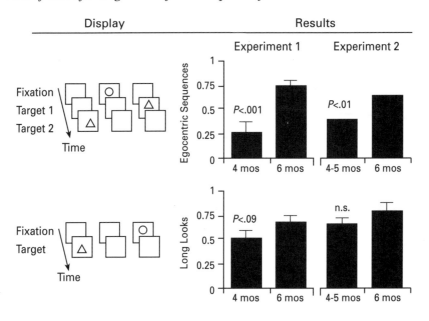

In a second study, we examined the patterns of saccade sequences made by 3- and 7-month-old infants performing a more challenging two-dimensional version of the double-step task.[40] In this experiment (see Fig 4), separate groups of 3- and 7-month-old infants observed double-step visual events. In each trial, a fixation stimulus appeared in one of four positions on the screen (up, down, left, or right). Subsequently, two targets appeared on the screen, one following the other, with no period of overlap. The amount of time each target was on the screen was chosen so that on most trials, both targets would have disappeared prior to the onset of the first saccade. A 1.5-second response interval followed each double-step trial. Saccade sequences were coded as indicated in Fig 4B.

Fig 4. Design of infant double-step saccade experiment.
(A) Stimulus sequence. (B) Response classification. An egocentric sequence consisted of two saccades, one to each target location, and a retinocentric sequence consisted of two saccades, each equivalent to the positions of the targets at the time of presentation relative to the retina.

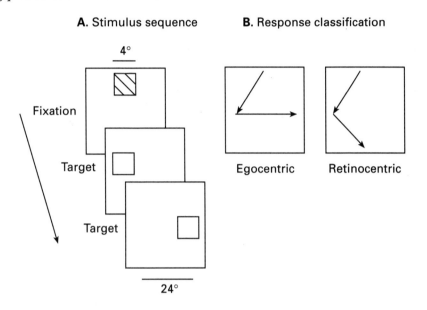

Reprinted from *Cognition.* Vol 65. Gilmore RO, Johnson MH. Body-centered representations for visually-guided action emerge in early infancy. B1-B9. Copyright 1997, with permission from Elsevier Science.

The results of this study are shown in Fig 5. On trials in which babies made initial saccades to the first target, younger babies made fewer second saccades overall (3 months old, 60%; 7 months old, 71%). When they did respond, 3-month-olds made more second saccades (Fig 5B) to the retinocentric screen location where no stimulus flashed (3 months old, 43% of sequences; 7 months old, 25%) and fewer body-centered sequences to the actual target locations (3 months old, 8% of sequences; 7 months old, 42%). Several additional analyses ruled out alternative hypotheses that the results stemmed from improved accuracy or memory for the target locations.[38]

Thus, in three separate experiments, we observed an increase with age in the prevalence of body-centered saccade sequences. The combined results

Fig 5. Results of infant double-step saccade experiment.

(A) Proportion of initial eye movements directed to each of the nine screen locations. T1 and T2 indicate the location of the first and second targets respectively. (B) Proportion of second saccades that followed an initial look to T1. Most second saccades were directed toward either the retinocentric or egocentric (T2/Body) location.

A

Display & location grid

	+	
T1		T2

Mean % valid first saccades

3 mo

2 (1)	+	2 (1)
50 (5)	15 (3)	22 (3)
4 (1)	2 (1)	4 (1)

7 mo

1 (1)	+	0 (0)
59 (5)	5 (2)	30 (4)
2 (1)	1 (0)	1 (1)

B

First saccade to T1

	+	
T1		T2/ Body
	Retino- centric	

Mean % valid second saccades

3 mo

1 (1)	5 (2)	1 (1)
	15 (6)	8 (3)
15 (4)	43 (8)	13 (3)

7 mo

4 (2)	5 (2)	1 (1)
	10 (3)	42 (7)
3 (2)	24 (5)	11 (4)

Reprinted from *Cognition*. Vol 65. Gilmore RO, Johnson MH. Body-centered representations for visually-guided action emerge in early infancy. B1-B9. Copyright 1997, with permission from Elsevier Science.

supported our initial hypothesis that the representations of the location of visual targets for saccades shifts from being eye centered to head or body centered in the first several postnatal months. This coincides with a period of rapid development in the brain's circuitry for action planning.

We interpreted these results to mean that a retinocentric representation of space usually dominates saccade planning in the youngest of infants, but gradual development of cortical circuitry permits functional body-centered representations to emerge subsequently. (These circuits are likely in the parietal lobe because it is associated with processing information about movement and retina and body position.) Our data cannot rule out the possibility, however, that gradual development in subcortical components of the oculomotor system could contribute to the observed shift in representation,[41] nor, because head movements were neither eliminated entirely nor systematically varied, can we distinguish between the possibly separate influences of head- or body-centered coordinates in planning saccades.

Conclusion: The Development of Representations for Perception and Action

Even the simplest visually guided actions depend on representations of locations in which visual and nonvisual sources of information are combined systematically. Available evidence in adults suggests that the systematic combination of visual and proprioceptive sources of information occurs in circuits of the cerebral cortex, particularly in perception- and action-planning areas of the occipital, parietal, and frontal lobes. However, perceptual, motor, and neurological factors suggest that young infants' spatial-processing systems are less highly tuned than in adults. Results of three experiments provided evidence for a gradual shift in the representation of visual location between 3 and 7 months of age. It appears that at least some forms of spatial behavior early in life are guided by simple, visually dominated representations of spatial location and that more stable and flexible body- and environment-centered representations emerge gradually in the first year. Consequently, while eye-, head-, trunk-, arm-, and even object-based representations underlie visually guided action in adults, far simpler frames of reference may be most influential early in life. The development of mature representations for action may be driven both by the infant's perceptual and movement experiences and by the development of circuitry in the brain devoted to action planning.

This evidence pertains directly to the development of spatial information for saccadic eye movements, and it is possible that the shift from eye- to head- or body-centered representations of visual locations does not easily generalize to other perception-action systems. The gradual emergence of body-centered representations to control saccades (during the first 6 months of life) is consistent with the development of other visually guided behaviors that emerge around this age and that may also depend on multimodal, body-centered representations of space. For example, infants between 2 and 6 months of age show increasing sensitivity to self- versus object-patterns of motion,[42] accuracy in orienting toward the location of sounds,[43] and precision in reaching with visual feedback or without it.[44,45] From 6 to 12 months of age, spatial processing continues to develop – infants show increasing sensitivity to landmarks when searching for hidden objects or predicting events. Determining how infants develop integrated representations of space that combine visual, auditory, olfactory, and proprioceptive sources of information remains a challenging and exciting topic for future research.

Another central problem that future research will have to consider concerns the role of early experience. A number of sources suggest that self-produced movements play a powerful role in the normal development of perception and action systems.[46,47] Moreover, a number of factors argue for the importance of experience-dependent plasticity in human infants' visual perception systems, including postnatal changes in the size of the eyes and head, the migration of retinal photoreceptors toward the fovea, and improvements in eye movement control.[23,34] We are beginning to assess individual differences in experiential factors that may contribute to the development of representations for perception and action. At this time, however, we cannot yet say with certainty whether one form of visual experience or another is critical for the development of mature, flexible representations for visually guided action.

It is tempting to speculate that the simple spatial representations that seem to influence eye-movement planning in young infants are truly adaptive. These simple sensorimotor systems may provide the neonate with opportunities to gather information from experience – by looking at a rich, patterned visual world. This experience may be necessary to calibrate the relationship between visual information and motor commands, such as those that drive saccades, and, ultimately, to contribute to the construction of mature representations of space. These representations are subsequently encoded in the newly maturing, powerfully flexible cerebral cortex, and, in turn, they provide new opportunities for action and learning. While this view is speculative, I believe that it will help guide future research into the earliest underpinnings of infants' visuomotor behavior, the results of which promise to illustrate the nature of infants' changing spatial representations and the processes that transform them.

References

1. Andersen RA, Snyder LH, Li CS, Stricanne B. Coordinate transformations in the representation of spatial information. *Current Opinion in Neurobiology.* 1993;3:171-176.

2. Graziano MSA, Yap GS, Gross CG. Coding of visual space by premotor neurons. *Science.* 1994;266: 1054-1057.

3. Stein JF. The representation of egocentric space in the posterior parietal cortex. *Behavioral and Brain Sciences.* 1992;15:691-700.

4. Farah MJ, Brunn JL, Wong AB, Wallace MA, Carpenter PA. Frames of reference for allocating attention to space: evidence from the neglect syndrome. *Neuropsychologia.* 1990;28(4):335-347.

5. Moscovitch M, Behrmann M. Coding of spatial information in the somatosensory system: evidence from patients with neglect following parietal lobe damage. *Journal of Cognitive Neuroscience.* 1994;6(2): 151-155.

6. Goodman SJ, Andersen RA. Microstimulation of a neural network model for visually guided saccades. *Journal of Cognitive Neuroscience.* 1989;1:317-326.

7. Guenther FH, Bullock D, Greve D, Grossberg S. Neural representations for sensorimotor control. III. Learning a body-centered representation of a three-dimensional target position. *Journal of Cognitive Neuroscience.* 1994;6(4):341-358.

8. Olson CR, Hanson SJ. Spatial representation of the body. In: Hanson SJ, Olson CR, eds. *Connectionist Modeling and Brain Function: The Developing Interface.* Cambridge, Mass: MIT Press; 1990:193-254.

9. Zipser D, Andersen RA. A back-propagation programmed network that simulates response properties of a subset of posterior parietal neurons. *Nature.* 1988;331:679-684.

10. Acredolo L. Behavioral approaches to spatial orientation in infancy. *Annals of the New York Academy of Sciences.* 1990;608:596-612.

11. Bremner JG. Egocentric versus allocentric spatial coding in nine-month-old infants: factors influencing the choice of code. *Developmental Psychology.* 1978;14:346-355.

12. Piaget J; Cook M, trans. *The Construction of Reality in the Child.* New York, NY: Basic Books; 1954.

13. Piaget J, Inhelder B; Landon FJ, Lunzer JL, trans. *The Child's Conception of Space.* London, England: Routledge & Kegan Paul; 1948.

14. Marr D. *Vision.* San Francisco, Calif: W Freeman; 1982.

15. von Helmholtz H. *Treatise of Physiological Optics.* New York, NY: Dover; 1925.

16. Becker W, Jürgens R. An analysis of the saccadic system by means of double step stimuli. *Vision Research.* 1979;19:967-983.

17. Hallett PE, Lightstone AD. Saccadic eye movements to flashed targets. *Vision Research.* 1976;114: 107-114.

18. Hallett PE, Lightstone AD. Saccadic eye movements towards stimuli triggered by prior saccades. *Vision Research.* 1976;16:99-106.

19. Matin L, Pearce DG. Visual perception of direction for stimuli flashed during voluntary saccadic eye movements. *Science.* 1965;148:1485-1488.

20. Matin L, Stevens JK, Picoult E. Perceptual consequences of experimental extraocular muscle paralysis. In: Paillard J, ed. *Brain and Space.* Oxford, England: Oxford University Press; 1991.

21. Behrmann M, Tipper SP. Object-based attentional mechanisms: evidence from patients with unilateral neglect. In: Umilta C, Moscovitch M, eds. *Attention and Performance XV: Conscious and Nonconscious Information Processing.* Cambridge, Mass: MIT Press; 1994:351-375.

22. Banks MS, Dannemiller JL. Infant visual psychophysics. In: Salapatek P, Cohen LB, eds. *Handbook of Infant Perception: From Sensation to Perception.* New York, NY: Academic Press; 1987:115-184.

23. Aslin RN. Motor aspects of visual development in infancy. In: Salapatek P, Cohen LB, eds. *Handbook of Infant Perception: From Sensation to Perception.* New York, NY: Academic Press; 1987:43-113.

24. Johnson MH. Cortical maturation and the development of visual attention in early infancy. *Journal of Cognitive Neuroscience.* 1990;2(2):81-95.

25. Aslin RN, Salapatek P. Saccadic localization of visual targets by very young infants. *Perception and Psychophysics.* 1975;17:293-302.

26. Salapatek P, Aslin RN, Simonson J, Pulos E. Infant saccadic eye movements to visible and previously visible targets. *Child Development.* 1980;51:1090-1094.

27. Hainline L. Oculomotor control in human infants. In: Groner R, McConkie GW, Menz C, eds. *Eye Movements and Human Information Processing.* Amsterdam, Netherlands: Elsevier; 1985.

28. Aslin RN. Development of smooth pursuit in human infants. In: Fisher DF, Monty RA, Senders JW, eds. *Eye Movements: Cognition and Visual Perception.* Hillsdale, NJ: Erlbaum; 1981:31-51.

29. Gwiazda J, Bauer J, Held R. From visual acuity to hyperacuity: a 10-year update. *Canadian Journal of Psychology.* 1989;43:109-120.

30. Birch EE, Gwiazda J, Held R. Stereoacuity development for crossed and uncrossed disparities in human infants. *Vision Research.* 1982;22:507-513.

31. Regal DM, Ashmead DH, Salapatek P. The coordination of eye and head movements during early infancy: a selective review. *Behavioral and Brain Research.* 1983;10:125-132.

32. Reisman JE, Anderson JH. Compensatory eye movements during head and body rotation in infants. *Brain Research.* 1989;484(1-2):119-129.

33. Daniel BM, Lee DN. Development of looking with head and eyes. *Journal of Experimental Child Psychology.* 1990;50(2):200-216.

34. Aslin RN. Perception of visual direction in human infants. In: Granrud CE, ed. *Visual Perception and Cognition in Infancy.* Hillsdale, NJ: Lawrence Erlbaum Associates; 1993.

35. Atkinson J. Human visual development over the first six months of life: a review and a hypothesis. *Human Neurobiology.* 1984;3:61-74.

36. Bronson GW. The postnatal growth of visual capacity. *Child Development.* 1994;45:873-890.

37. Huttenlocher PR. Morphometric study of human cerebral cortex development. *Neuropsychologia.* 1990;28:517-527.

38. Chugani HT, Phelps ME, Mazziotta JC. Positron emission tomography study of human brain functional development. *Annals of Neurology.* 1987;22:487-497.

39. Gilmore RO, Johnson MH. Egocentric action in early infancy: spatial frames of reference for saccades. *Psychological Science.* 1997;8:224-230.

40. Gilmore RO, Johnson MH. Body-centered representations for visually-guided action emerge in early infancy. *Cognition.* 1997;65:B1-B9.

41. Mays LE, Sparks DL. Dissociation of visual and saccade related responses in superior colliculus neurons. *Journal of Neurophysiology.* 1980;43:207-232.

42. Kellman PJ, von Hofsten C. The world of the moving infant: perception of motion, stability, and space. In: Rovee-Collier C, Lipsitt LP, eds. *Advances in Infancy Research.* Vol 7. Norwood, NJ: Ablex Publishing Corp; 1995:147-185.

43. Muir DW, Field J. Newborn infants orient to sounds. *Child Development.* 1979;50:431-436.

44. von Hofsten C. Developmental changes in the organisation of prereaching movements. *Developmental Psychology.* 1984;20:378-388.

45. Clifton RK, Muir DW, Ashmead DH, Clarkson MG. Is visually guided reaching in early infancy a myth? *Child Development.* 1993;61(1):1098-1110.

46. Bertenthal B, Campos J, Barrett K. Self-produced locomotion: an organizer of emotional, cognitive, and social development in infancy. In: Emde R, Harmon R, eds. *Continuities and Discontinuities in Development.* New York, NY: Plenum Press; 1984:175-210.

47. Held R, Hein A. Movement produced stimulation in the development of visually guided behavior. *Journal of Comparative Physiological Psychology.* 1963;56(5):872-876.

The Emergence of Future-Oriented Thinking in the Early Years

Marshall M. Haith, PhD

Introduction

This paper will address a cluster of psychological processes in infants and young children that I believe underlies the development of children's ability to think about the future. This cluster is referred to as future-oriented processes (FOPs), a term that includes such processes as perceptual set, prospective motor processes, expectations, forecasting, intentionality, planning, and goal setting – any process that is oriented to events that have not yet occurred. My colleagues and I have taken three approaches to this phenomenon (Table 1). The first is an experimental approach with infants who are usually in the first 3 months of life but may be as old as 7 months. The second involves an interview and questionnaire to obtain parents' reports of their children's understanding about the future, when the children are 9 to 42 months of age. The third consists of longitudinal analyses of transcripts of parents' utterances with their children to examine to what extent parents talk to their children about the past, present, and future at 14, 20, and 32 months of age.

If one were to ask most people how much time they spend thinking about the past, present, and future, the most common answer would be that future-oriented thought occupies an enormous amount of mental energy, typically much more than past thought. A few examples are your thoughts about what you are going to wear in the morning, with whom you will have lunch, when you plan to work on a report, how you can set aside enough money for retirement, and when you should call your physician to make an appointment.

Nonetheless, psychology has paid very little attention to future-oriented thought, certainly in comparison to past-oriented thought, or what is referred to as memory. For memory, there are several cognitive, neurophysiological, and biochemical models, a highly developed terminology (eg, short- and long-term memory, working memory, episodic memory, and semantic memory), and a large number of accepted paradigms for studying these domains. This is not true for future-oriented thought. That is not to say that people

Table 1. Three Approaches to Studying the Development of Future-Oriented Processes

Experimental

Initial findings with 3-month-olds

Expectations for nonalternating events

Adaptive function of expectations

Role of constraints in infant expectations

Individual differences in expectation formation and prediction of later cognitive functioning

Questionnaire

Dimensions of future-oriented thinking

Development from 9 months to 3 years in understanding

Parents' report of their talk about the future

Observational

Categorizing time talk

Percent of parents' utterances about past, present, and future

---

have ignored phenomena that involve future-oriented thinking; future thinking is embedded in virtually everything we do. Research on planning and problem solving are prime examples. Nevertheless, the spotlight has not been turned on FOPs in the same way that it has illuminated research on memory; there has not been a focus on future-oriented thought processes per se.

This neglect is even more severe in the area of child development, so my colleagues and I have spent the last decade or so doing what we can to bring this issue into focus. Our belief is that FOPs are crucial to adaptation of any organism to the world. In fact, the irony is that the adaptive function of memory is to foster better future-oriented action. Memory benefits us by enabling more effective functioning in future situations; to paraphrase the Boy Scouts, "Preparation is all."

Where do FOPs come from? To address this question, we have been conducting a research program with infants mostly in the first 3 months of life. At this age, infants' motor control is not sophisticated enough to permit them to press buttons or pull levers and, even if they could, their ability to understand instructions is nonexistent. Therefore, we engineered studies to take advantage of their visual behavior and eye movements to tell us what the brain is doing, specifically the expectations they form for what comes next. Eye movements are well controlled by alert infants almost from birth; in fact, this infant motor system more closely parallels that of the adult than any other action system.

The Basic Visual Expectation Paradigm and Initial Findings

The video setup that we use to record infant eye movements is shown in Fig 1. Infants lie on their backs and watch displays on the television screen reflected in a mirror angled at 45°, while we record the image of their eye with infrared light through the mirror. Attractive pictures appear to the left and the right of center, for example, checkerboards, faces, and bull's-eyes.

Fig 1. Infant recording apparatus.

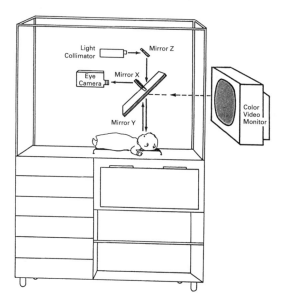

Fig 2 shows typical timing for an alternating sequence with, for example, a picture on the left for 700 msec, followed by an interpicture interval (IPI) of 1000 msec, then a picture on the right for 700 msec, and so on. Later, we decode the infants' eye orientation, frame by frame, 30 times each second, to determine where they are looking at each moment. We do this either manually or through a custom-built computerized eye tracker.

Fig 2. Timeline for a typical study.

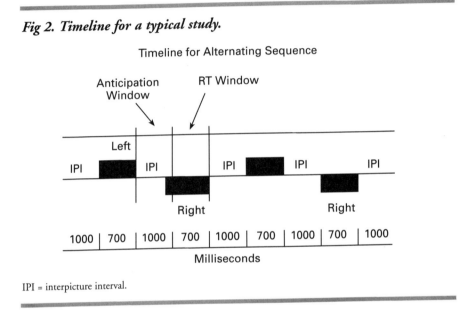

IPI = interpicture interval.

We use these important concepts in these studies: expectation, anticipation, and facilitation. *Expectation* is a construct that we infer from specific behaviors of the infant. We cannot see expectations, but we can see their effect. The most obvious effect is *anticipation,* which we define as an eye movement to the location where an event is going to happen before it begins – during the interpicture interval or so quickly after a picture appears that the eye movement must have been programmed beforehand. *Facilitation* is another indicator of expectation – most of the time, infants do not actually anticipate the next event, but their reaction times to picture onsets are so quick that they appeared ready for them to occur, as though they forecast what was coming next. We calculate response time (RT) from the time of picture onset to the beginning of a reactive eye movement. With proper control conditions, one can ask whether infants form expectations from their RT data – their efficiency of response indicates preparedness just as the efficiency of an adult's driving behavior (braking) is enabled by seeing a school-zone sign before seeing a ball bounce into the street.

Fig 3. Infant visual tracking record.

Shown here is a sequence of picture onsets, indicated by the rectangular boxes, that are separated by blank display interpicture intervals; time proceeds from top to bottom. Overlaid on this picture sequence are an infant's fixations and eye movements (dotted line). One can see that for the first several pictures of the eye-tracking record of the 3-month-old infant, the eye movements are reactive. For the fifth and sixth pictures, the infant anticipates picture onset and also does so for several other pictures. On average, infants who show any anticipations at all make their first anticipation within 17 seconds of the beginning of the series.

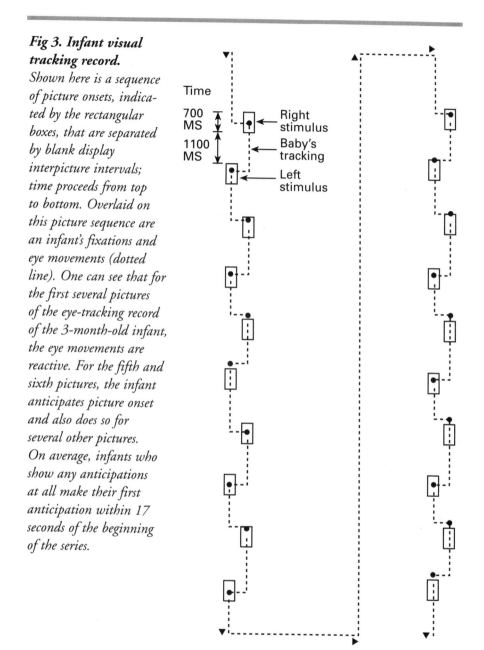

Time

700 MS

1100 MS

Right stimulus

Baby's tracking

Left stimulus

Adapted from Haith MM. The early development of visual expectations. In Granrud C (ed), *Carnegie-Mellon Symposium on Visual Perception and Cognition in Infancy.* Lawrence Erlbaum Associates; 1993. Courtesy of the author.

Table 2 displays some RT and anticipation data for the experiment.[1] We typically present 10 baseline pictures at the beginning in randomly sequenced locations to get an indication of infants' "raw" RT before they have learned anything about the patterns. These baseline RTs were longer than RTs in the subsequent predictable, alternating series. For infants who saw a nonpredictable, irregular series, however, the RTs did not decrease following baseline. Infants in the alternating group also displayed significantly more fixation shifts to the opposite side during the interpicture interval than did those in the irregular group.

Table 2. Median Reaction Times and Percent of Anticipations.

	Predictable Alternating Display	Nonpredictable Irregular Display
Reaction Time: Baseline	468 msec	462 msec
Reaction Time: Experimental	391 msec	462 msec
Anticipations	22%	11.1%

Adapted from Haith MM, Hazan C, Goodman GS. Expectation and anticipation of dynamic visual events by 3.5 month-old babies. *Child Development.* 1988;59:467-479.

Expectations for More Complex Event Sequences

One of the limitations of this experiment is its simplicity. One might suppose that infants somehow become trained to a pendulum-like sequence and for some reason just sped up a bit, eventually moving ahead of each picture appearance, displaying a kind of mental short-circuiting. Digging deeper, Richard Canfield and I carried out a separate experiment that showed why this was not the case.[2] Fig 4 shows the four groups that were used. One group saw an alternating series (as in the previous study [the 1/1 group]), a second group saw a repeating series of two pictures on the left side, followed by one on the right side (the 2/1 group), and a third group saw a repeating series of three pictures on the left, followed by one on the right (the 3/1 group). A fourth, control, group saw a random series with embedded 1/1, 2/1, and 3/1 series, but the location of the next picture at any moment was unpredictable.

Fig 4. *Complex event sequences schematic conditions.*

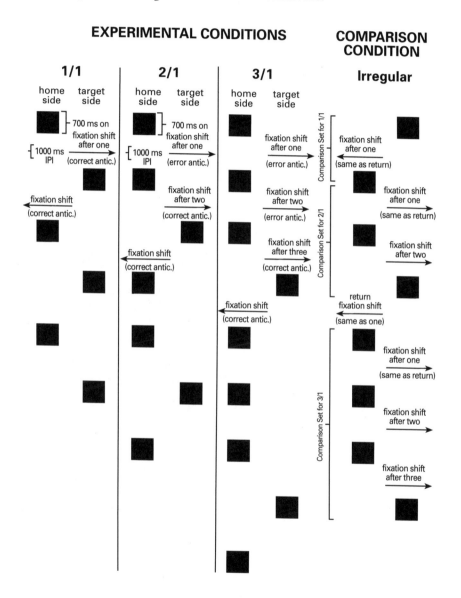

Fig 5. Infant visual tracking record for the 2/1 sequence.

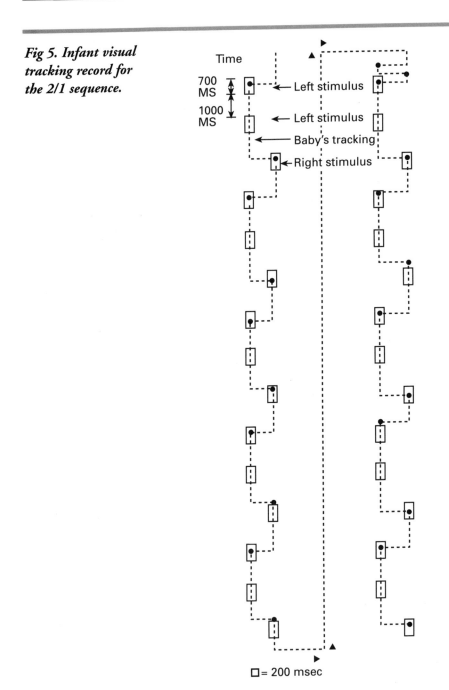

Time

700 MS

1000 MS

Left stimulus

Left stimulus

Baby's tracking

Right stimulus

□ = 200 msec

Adapted from Haith MM. The early development of visual expectations. In Granrud C (ed), *Carnegie-Mellon Symposium on Visual Perception and Cognition in Infancy.* Lawrence Erlbaum Associates;1993. Courtesy of the author.

Fig 5 displays a tracking sequence for an infant in the 2/1 condition. One can see again that the infant first only reacts to pictures as they are presented but then quickly begins to anticipate forthcoming pictures (eg, pictures 9 and 12). Fig 6 shows the data for the whole experiment in terms of RT decline from baseline. For 3-month-olds, as the complexity of the sequence increased, the RT savings diminished. Infants in the 2/1 condition had a reliably greater decline than did control infants, and they had more frequent anticipations. The RT of the 2-month-old group did not benefit from predictability in any of the series.

This study demonstrates that, by 3 months of age, infants not only form expectations for sequences that are nonpendular but also that they are capable of quickly forming expectations when different numbers of events occur in one location than another.

Fig 6. Change in reaction times and sequence complexity.

The simple sequences had shorter reaction times.

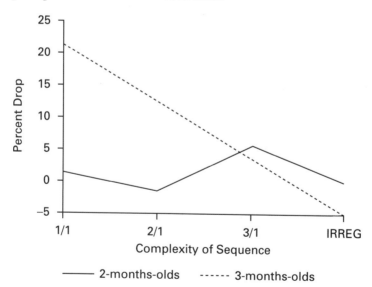

As stated earlier, the benefit of memory is more efficient performance in future situations to which experience can be applied. The above experiments have only demonstrated that an infant can learn in a single session to form expectations for what comes next in that situation. Can infants utilize expectations they form for situations in which they later find themselves?

The Adaptive Function of Expectations

Denise Arehart and I observed 3-month-olds in two sessions, separated by about 1 week.[3] On the first visit, two groups saw different sequences; Group 1 saw a regular alternating sequence, Group 2 saw a random irregular sequence. On the second visit, both groups saw a regular alternating sequence. The data presented here are for only the second visit, when both groups saw the same display. As shown in Fig 7, the group that saw the alternating sequence on week 1 was much faster to respond in the first blocks of 10 pictures than the group that saw the random series. After three blocks of trials, the irregular group caught up, but they slowed down in blocks 5 and 6. Fig 8 shows the data for anticipations. Again, the group that saw the alternating sequence produced more anticipations at the beginning and, in fact, throughout the test session. This study illustrates that infants can use their experience as an aid for forming expectations for similar situations at a later time.

Fig 7. Median reaction times on Visit 2.

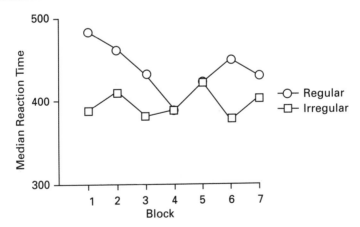

Adapted from Haith MM, Wentworth N, Canfield RL. The formation of expectations in early infancy. In: Rovee-Collier C, Lipsitt LP (eds) *Advances in Infancy Research.* Norwood, NJ; Ablex: 1993.

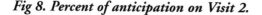

Fig 8. Percent of anticipation on Visit 2.

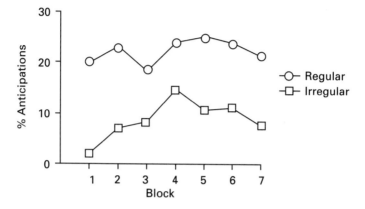

Adapted from Haith MM, Wentworth N, Canfield RL. The formation of expectations in early infancy. In Rovee-Collier C, Lipsitt LP, eds. *Advances in Infancy Research.* Norwood, NJ: Ablex; 1993.

The situations discussed so far are fairly limited. After all, how often is it that we know exactly what will happen next? In the non-laboratory world, we tend to form expectations for classes of events rather than for specific things to happen. In listening or reading, for example, when we hear the sentence "Jane picked up the…" we know that the next word will be a noun and that it will be something that is graspable (ie, not a football field, fire, water, air, etc), even though we do not know exactly what the object will be. We use constraints such as these in language to facilitate both reading and listening. Are babies only capable of benefitting from expectations for something that will certainly happen, or can they benefit also from expectations for events that are only likely to happen? Stated differently, are infants able to benefit from knowing what *can* happen as well as exactly what *will* happen?

The Role of Constraints in Infant Expectation

Thomas Dougherty addressed this question in an experiment that modified our usual paradigm.[4] Instead of using a continuing flow of pictures, he used what looks like a more traditional trial format. Each trial started with an attractive picture that appeared in the center of the screen to get the infant's attention. Infants participated in one of three groups at 7 months of age (see Fig 9). For the perfectly predictable group (0 bits, in information-theory terminology), the center picture disappeared, and, a variable time later, a peripheral target picture appeared, always in the same place. For different infants, this target picture could appear in one of four locations – up-left, up-right, down-left, or down-right. For the two-location group, the target picture could appear in either of two places (either up-left or down-right, for example), but on any trial the infant had no way to predict which would occur. Thus, this group had constraints on where things could happen, but infants did not know exactly where something would appear next. For the four-location group, a picture could appear in any of four locations, up-left, up-right, down-left, or down-right, again unpredictably.

The results were consistent with the hypothesis that infants can use constraints on what can happen even when they cannot predict exactly what it will be. Response times improved (difference between baseline and postbaseline; see Fig 10) when the infants were more constrained and had fewer possi-

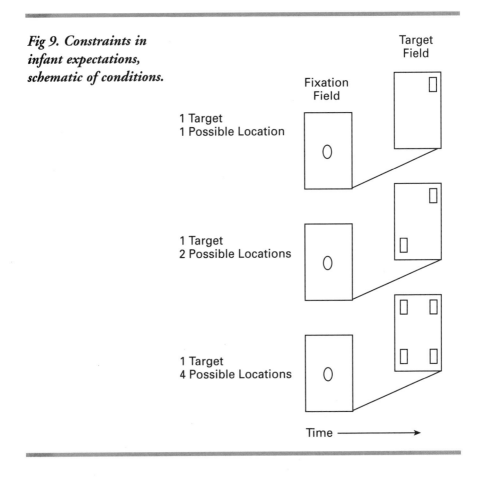

Fig 9. Constraints in infant expectations, schematic of conditions.

Target Field

Fixation Field

1 Target
1 Possible Location

1 Target
2 Possible Locations

1 Target
4 Possible Locations

Time ⟶

Fig 10. Facilitation of reaction times for the three conditions.

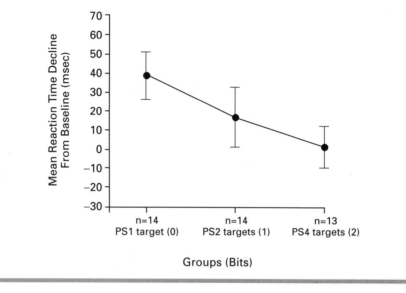

bilities that could occur. Importantly, there was significantly greater facilitation for the two-location than for the four-location condition, even though precise predictability was not present for either. Data from anticipatory fixations supported the RT data. In the two-location group, when infants did anticipate the next picture, they usually looked at a possible location rather than at an impossible location; this was true for eight of nine infants, indicating that they were sensitive to where things could happen even if they did not know exactly when. Thus, as for adults, young infants can use constraints in the environment to form expectations for likely but not certain events.

Individual Differences

The question always arises about whether we are really tapping cognitive functioning with this paradigm and, if so, whether there are individual differences in performance. The quick answer is "yes" to both questions. In one study, we brought 3-month-old infants back to the lab a little less than 1 week after they had seen an alternating left-right sequence and showed them the same sequence again.[5] We obtained both stable within-session and between-session performance for RTs, with between-session correlations typically in the .60s. Individual stability was somewhat less evident for anticipations, with the between-session correlation falling in the mid-.30s.

Indications that we are tapping a cognitive process and that infant performance is predictive of later cognitive functioning come from three studies. One
yielded stable correlations between performance on the Visual Expectation
Paradigm at 8 months of age and performance on the Stanford-Binet at
3 years of age, and a second study produced a similar finding between infant
performance and midparent IQ (as a proxy for the eventual infants' IQ).[6,7]
More recently, Thomas Dougherty and I followed up infants whom we had
seen at 3 months of age to assess their RT and intellectual performance at
around 4 years of age.[8] We obtained the first somewhat surprising evidence
that there is a fairly strong relation between infant RT and childhood RT but,
more relevant, that RT and percent of anticipations correlated with infants'
full-scale IQ at 4 years of age (see Fig 11). We also examined whether variability in infants' RTs was predictive and found that the amount of variability
correlated reliably with childhood full-scale IQ.

It is not clear what processes are responsible for the continuity that we
found between early infancy and childhood. Our best guess is that RT taps

---

***Fig 11. Relation between infant performance in the Visual Expectation
Paradigm and childhood RT, anticipations, and IQ.***

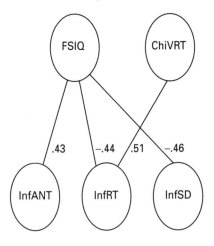

FSIQ = Full Scale IQ
ChiVRT = Childhood Visual Reaction Time
InfANT = Infant Percent Anticipations
InfRT = Infant Reaction Time (eye movement)
InfSD = Infant Standard Deviation of Reaction Times

processing speed, anticipations tap memory, and RT variance taps maintenance of attention. These are all processes that have been implicated in intelligence tests, but we are speculating at this point, and a lot more research must be done to validate or refute these possibilities.

Summary: Reaction Time Studies

We have seen that infants form visual expectations as early as 3 months of age, and they do so very quickly – typically within only a few seconds of exposure to a regular spatiotemporal visual display. This ability can be demonstrated not only for simple left-right sequences but also for sequences that require the infant to remember a complete spatial pattern and where the infant is in that pattern at each moment (eg, the 2/1 sequence). Thus, it seems quite easy and natural for infants to form expectations for predictable events. Moreover, we have seen that infants can remember the events for which they formed expectations and can utilize that stored information in a later, similar task. They also appear to be able to detect constraints on what can happen next, so they are not limited to forming expectations only for perfectly certain events. Finally, there are reliable individual differences between infants both in RT and in their tendency to form expectations. These individual differences are predictive of moderate variance in cognitive performance in later childhood, so it appears that the Visual Expectation Paradigm is tapping processes that are important for cognitive development. We believe that candidate processes are processing speed, memory, and the ability to sustain attention. Regardless, the roots of future-oriented processing seem to be established in the very early months of life.

The Questionnaire Approach

While the approximately 20 years that we have put into developing and exploiting the Visual Expectation Paradigm have been fruitful in tapping a domain of future-oriented processing in early childhood, we also knew that we were missing many other aspects of future thinking that occur outside the lab in everyday life. To get a feeling for what these domains might be, we adopted a very different approach, consisting initially of interviews with mothers of infants which led to developing and using questionnaires. The effort was enlightening both in terms of the difficulty of conceptual bootstrapping in an undeveloped area and in terms of how much effort is required to develop a useful, understandable, and reliable instrument from scratch.[9]

We are close to submitting a more complete report of our findings from follow-up studies.

The questionnnaire consists of two parts (see Table 3). The first part deals with family-context factors – parents' beliefs about what their children understand about the future, parent theories about how children learn about the future, family practices that promote future understanding (regular routines, traditions, etc), and how the parents were raised along these dimensions. The second part involves the domains of future-oriented processing that represent our initial approach to conceptualizing the dimensions of future thinking in young children. These domains are Order (ordering of events), Routines (knowing what follows what in a routine), Planning, Expectation, Time, and Problem Solving. Examples of these domains are shown in Table 4. In later work, we added a section that we call an Emotional/Compliance domain, which addresses social negotiation in rule situations (eg, "if you jump on the bed, you'll go to time out").

Table 3. The Future-Oriented Processes Questionnaire (9-36 Months) Demographic Information.[9]

Part I: Contextual Influences

- Parental beliefs: what child knows about near- vs far-term future (4-point scale: Understands Well – Does Not Understand)
- Parental theories: how child knows about the future (4-point scale: Importance Ranking)
- Family practices (4-pt scale: Almost Always – Almost Never)
- Precedent family practices (4-pt scale: Almost Always – Almost Never)

Part II: Domains (and Subdomains) of Future Orientation
(4-point scale: Very True – Not at All True)

- Order
- Routine
- Planning
- Expectation (cues; violations; language; comprehension; production)
- Time (terms; duration; verbs; tools)
- Problem solving (flexibility; goal-orientation; social)

Table 4. Example Questions for the Six Domains.[9]

(Possible Answers: Very true, Sometimes true, Once in a while, Not at all true)

- **Order**
  My child understands that some things must happen before other things. (Example: "You must wash before eating" means wash your hands and then eat lunch.)

- **Routine**
  My child wants some things done the same way every time. (Example: Having a snack before bedtime.)

- **Planning**
  My child does things that show preparation for the future. (Example: My child gets a toy to take to Grandma's.)

- **Expectation** (cues; violation; language; comprehension; production)
  My child has expectations for things that happen. (Example: My child expects someone to enter the house when hearing the doorbell.)

- **Time** (terms; duration; verbs; tools)
  My child understands time if I compare it to something familiar. (Example: "It will take as long as 'Sesame Street' for the cookies to be ready.")

- **Problem-solving** (goal orientation; flexibility; social agent)
  My child tries to get help from others to get something done. (Example: Putting my hand on the music box to make it play.)

In our first study, 68 parents participated who had children ranging in age from 9 to 36 months. We carried out an additional study with 286 more parents of 12- to 42-month-olds with a revised survey, but the initial findings are not materially different from the earlier findings, which are reported here.

First, we ran alpha statistical tests to give us some indication of the coherence of questions within domains and their separability from other domains, and these turned out satisfactorily, ranging from the mid-.60s to the mid-.90s (Table 5).

Table 5. Item Internal Consistency (Alpha) for Future-Orientation Domains.[9]

DOMAIN	N	ALPHA	# OF ITEMS
Order	66	.85	2
Routine	68	.67	2
Planning	66	.80	2
Expectation	61	.92	13
Time	63	.86	8
Problem solving	66	.79	8

Second, there was more clear development for some of the domains than for others, as shown in Fig 12. We worried about whether parents' judgment would be influenced by their children's language development, but the change in domains does not parallel language changes very closely. The level of performance for some domains is high throughout the age range; for others, the level changes dramatically, and for still others performance remains relatively low while yet improving with age. Thus, the different domains of future orientation do not follow the same developmental course.

Third, very surprisingly, parents' reports of how much they talked to their children about the future did not vary much across the age range of 9 months to 36 months, a wide developmental span. The reports at least seemed to have some validity, because parents gave sensible answers when asked how much they talked about the future as a function of time. That is, they reported less talk about more distant future events (eg, months away) than about more proximal events (eg, tomorrow; see Fig 13).

This does not seem reasonable, however. We all know that infants understand more of what one says to them when they are 3 years old than when they are 9 months old. Are parents really unaware of what their own children understand? Fig 14 shows what parents think their children understand about what they are being told; I have superimposed the data from Fig 13 on this graph. In fact, parents know very well that their 9-month-olds do not understand what they are saying and that their children understand more as they grow older. This knowledge does not seem to affect how much they talk to their children about the future – at least, that is what they report.

Fig 12. Age trends for the major domains of the Future-Oriented Processes Questionnaire.

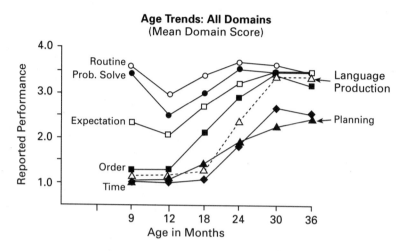

Adapted from Benson JB. The origins of future orientation in the everyday lives of 9- to 36-month-old infants. In Haith MM, Benson JB, Roberts RJ Jr, Pennington BF, eds. *The Development of Future-Oriented Processes.* Chicago, IL: University of Chicago Press; 1994.

Fig 13. Future time talk by parents to their children at different ages.

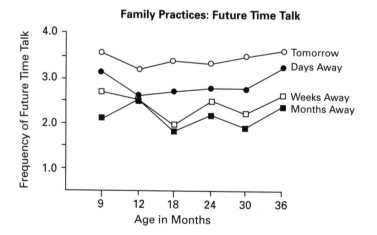

Adapted from Benson JB. The origins of future orientation in the everyday lives of 9- to 36-month-old infants. In Haith MM, Benson JB, Roberts RJ Jr, Pennington BF, eds. *The Development of Future-Oriented Processes.* Chicago, IL: University of Chicago Press; 1994.

Fig 14. Parental beliefs about their children's understanding of time talk.

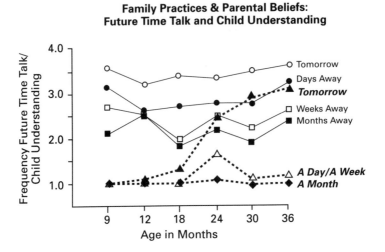

Adapted from Benson JB. The origins of future orientation in the everyday lives of 9- to 36-month-old infants. In Haith MM, Benson JB, Roberts RJ Jr, Pennington BF, eds. *The Development of Future-Oriented Processes.* Chicago, IL: University of Chicago Press; 1994.

There appear to be two factors in operation here. One is that parents do not know precisely what their infants understand, but they do know that their understanding about the future will grow. They talk to their children about future events, because they know that understanding emerges gradually and that their children will come to grasp what is going to happen next as they connect language to action – hearing about something that will happen and then actually seeing it happen. In brief, the parent scaffolds the child's accumulating grasp of future events through talk; like chicken soup for the common cold, future talk may not help, but it can't hurt. The second factor is that the parent is constantly thinking about what she has to do next or about planning for future events and is simply talking out loud, about events such as errands, dinner, or picking up an older sibling from school. Perhaps adults would do the same if we had only a dog as a companion. Nevertheless, the potential scaffolding effect is the same.

This branch of our research effort has broadened our horizons about the various planes on which future thinking develops. There are three conclusions to be drawn from this brief description. First, the span of FOPs is quite broad in early childhood, certainly a lot broader than expectation formation in the lab in young infants. Second, not all domains advance at the same pace. Third, the scaffolding of infants' learning about the future can be quite extensive, with parent speech being a major component.

Observation of Future-Oriented Talk

We were troubled by the lack of direct empirical support for the information we were getting from parents. Do parents really talk to their children about the future as much as they say? Wouldn't we expect parent talk to be mostly about the present and the past, leveraging on young children's direct experience? If so, perhaps future-oriented talk just slips in as a minor fraction of parent-child dialogue, because, in fact, it is important only to the parent.

To address this question, we used the Child Language Data Exchange System, which was pioneered by Brian MacWhinney at Carnegie-Mellon University. This is a large database of coded transcripts of parent-child narratives. We analyzed data from a longitudinal project headed by Catherine Snow based on mother-infant dialogues when the child was 14, 20, and 32 months of age.[10,11] The setting consisted of free play and the presentation of several play objects. Each of the mother's utterances was categorized in terms of orientation to the past, the present, or the future (with more emphasis on event time than on tense; see Table 6 for examples). Utterances that were categorized as naming, imperatives, or ambiguous were not included. Thus our analysis for future events is somewhat conservative, as other investigators consider imperatives to be future oriented.

We expected a small change in future talk with age, consistent with the questionnaire data we collected. We also thought that talk about the past would increase with age as the child's memory improved and that overall time talk would increase also.

Fig 15 displays the results of our analyses. Across all ages, we found that utterances most often could be categorized as dealing with the present, but we also found a substantial fraction of utterances that dealt with the future, and these increased with age. Counterintuitive to what most people might expect,

Table 6. Sample Adult Utterances, Coding Category, and Rationale.

Adult Utterance	Coding Category Type	Rationale
Time Talk:		
"We danced at ballet class yesterday."	Past	past event, past tense
"I put that on chicken when I make some dishes."		past event, current tense
"Now here we are."	Current	current event, current tense
"You've got too much in it."		current event, current tense
"We need to write it down."	Future	future event, future tense
"Let me see if I can do that myself."		future event, future tense
Other Talk:		
"This is a duck."	Naming	naming an object
"Elmo is playing soccer."		naming an action
"Put the chicken to bed."	Imperative	command statement
"Let me see your finger."		
"What?"	Ambiguous	unsure of the reference of the utterance
"Hmmm."		

there were many more utterances that referenced the future than the past. These data support what parents have been telling us. Parents spend a significant amount of time talking to their children about the future. Of all utterances that we categorized as time talk, around 30% were about the future over all ages and close to 5% were about the past. Again, we did not include imperatives; if we had, the discrepancy between the percentages of past and future talk would be even greater.

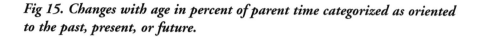

Fig 15. Changes with age in percent of parent time categorized as oriented to the past, present, or future.

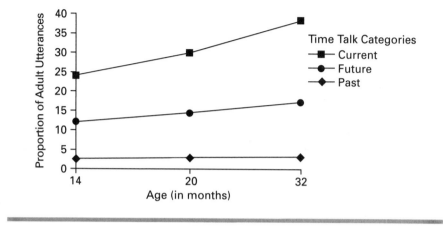

Conclusions

Future events play an important role in the life of the young child. Even in the first months of life, infants are aware of what comes next, and they organize their mental activity and behavior around what is going to happen for predictable events rather than just reacting to them. After the fact, one can ask how it could be otherwise. A world without expectations would be chaotic. We have shown several aspects of this future-oriented process, including its importance in maximizing efficiency for later behavior, its status as a cognitive process, and its relation to stable processes that underlie intellectual performance in the early years. The questionnaire work has helped us to dimensionalize the domains that constitute early future-oriented thinking beyond the laboratory into everyday life. Finally, the language analyses support our intuitions and parents' reports that at least the children in our sample are surrounded by influences, both linguistic and nonlinguistic, that support their learning about the future.

It is not difficult to make the case that future thinking during childhood, in adolescence, and, indeed, throughout life is critical to one's development, welfare, and successful adaptation to the world. One hears repeated claims about how critical it is for children to understand the future consequences of their current action, whether we talk about morals, smoking, saving money, or risk avoidance. We do not really know what the effects on the development of future thinking might be of growing up in a relatively chaotic home where events are less predictable and less supportive of future thinking than in the middle-class samples we studied, nor do we know what the effects might be of limited opportunity for children to discuss future events with their parents. We do believe that a child's ability to think about the future depends on environmental regularity, such as family routines and rituals, and parental scaffolding through talk and action.

We have just scratched the surface in developing a scheme for conceptualizing this important area of inquiry and how contextual factors could affect its development. More fundamentally, the recognition that future-oriented processes are central to cognitive development is a necessary first step for making progress in this area. We hope that the work discussed here will help foster that recognition and form a foundation for further investigation.

References

1. Haith MM, Hazan C, Goodman GS. Expectation and anticipation of dynamic visual events by 3.5 month-old babies. *Child Development.* 1988;59:467-479.

2. Canfield RL, Haith MM. Active expectations in 2- and 3-month-old infants: complex event sequences. *Developmental Psychology.* 1991;27:198-208.

3. Arehart DM, Haith MM. Memory for space-time rules in the infant visual expectation paradigm. Poster presented at the *International Conference on Infant Studies,* Montreal, Canada, April 1990.

4. Dougherty T. *Processing Speed and Working Memory in Infancy.* Denver, Colo: University of Denver; 1998. Dissertation.

5. Haith MM, McCarty M. Stability of visual expectations at 3.0 months of age. *Developmental Psychology.* 1990;26:68-74.

6. Benson JB, Cherny SS, Haith MM, Fulker DW. Rapid assessment of infant predictors of adult IQ: midtwin/midparent analyses. *Developmental Psychology.* 1993;29:434-447.

7. DiLalla LF, Thompson LA, Plomin R, et al. Infant predictors of preschool and adult I.Q.: a study of infant twins and their parents. *Developmental Psychology.* 1990;26:759-769.

8. Dougherty T, Haith MM. Infant expectations and reaction time as predictors of childhood speed of processing and IQ. *Developmental Psychology.* 1997;33:146-155.

9. Benson JB. The origins of future orientation in the everyday lives of 9- to 36-month-old infants. In: Haith MM, Benson JB, Roberts RJ Jr, Pennington BF, eds. *The Development of Future-Oriented Processes.* Chicago, Ill: University of Chicago Press; 1994.

10. Snow CE. Imitativeness: a trait or a skill? In: Speidel G, Nelson K, eds. *The Many Faces of Imitation.* New York, NY: Reidel; 1989.

11. Benson JB, Talmi A, Haith MM. Analyzing adult time talk to infants and toddlers. Poster presented at the *International Society for the Study of Behavioral Development,* Atlanta, Ga, April 1998.

Section 5:
Biosocial Development

Abstracts From Section 5. Biosocial Development

Hormones May Influence Both Social Attachment and Reactivity to Stress

C. Sue Carter, PhD

Social attachments, especially pair bonds, are important to survival and reproduction. They provide a sense of safety, reduce anxiety, and facilitate maternal behaviors. Hormonal processes can be causally important in the formation of these attachments. A dynamic interaction between oxytocin and vasopressin is part of a larger system that integrates neuroendocrine and autonomic changes associated with social behaviors.

The Role of Early Experience in Infant Development – Enhancing Outcome After Extremely Preterm Birth

Neena Modi, MB, CHB, MD, FRCP, FRCPCH

One of the major challenges confronting a preterm infant is immaturity of the neonatal brain, responsible for a number of immediate and long-term impediments to normal development. It is plausible that morbidity from preterm birth can be either reduced or increased by the infant's early experiences, including the nature of environmental stimuli. Ongoing clinical research seeks to find the optimal treatment strategies that will ensure survival without disability.

Effects on Mother and Infant of Oxytocin Released in the Postpartum Period

Kerstin Uvnäs-Moberg, MD, PhD

The interaction between mothers and infants immediately following birth has been shown to cause mutual behavioral and physiologic effects. These effects, including breastfeeding and attachment behavior, may involve endogenous oxytocinergic mechanisms. Routine clinical care in the perinatal period can affect oxytocin secretion and activity, and thereby influence behavior.

Hormones May Influence Both Social Attachment and Reactivity to Stress

C. Sue Carter, PhD

Introduction

Social bonds are of major importance to survival and reproduction. Social attachments, and especially pair bonds, provide a sense of safety, reduce anxiety or stress, and facilitate sexual and maternal behaviors. However, selective social behaviors, including those that comprise social bonds, are uncommon in laboratory animals. Nonhuman primates and some domestic animals do exhibit selective social behaviors, but are difficult to study in the laboratory. In addition, it is sometimes assumed that the development of selective social bonds is based on complex or "higher" cognitive processes. For these reasons the study of social attachments has remained largely within the domain of social and behavioral sciences.

There is accumulating evidence that biological, and specifically hormonal, processes can be causally important in social behavior in general, and more specifically in the formation of social attachments. One purpose of this paper is to describe an animal model that is now helping to advance our understanding of the endocrinology of social attachment. Research in animals has highlighted the hypothesis that hormones, and specifically oxytocin and vasopressin, may act within the nervous system to facilitate social bonding. Social bonds and other positive social experiences may buffer the response to stressors and convey a survival advantage. Hormones (especially oxytocin) that are capable of influencing social bonding also have been implicated in the regulation of hypothalamic-pituitary-adrenal (HPA) or "stress" axis.

Gender differences exist in the processes that regulate social bonding and the effects of stress on the development of attachments. In addition, studies of lactating females with high oxytocin levels (including humans) support the hypothesis that the hormonal systems that regulate social attachment also may coordinate the activities of the HPA axis. The effects of oxytocin are facilitated by estrogen and may be more pronounced in females. Oxytocin facilitates positive social behaviors and also may coordinate the behavioral and health benefits of positive behaviors by its additional capacity to down-regulate the HPA axis. Vasopressin synthesis is androgen-dependent; vasopressin can facilitate alertness and territorial aggression and does not down-regulate the HPA axis. Differential effects of oxytocin and vasopressin may contribute to male-female differences in the vulnerability to stress-related illnesses, including those that are influenced by the social environment.

Animal Models and Analysis of the Endocrinology of Social Bonding

Monogamy in Prairie Voles

Monogamous rodents, such as prairie voles *(Microtus ochrogaster)*, form long-lasting pair bonds with many of the characteristics of human social attachments. Prairie voles are small, mouse-sized rodents from the midwestern United States. Males and females of this species live in pairs in nature and show well-defined behavioral preferences for their familiar partners.[1,2] Pair bonding in this species is assessed by allowing an experimental animal to chose between a stimulus animal made familiar by association or cohabitation and a comparable stranger.[3] Within about 24 hours following the onset of mating, male prairie voles become very aggressive to strangers.[4] Aggression in females takes longer to appear (8 to 12 days) and is not directly affected by mating (Bowler and Carter, unpublished data). The study of prairie voles has offered a unique opportunity to examine mechanisms underlying the formation of social bonds. This research has revealed that specific peptide hormones, including oxytocin and vasopressin, may help regulate pair bonding.

Neuropeptides: Structure and Synthesis

Oxytocin and vasopressin are small neuropeptides, consisting of nine amino acids configured as a six-amino acid ring with a three-amino acid tail as shown in Fig 1. These two peptides are identical with the exception of one amino acid in the ring and one in the tail of the molecules. Oxytocin and vasopressin are synthesized primarily within large, magnocellular neurons in the supraoptic nucleus and paraventricular nucleus; peptides manufactured in these cells are released into the systemic circulation at the posterior pituitary gland. In addition, both peptides are released within the central nervous system (CNS) from smaller, parvocellular neurons located in the paraventricular nucleus and other brain areas. Cervical stimulation during parturition and nipple stimulation during nursing are proximate stimuli for the release of oxytocin. Social signals, including tactile and olfactory cues that may be present in positive social interactions, play a major role in the release of oxytocin. Vasopressin is released by various stressors, including dehydration, and may be released with a novel social partner during the early stages of pair bonding. The release of peptides within the CNS and posterior pituitary can occur independently, although central and peripheral release patterns also may be coordinated.[5]

Within the CNS, oxytocin and vasopressin receptors are found in the olfactory system, limbic-hypothalamic system, brainstem, and spinal cord areas that regulate reproductive and autonomic functions. The distribution of the receptors for these peptides within the CNS varies across development and among mammalian species. The densities and binding patterns for oxytocin and vasopressin also can be influenced by steroid hormones, including estrogen, progesterone, androgens, and glucocorticoids.[6] Some of the major effects of oxytocin and vasopressin are summarized in Table 1.

Fig 1. Oxytocin and vasopressin.

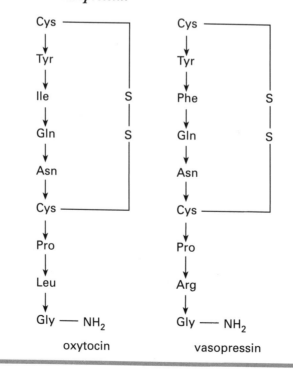

Oxytocin, Vasopressin, and Pair Bonding

Reliable partner preferences, a core component of pair bonding, can develop following a period of nonsexual cohabitation, but preferences occur more quickly when a male and female are allowed to mate. Mating, or vaginal/cervical stimulation, is known to cause the release of oxytocin. In addition, we have observed increased social contact in female prairie voles treated with vasopressin or oxytocin (by intracerebroventricular injection, ICV). We initially hypothesized that treatment of females with oxytocin or of males with vasopressin might facilitate pair bonding, and this hypothesis was confirmed. In addition, we found that in both males and females, either peptide at high ICV doses could hasten the onset of partner preferences. Conversely, oxytocin antagonists or vasopressin antagonists (for the V1a receptor) interfered with partner-preference formation following either oxytocin or vasopressin treatments in both sexes. These results suggested that at high doses both peptides could facilitate pair bonding in both sexes, and that blocking the central receptors for either oxytocin or vasopressin interfered with pair bonding.[7] These unexpected findings suggest that both oxytocin and vasopressin can affect pair bonding in both sexes. The effects of steroids on binding patterns for both receptors, however, are species specific and, especially for oxytocin, gender specific. In addition, these same peptide hormones play a role in the regulation of the hypothalamic-pituitary-adrenal (HPA) axis.

Stress Responses and Pair Bonds

The most abundant and commonly measured "stress" hormones are the glucocorticoid steroids, cortisol (predominant in primates), and corticosterone (predominant in rodents), herein described collectively as "CORT." Glucocorticoids are synthesized in the adrenal cortex and usually released in response to psychological and physical challenges. Basal levels of CORT vary widely among different species and may differ among individuals within species. Furthermore, reactions to stressful experiences differ among species and individuals. In highly social or monogamous mammals, social separation or isolation may be followed by increased release of CORT, indirectly suggesting that such experiences are stressful.[8,9]

Stressful experiences or injections of CORT can directly promote social bonds in prairie voles. Positive social behaviors and social bonds in turn may reduce HPA axis activity or have "antistress" effects. In socially naive prairie voles, treatment with exogenous oxytocin or vasopressin is capable of increasing positive social behaviors and the formation of pair bonds. Both oxytocin and social interactions reduce activity in the HPA axis. Central vasopressin is androgen dependent, and vasopressin increases aggression in male prairie voles. Vasopressin does not significantly inhibit or increase HPA axis activity, as measured by CORT secretion.

Male prairie voles form new partner preferences quickly following either exposure to a stressor (3 minutes of swimming) or corticosterone injections. Under comparable conditions, stressed females did not form new pair bonds with males but did develop preferences for females that were present immediately following exposure to the stressor. Prairie voles are both monogamous and communal. Males have no opportunity to mate within their natal families, and must leave their families to reproduce. For female prairie voles, conditions of environmental stress could produce physiologic signals encouraging a return to the security of the family nest; unlike males, females may produce litters within the family nest. Thus, stress may encourage the rapid formation of social preferences in both sexes, even when the object of the attachment is not necessarily a member of the opposite sex.

Table 1. Oxytocin and Vasopressin: Mediators of Social Interaction.

	Major Effects	Triggers	Sex Hormone Interaction	HPA Axis Effects	Pair Bonding
Oxytocin	"Social" attachment, pair bonding	Tactile, olfactory	Augmented by estrogen	• ↓HPA axis • Inhibits CORT secretion	• High doses ↑bonding in males and females • Antagonists block bonding
Vasopressin	"Defensive" arousal, agitation, vigilance	Stress, dehydration	Androgen dependent	• No documented effect on HPA or CORT secretion • *Possibly* releases CORT and ACTH	• High doses ↑bonding in males and females • Antagonists block bonding

Species Variation in Adrenal Corticoids

Species differences in the tendency to form selective social bonds may be related in part to variations in HPA axis activity. For example, prairie voles are glucocorticoid resistant and have serum levels of adrenal corticoids that are 5 to 10 times higher than those found in other vole species that are nonmonogamous. In many cases, exceptionally high levels of activity in the HPA axis, measured as increased CORT secretion, are associated with or precede well-defined patterns of social attachment. Correlations between HPA axis activity and attachment offer further support for the role of HPA axis hormones, and specifically CORT, in the events that eventually lead to pair bonding.

When previously unpaired and unfamiliar male and female prairie voles are first introduced to each other, both sexes show a rapid decline in serum levels of CORT (Fig 2a). This change occurs slightly more quickly in males and lasts slightly longer in females. Since mice and other rodents show increased HPA axis activity (higher levels of CORT) under conditions of social novelty, we did not expect this change. Similar socially induced declines in HPA activity have been observed in monogamous primates (common marmosets), which are also glucocorticoid resistant.

Oxytocin Reduces HPA Axis Activity in Voles

Intracerebrovascular injections of oxytocin (but not vasopressin) inhibit CORT secretion in both male and female prairie voles (Fig 2b). The effects of oxytocin are similar to those observed during pairing. In addition, pairing no longer reduces CORT levels if males or females are pretreated with oxytocin antagonists, suggesting that the antistress effects of pairing are mediated by oxytocin.

Steroid Effects on Peptides

Steroid hormones can influence oxytocin-receptor binding in the CNS, particularly in the olfactory-limbic-hypothalamic area, which has been implicated in social and sexual behaviors. For example, there is evidence from the research of Zingg and associates that progesterone is capable of binding to the rat oxytocin receptor, potentially inhibiting the functions of oxytocin. The concurrent presence of multiple steroid and peptide receptors in a given neural system (or within the same cell) offers mechanisms through which steroid hormones may regulate peptide functions. Gonadal and/or adrenal steroids

Fig 2. The interrelation of oxytocin, corticosterone, and pair bonding.

A. Cohabitation involved caging with an unfamiliar member of the opposite sex for 60 min prior to blood collection. Both cohabitation or oxytocin inhibited corticosterone secretion in male and female prairie voles.

B. In a separate study, oxytocin or a control injection was administered 60 min prior to blood collection. Animals that received oxytocin had significantly lower levels of corticosterone than controls (P <.05).

C. Prairie voles were injected with oxytocin or control and allowed to cohabit with an assigned partner of the opposite sex for 1 hour. Subsequently, the animals were given a 3-hour preference test in which they could elect to spend time with either the familiar partner or an unfamiliar but otherwise comparable stranger. Animals receiving oxytocin showed a significant preference for the familiar partner (P <.05), and control-injected animals were equally likely to select the familiar animal or a stranger.

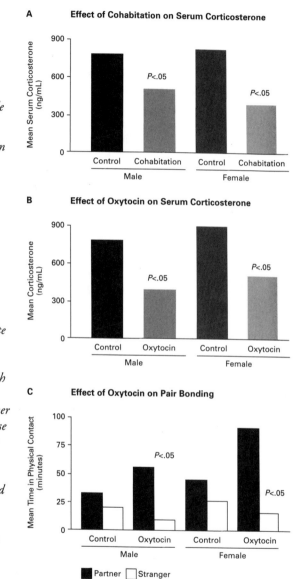

Adapted from Carter CS. Neuroendocrine perspectives on social attachment and love. *Psychoneuroendocrinology.* 1998;23:779-818.

also can cause site-specific changes in peptide activity. Modulation of peptide binding by specific steroid hormones or combinations of steroid hormones could account for at least some of the regulatory effects of stress on behavior.

A Working Model for the Role of Peptides and Adrenal Steroids in Pair Bonding

Stressful experiences (such as pregnancy and parturition), anxiety, neophobia, and isolation often precede the formation of social attachments. These circumstances may increase social drive or motivation and subsequent social interaction.[10] Positive social interaction in turn could be rewarding, and, in species that form attachments, positive social bonds would follow. Both positive social interaction and social bonds could function to provide a sense of safety and reduce anxiety or the negative feelings associated with stressful experiences. The stress-reducing effects of social interactions may be especially important for females.

Traits

The tendency to form attachments is a species-typical trait. Based on somewhat limited mammalian data, it appears that social bonding is particularly common in species that are glucocorticoid resistant and thus capable of producing exceptionally high serum levels of CORT. At present, the best-known animal models of glucocorticoid resistance are New World primates and rodents, many of which, such as prairie voles or marmosets, also are capable of developing selective social attachments or pair bonds.

States

Attachment formation and other forms of social behavior also are state dependent. For example, mother-infant attachment usually follows the extreme physiologic challenges associated with pregnancy and parturition. Metabolically demanding behaviors, such as sexual activity or exercise, may precede attachment formation. In addition, both glucocorticoids and oxytocin can be anxiolytic in rats. High levels of steroids and/or oxytocin may induce physiologic processes that cause motivation, and increase the probability of social interaction. Our research with prairie voles indicates that oxytocin increases both social contact and social preferences.

Positive social interaction is associated with increased oxytocin secretion and a state-dependent decline in HPA axis activity. Oxytocin is capable of facilitating both social contact and social attachment, at least in prairie voles. In addition, positive social behaviors, perhaps mediated in part through oxytocin, may feed back to inhibit HPA axis activity and reduce sensations of anxiety or fear. There is a recurrent association between increased activity in the HPA axis and the subsequent expression of social behaviors and attachments. The HPA axis and adrenal steroids are particularly responsive to social and environmental demands. Under certain conditions, stressful experiences and HPA axis activity are followed by increased sexual, parental, and social behaviors and the formation of social bonds. Adrenal steroid-neuropeptide interactions involving oxytocin or oxytocin receptors may regulate the development of social attachments while concurrently modulating the HPA axis. Positive social behaviors, perhaps mediated through a central oxytocinergic system, may modulate the activity of the HPA axis and the autonomic nervous system, accounting for health benefits that are attributed to attachment.

Gender and Social Attachment

Research with prairie voles suggests that the neuroendocrinology of social attachment is sexually dimorphic, with males more likely than females to form heterosexual pair bonds in the presence of a stressful experience or high levels of HPA activity. In male prairie voles the induction of aggression toward strangers, which accompanies mating and pair bonding, is regulated by a second neuropeptide, vasopressin. Vasopressin shares some functions with oxytocin, including the induction of pair bonds, but in other contexts vasopressin has effects that oppose those of oxytocin. For example, vasopressin does not inhibit the HPA axis, and there is evidence in rats (not yet studied in voles) that vasopressin releases corticotropin (ACTH) and CORT. The fact that vasopressin synthesis, especially in the limbic system, is androgen dependent makes vasopressin a particularly likely candidate for social processes that are sexually dimorphic. Male voles remain capable of forming pair bonds under stress and following treatments with CORT.

Although both males and females can respond to exogenous oxytocin, sex differences exist in the endogenous regulation of both social behavior and the HPA axis. Sex differences are adaptive in an evolutionary sense, and males and females are under different selection pressures. Sex differences in neuropeptides may permit males to form new pair bonds and mate in the face of environmental challenges but also may account in part for gender differences in vulnerability to stress-related illnesses, which tends to be higher in males.

Summary: Pair Bonding, Neuropeptides, Adrenal Steroids

Studies of monogamous prairie voles provide an opportunity to examine the neuroendocrinology of both social behavior and the HPA axis. Neuropeptides, including oxytocin and vasopressin, have emerged as central regulators of both systems, playing an important role in the adaptive coordination of social behavior and physiologic systems such as the HPA axis. The analysis of positive social behaviors suggests new insights regarding the mechanisms responsible for both stress and antistress. The activity of the HPA axis has been implicated in a variety of mental and physical illnesses.[11] Understanding of the role of social behaviors and neuropeptides in control of the HPA axis may be particularly important in understanding sex differences in vulnerability to stress-related illnesses.

Peptides and Human Behavior

Peptide hormones, including oxytocin and vasopressin, do not readily cross the blood-brain barrier and must be administered centrally (ICV) to reach the brain. Nasal sprays have been used to promote milk letdown and have been used in a few behavioral studies, but the extent to which such compounds reach the brain is not known. Therefore, virtually nothing is known regarding the effects in humans of centrally administered oxytocin.

Naturally Occurring Changes in Peptides

Two aspects of mammalian life, birth and breast-feeding, are clearly associated with the release of oxytocin. The naturally occurring changes in peptides associated with birth and lactation offer opportunities to correlate behavioral and hormonal events. Among the neuroendocrine adaptations that accompany both birth and subsequent lactation are hormonal changes that may promote selective social interactions, including maternal behaviors and high levels of physical contact.

Birth and Breast-feeding

Birth is a difficult-to-study hormonally complex event, and giving birth undoubtedly plays a role in the particularly strong form of social bonding that is recognized as mother love. Studies in sheep have demonstrated (at least for sheep) a major role for oxytocin in maternal bonding.[12] Although the experiences associated with birth may play a role in maternal bonding in humans, studies of the physiology of mother-infant interactions are at present primarily correlational.[13,14]

Lactation is the defining characteristic of mammalian existence and oxytocin has a central role in lactation and milk letdown.[15] The study of human lactation, in conjunction with animal research, provides an opportunity to begin developing viable hypotheses regarding the behavioral effects of oxytocin (Table 2). It has been found that lactating women interact more positively with their babies, touching and smiling at their infants more than bottle-feeding mothers. It also is reported that nursing mothers are more likely than bottle-feeding women to describe positive mood states.

Table 2. Some Effects of Oxytocin/Lactation on Behavior in Mothers.

↑ Smiling toward infant

↑ Touching infant

↑ Positive moods

↓ Response to stress

↓ ACTH and CORT concentrations

↓ Symptoms of panic disorder

Wiesenfield and associates measured reduced autonomic reactivity in response to infant cries in lactating women.[16] Both skin conductance and heart rate showed indications of lower levels of sympathetic arousal in lactating than in nonlactating mothers. The reduced responsivity to stressful experiences associated with lactation may be viewed as an adaptive response that protects a nursing woman from overreacting to stressful stimuli and promotes successful lactation.

In general, neuroendocrine reactivity of the adrenal axis is reduced during lactation.[17] Successful lactation involves the nervous system and neuroendocrine adaptations of the HPA and gonadal axes. Oxytocin plays a pivotal role in the integration of the behavioral and physiological processes unique to female physiology. Based primarily on research with animals, we speculate that oxytocin and vasopressin, and interactions between these hormones and steroid hormones, might regulate dynamic behavioral states, including the capacity of an individual to respond to both social and physical challenges. It has been known since the early 1970s that lactating female rodents showed reduced adrenal reactivity, often indexed by reduced corticosterone secretion, following exposure to stressors such as ether, surgical trauma, and electric shock. In rats, injections of hypertonic saline normally are considered stressful and are expected to cause glucocorticoid release. During lactation, however, there is selective inhibition of normal hypothalamic stress responses. In women, both ACTH and CORT levels fall during a period of breast-feeding. There also is evidence that peripheral injections of oxytocin can inhibit ACTH and CORT release in both men and women. In addition, oxytocin injections can inhibit the release of ACTH and/or CORT, which normally follows treatments with ACTH-releasing hormone, vasopressin plus ACTH-releasing hormone, or exercise.

Carter and Altemus examined the effects of physical stress in lactating versus recently delivered, bottle-feeding women.[17] In that study, women were given treadmill exercise to 90% of their maximum oxygen consumption. The two groups were matched in age and weeks postpartum. The peak blood lactate level, a measure of exercise intensity, was similar in both groups, and lactating and nonlactating women had similar basal levels of ACTH and CORT. ACTH, CORT, and vasopressin increased following exercise in bottle-feeding women, as would be expected in normal controls. The magnitude of the increase in ACTH, CORT, and vasopressin in response to exercise stress was blunted in the lactating women. Thus, lactating women show a marked inhibition of stress hormone secretion in response to exercise, which was not seen in postpartum women who bottle-fed their infants. Taken together, these studies suggest, for humans and other mammals, that lactation and/or oxytocin can reduce physiologic reactivity to various stressors.

Lactation also influences the activity of other neural systems that have been implicated in the management of psychological stress. For example, catecholamine responses to stress are reduced in lactating rats. Suckling also increases central production of gamma-aminobutyric acid (GABA) in rats and sheep. GABA is an inhibitory neurotransmitter known to play an important role in the regulation of anxiety and behavioral reactivity. Lactating females do not show the expected neuronal activation in cortical neurons following exposure to an excitatory amino acid, suggesting that the functional modifications associated with lactation extend beyond the hypothalamus to include cortical functions.

Since oxytocin and lactation may alter adrenal function and glucocorticoid secretion, it is to be expected that this might have immunologic consequences. There is not much recent research on the effects of lactation on immunologic parameters in animals or humans. Among the few studies available is work indicating that lactation is associated with enhanced inflammatory reactions to endotoxin and ozone in rats. We recently observed that the responses of lymphocytes (an important component of the immune system) to mitogen stimulation are altered in lactating women and rats (Redwine et al, unpublished data).

Clinical research also indicates that biologic changes associated with pregnancy and lactation may protect some women from mental disorders. In women with histories of panic disorder, panic symptoms tend to decline in pregnancy and remain low during lactation. These results suggest that patterns of infant feeding may influence a mother's mental health and thus her ability to deal with the demands of child rearing.

For mammalian reproduction to succeed, self-defense and reactivity to stress must be subjugated to positive social behaviors, at least during birth, lactation, and sexual behavior. Perhaps the important task of regulating interaction between social behaviors is managed, in part, by interactions between two related neurochemical systems that incorporate oxytocin and vasopressin in their functions.

Conclusions

The neuropeptides oxytocin and vasopressin participate in important reproductive functions, such as parturition and lactation, and in homeostatic responses, including modulation of the HPA axis. Recent evidence also implicates these hormones in social behaviors. Natural conditions associated with high levels of oxytocin may facilitate both social contact and selective social interactions associated with social attachment, pair bonding, and reduced HPA reactivity. Vasopressin, in contrast, is associated with behaviors that might be broadly classified as "defensive," including enhanced arousal, attention or vigilance, increased aggressive behavior, and a general increase in HPA reactivity. Based on the literature regarding the functions of these hormones and on our own recent findings, we propose that dynamic interactions between oxytocin and vasopressin are components of a larger system that integrates neuroendocrine and autonomic changes associated with mammalian social behaviors and the concurrent regulation of the stress axis. In addition, studies of lactating females provide a valuable model for understanding the more general neuroendocrinology of the stress axis.

References

1. Getz LL, Carter CS. Prairie-vole partnerships. *American Science.* 1996;84:56-62.

2. Carter CS, DeVries AC, Getz LL. Physiological substrates of mammalian monogamy: the prairie vole model. *Neuroscience Biobehavioral Reviews.* 1995;19:303-314.

3. Carter CS, Getz LL. Monogamy and the prairie vole. *Scientific American.* 1993;268:100-106.

4. Winslow JT, Hastings N, Carter CS, Harbaugh CR, Insel TR. Selective aggression and affiliation increase following mating in a monogamous mammal: a role for central vasopressin in pair bonding. *Nature.* 1993;365:545-548.

5. Englemann M, Wotjak CT, Neumann I, Ludwig M, Landgraf R. Behavioral consequences of intra-cerebral vasopressin and oxytocin: focus on learning and memory. *Neuroscience Biobehavioral Reviews.* 1996;20:341-358.

6. Insel TR. A neurobiological basis of social attachment. *American Journal of Psychiatry.* 1997;154: 726-735.

7. Cho MM, DeVries AC, Williams JR, Carter CS. The effects of oxytocin and vasopressin on partner preferences in male and female prairie voles (Microtus ochrogaster). *Behavioral Neuroscience.* In press.

8. Keverne EB, Nevison CM, Martel FL. Early learning and the social bond. *Annals of the New York Academy of Science.* 1997;807:203-209.

9. Hennessy MB. Hyppothalamic-pituitary-adrenal responses to brief social separation. *Neuroscience Biobehavioral Reviews.* 1997;21:11-29.

10. Carter CS. Neuroendocrine perspectives on social attachment and love. *Psychoneuroendocrinology.* 1998;23:779-818.

11. Chrousos GP, McCarty R, Pacak K, Cizza G, Sternberg E, Gold PW, Kvetnansky R. Stress basic mechanisms and clinical implications. *Annals of the New York Academy of Science.* 1995; volume 771.

12. Keverne EB, Nevison CM, Martel FL. Early learning and the social bond. *Annals of the New York Academy of Science.* 1997;807:329-339.

13. Uvnas-Moberg K, Windstrom AM, Nissen E, Bjorvell H. Personality traits in women 4 days post par-tum and their correlation with plasma levels of oxytocin and prolactin. *Journal of Psychosomatic Obstetrics Gynaecology.* 1990;11:261-272.

14. Uvnas-Moberg K. Oxytocin may mediate the benefits of positive social interaction and emotions. *Psychoneuroendrocriniology.* 1998;23:819-835.

15. Russell JA, Leng G. Sex, parturition and motherhood without oxytocin? *Journal of Endocrinology.* 1998;157:343-359.

16. Wiesenfield AR, Malatesta CZ, Whitman PB, Grannose C, Vile R. Psychosocial response of breast- and bottle-feeding mothers to their infant's signals. *Psychophysiology.* 1985;22:79-86.

17. Carter CS, Altemus M. Integrative functions of lactational hormones in social behavior and stress management. *Annals of the New York Academy of Science.* 1997;807:164-174.

Acknowledgements.

Support from the Department of Defense, National Science Foundation (BNS 7925713, 8506727, 8719748), the National Institutes of Health, including the Institute of Child Health and Human Development (HD 16679), and the National Institute of Mental Health (MH 45836) has been essential to this research.

The Role of Early Experience in Infant Development – Enhancing Outcome After Extremely Preterm Birth

Neena Modi, MB, ChB, MD, FRCP, FRCPCH

Introduction

Survival rates for extremely immature infants have improved steadily over the last decades, and more than 80% of infants born weighing less than 1500 g now survive.[1] In the early days of neonatal intensive care in the late 1970s and early 1980s, survival was a major goal. Survival as a key objective, however, has been overtaken by the goal of survival without disability. There was great optimism at the beginning of the 1990s that the rapidly falling rates of major cerebral injury, so prevalent in the previous decade, would lead to improved quality of survival. In our practice, extensive periventricular hemorrhagic infarction, porencephaly, multicystic periventricular and subcortical leucomalacia, and obstructive ventriculomegaly are now rarely seen. Yet in the developed world, disability rates among very-low-birth-weight survivors have remained disappointingly static. Currently, between 5% and 15% of very-low-birth-weight survivors develop cerebral palsy.[1]

There are also growing concerns about the substantial proportion of these infants who develop subtle deficits in the absence of markers of cerebral injury. It has been estimated that between 25% and 50% of very-low-birth-weight survivors develop abnormalities of cognition and behavior with resulting learning difficulties.[2] Additionally, we now recognize that these infants are at greater risk for other long-term problems, including poor growth in childhood, increased anxiety, psychological morbidity, and, in some cases, increased risk of cardiovascular and other diseases in adult life.[3,4] A major focus of research is the cause of these often subtle yet frequently disabling conditions. There is great interest in the possible role of early experience and environmental influences.[5,6] Certainly, better understanding of these issues would enable us to move forward to a new goal for the next decade of neonatal intensive care, namely survival not only without disability but also with preservation of full potential.

Development of the Preterm Brain

The human brain undergoes remarkable organizational changes during intrauterine and early postnatal development and generates many more neurons than will be needed in adult life. The final population of neurons in the adult brain is due to both production and programmed cell death. A surplus of interneuronal connections is similarly pruned during infancy. For example, there are approximately twice as many synapses present in parts of the cortex during early postnatal life than during adult life.[7] Certain of these changes not only create particular patterns of vulnerability but also underpin the concept of plasticity of the developing brain.[8] This long-established concept has been given a firm basis in recent years via techniques such as transcranial focal magnetic brain stimulation.[9] When damage is sustained early in development, remarkable brain reorganization is possible. Clearly, there is great potential for both adverse and beneficial influences during this period of rapid cerebral organization.

The healthy preterm baby upon reaching full term is not the same as a baby born at full term; this gives credence to the possibility that the postnatal environment has affected brain development. Healthy preterm babies have been found to differ from their full-term counterparts in structural brain development, assessed via magnetic resonance imaging, as well as in neurobehavioral parameters. Hüppi et al studied 18 healthy preterm babies born at a mean gestational age of 32 weeks.[10] At full term, comparison was made with 13 infants born at term. The preterm infants at term showed significantly less gray/white matter differentiation and myelination as well as significantly poorer neurobehavioral performance. My colleagues at Hammersmith Hospital have preliminary evidence that cortical folding is reduced in preterm infants (born at gestational ages from 24 to 29 weeks) on reaching term compared with infants born at term.[11] At term, the overwhelming majority of these infants also have evidence of subtle white matter disease or white matter loss in the absence of major markers of brain injury.[12]

Evidence for Early Environmental Experience Affecting Neural Development

The evidence that early experiences may affect future neural development in both beneficial and detrimental ways comes from animal studies and a small but increasing amount of human research. Attention has focused on both intrauterine and early postnatal influences.

In rats, born at a stage equivalent to the late fetus in humans, early postnatal handling by humans results in altered endocrine and behavioral responses to stress throughout life.[13-15] Handling during the first postpartum week has greater long-term effects than handling in the subsequent 2 weeks.[14] Handling increases glucocorticoid receptor gene transcription in the hippocampus,[16] an effect that in turn appears to be mediated by an increase in serotonin activity.[17] The resulting permanent increase in hippocampal glucocorticoid receptors enhances negative feedback inhibition of subsequent glucocorticoid secretion and so protects the animal from glucocorticoid hypersecretion in later life.[18] In these rat models, the effect appears to be induced not by human handling itself but because human handling results in a much greater amount of licking and grooming by the mother. Tactile stimulation by mother rats also maintains growth hormone and ornithine decarboxylase levels in rat pups. Ornithine decarboxylase is thought to be a key regulator of cell proliferation and differentiation.[19] In contrast, rat pups subjected to the severe stress of prolonged maternal deprivation show an increased sensitivity to stress during adult life,[14,20] persistent changes in corticotropin-releasing factor,[21] impaired tissue growth,[22] altered circadian rhythms,[23] and deficits in learning ability and memory.[24]

The extent to which these observations may be transposed to the human condition remains unclear. Environmental-enrichment programs, applied predominantly beyond the period of hospitalization, have not appeared to provide benefit other than to children from socioeconomically deprived backgrounds.[25]

There is limited evidence for adverse effects of very early experience in humans. A prospective study of male babies circumcised in the immediate neonatal period found that they cried more and exhibited greater distress in response to routine immunization at 4 months than those who had not been circumcised.[26] Ramsay and Lewis observed differences in the cortisol response to routine immmunization at 2, 4, and 6 months of age between infants who had been in either "optimum" or "nonoptimum" condition at birth.[27] Stevenson and Aynsley-Green studied twin pairs discordant for surgery before the age of 5.5 years.[28] A twin who had experienced surgery had higher mean impulsivity and activity than his or her counterpart, although the authors pointed out that this study could not differentiate between the effects of different components of the experience of surgery on later behavior.[29] Grunau et al compared 36 extremely low-birth-weight infants with matched full-term controls at the age of 4.5 years.[30] The extremely low-birth-weight infants had had prolonged hospitalization and numerous painful interventions. They showed higher somatization (frequency of stomachaches, headaches, and leg pains) than the full-term controls.[30,31] Of particular interest was that within the extremely low-birth-weight group, the children with high levels of somatization were not more likely to be those experiencing continuing medical problems.

The Environment of Neonatal Intensive Care and Early Attempts at Manipulation

A striking feature of neonatal intensive care is the extent to which the environment differs from the popular view of what is appropriate for a newborn baby. Soft lights, soothing sounds, comforting touch, and gentle swaddling are not in great evidence in neonatal intensive care units. For almost 3 decades, researchers have attempted to investigate whether the neonatal intensive care unit environment affects outcome.

In 1993, Lacy and Ohlsson assessed all peer-reviewed "developmental" interventions published between 1980 and 1990 that attempted to reduce adverse biological and developmental effects on infants weighing less than 2250 g at birth.[32] Of 81 papers initially retrieved, 29 were finally accepted for inclusion in their review. Inclusion criteria were that the intervention both started and ended during hospitalization and that there was an appropriate control group. The interventions included a range of vestibular, auditory, and tactile stimulation, positioning, decreased handling, and decreased visual stimulation. Twenty-six of the 29 studies ascribed short-term benefit to the intervention, but all had serious methodological flaws. The three studies showing no benefit were also those with the largest sample sizes and the best design. Information on follow-up was disappointing, with only a single study reporting outcome at 2 years. This was a randomized, controlled trial of auditory stimulation and a rocking bed.[33] Eighty-seven infants were enrolled into four groups: control, stimulation at fixed intervals, stimulation after 90 seconds without activity by the infant, or stimulation only once per hour. The authors reported improved cognitive scores at 24 months in all groups, but concerns have been voiced that there may have been problems in the randomization process, because the fourth group, comprising only 10 infants, was formed by a mistake in the settings of the stimulation switches.

Five of the studies reviewed demonstrated improved weight gain over observational periods ranging from 4 days to 9 months, but the extent to which nutritional intake was controlled was largely unclear. More recently, Osborn and Henderson-Smart reviewed the effects of kinesthetic stimulation in preterm infants.[34] They found no evidence of benefit in development at 1 year. Massage therapy for preterm infants has also been subjected to systematic review.[35] Massage improves daily weight gain by 5 g (95% CI 3.5, 6.7) and appears to have a slight beneficial effect on weight at 4 to 6 months; however, evidence that massage improves developmental outcome for preterm infants remains weak.

Als and coworkers conducted a randomized, controlled trial of "individualized developmental care" involving 38 infants born at less than 30 weeks' gestation.[36] Specially trained nurses made detailed observations of the infants to construct so-called developmental-care plans. These involved the use of procedures such as gentle positioning, supportive holding, dark/light cycling, low sound levels, and parent support. The infants in the experimental group were said to have a significantly shorter duration of mechanical ventilation; earlier progression to oral feeding; reduced incidences of intraventricular hemorrhage, chronic lung disease, and pneumothorax; and enhanced neurodevelopmental outcome at 9 months. This study was not without problems, many of which have been discussed in correspondence columns. Morbidity rates in the control group were surprisingly high (for example, pneumothorax: 33% and grade III/IV intraventricular hemorrhage: 33%), suggesting that the two groups were not well matched for disease severity. Although randomization assignment was not revealed to the staff, it is difficult to understand how blinding could be achieved, given both the nature of the interventions and that each assessment took 3 to 4 hours to complete. Though not explicitly stated, the study also appeared to have been conducted prior to 1990, and the environment of neonatal intensive care has changed considerably since then. These effects have not been reproduced in recent research, and it is probably fair to say that so far, formal environmental manipulation has not impacted appreciably on neonatal intensive care.

How Might the Effects of Early Experience Be Mediated?

The early studies attempted to create an environment that conformed in some way to the popular notion of what was suitable for a newborn baby. There was little focus on the biological mechanisms that might underlie possible effects, adverse or otherwise, of early experience and thereby allow more precise targeting of interventions. What might these mediators be?

Programming

The concept of programming has influenced our understanding of how early experiences may have an impact on later well-being. Programming has been defined as the process whereby a stimulus, applied at a critical or sensitive period, causes long-lasting effects on structure or function.[37] Evidence in support of programming as an influence on outcome is mounting. Programming in fetal life may permanently affect blood pressure, glucose tolerance, and the risk of hyperlipidemia and coronary artery disease.[3,4,38] In babies born at term, reduced birth weight is associated with higher blood pressure in childhood and adult life, as well as glucose intolerance. The hypothesis linking fetal experience with later disease involves programming of the hypothalamic-pituitary-adrenal (HPA) axis resulting in glucocorticoid hypersecretion that persists into later life. These associations reflect powerful effects; for example, a small baby with a large placenta has a relative risk of adult hypertension approximately three times that of a large baby with a normal placenta,[3] whereas, in contrast, the angiotensinogen M235T genotype, a molecular marker of adult hypertension, is associated with a relative risk of only 1.6.[39] The extent to which preterm birth programs future events is an exciting and expanding area of research.

Nutrition

Early nutritional influences also appear to have long-lasting effects on neurodevelopment. Follow-up, so far to 8 years, of preterm infants recruited into randomized trials begun in the early 1980s has shown that a brief period of dietary manipulation involving human milk and/or nutrient enrichment improves mental and motor outcome.[40-43] In these studies, 424 preterm infants weighing less than 1850 g at birth were randomized to receive a nutrient-enriched preterm formula or standard infant formula, either as sole diet or as a supplement to maternal milk, for a mean of 1 month. Diet was shown to have an important impact on outcome, and there was a major gender difference. At 7½ to 8 years, boys who had received standard formula as sole diet had a 12.2-point disadvantage in verbal IQ (95% CI 3.7, 20.6). In the group that received no maternal milk, cerebral palsy was significantly more common in those fed standard rather than preterm formula (8/67 vs 1/66, P=.03).[43] Higher IQs were found in children who received diets that included their own mothers' milk.[41] The authors suggested that their findings support the hypothesis that nutrition during critical periods of growth can have a permanent effect on cognitive outcome. They speculated that because cerebral palsy in many preterm children is believed to originate antenatally, the brain's ability to achieve functional compensation might depend on the availability of adequate and appropriate nutritional substrates during the period of rapid growth and development. For example, human milk contains a range of polyunsaturated fatty acids, notably docosahexanoic acid (DHA, 22:6ω3). The brain and retina are rich in DHA,[44] and the addition of long-chain polyunsaturates to infant diets improves retinal function.[45] Breast milk also contains a number of growth factors and other biologically active polypeptides.

Mother/Infant Interaction

Children who were born preterm are at increased risk for anxiety and behavioral problems[46]; not surprisingly, mother/infant interaction during the first year after preterm birth is poorer than after birth at full term.[47] Mothers of preterm infants are more likely to develop mental health problems,[48] including postnatal depression, which is a risk factor for suboptimal mother/infant interaction.[49]

Part of the reason for this may be biochemical. At birth, the human adrenocortical system is highly responsive, and alterations in circulating cortisol can be demonstrated after even minor manipulations. At about 3 months after full-term birth, a marked decrease in responsivity occurs; in other words, HPA axis activity is buffered, with the result that the infant is protected from exposure to persistently elevated glucocorticoids. In human infants, the security of mother/infant attachment appears to dictate the degree of buffering of HPA axis activity. Spangler and Grossman demonstrated that adrenocortical activation during Ainsworth's strange situation paradigm occurred only in insecurely attached infants.[50] In contrast, securely attached infants appropriately utilized the strategy of maternal contact and showed no adrenocortical response. Similarly, 18-month-old infants who were wary or fearful of new experiences, such as approach by a clown, did not show elevation in cortisol if their attachment to their parents was secure; however, similarly fearful infants whose attachment was insecure showed significant elevations in cortisol.[51] The extent to which facilitating mother/infant interaction after extremely preterm birth might affect long-term outcome has not been systematically examined.

Neonatal Intensive Care and Hormonal Stress Responses

A common denominator for the experiences that together make up neonatal intensive care is that they impose stress on infants. The most immature of infants, including a fetus,[52] is able to mount a metabolic and endocrine stress response. Acutely stressful procedures appear to have the potential to affect outcome adversely. The observation that preterm infants mount considerable stress responses when undergoing surgery and that the administration of anesthesia during operations improves outcome had a landmark impact on physicians' attitudes to the stress of painful procedures during neonatal intensive care.[53]

Neonatal intensive care in its entirety might with reason be regarded as a model for chronic stress. To the stress of chronic illness is added that of a disordered environmental milieu, repeated painful procedures, lack of dark/light cycling, and over- or possibly understimulation. There is persuasive evidence not only that chronic stress is damaging but also that stress experienced early in development may program the HPA axis for life (for example, the risks of developing cardiovascular disease, hypertension, and adult glucose intolerance in infants experiencing intrauterine stress reviewed earlier). The rapid development of invasive techniques for the treatment and investigation of the fetus has meant that many now experience repeated intrauterine procedures. Chronically stressed fetuses, such as those who are anemic, tolerate vascular puncture less well than those with normal hematocrits.[54] In addition, preterm birth, with its associated prolonged period of intensive care, is a common sequel to such a clinical course. To our knowledge there have been no studies of neurobehavioral outcome after repeated fetal intervention.

Antenatal stress may also impact on the baby via maternal stress. Prenatal stress in pregnant rhesus monkeys has been shown to have long-term effects on the offspring, augmenting their hormonal and behavioral responses to new stressors.[55-59]

Adrenal glucocorticoid hormones represent the end product of stimulation of the HPA axis. This axis is largely controlled by corticotrophin-releasing factor, a peptide secreted by the neurons located in the paraventricular nuclei of the hypothalamus. The glucocorticoids comprise a major component of the mammalian stress response and are essential for survival. Excessive HPA activity is harmful, however, and an efficient response to stress is one that is effectively ended or "turned off" when no longer required.

We have observed a very wide range of cortisol output in timed urine samples (20 to 2000 nmol/L) and plasma samples (15 to 1500 nmol/L) in preterm babies receiving intensive care (unpublished observations). The highest levels were found in the most ill babies, but there was considerable variation in both well and unwell groups. Others have reported similar levels in well premature babies (31 to 306 nmol/L in the first 8 postnatal weeks), with a significant fall during this period.[60] Extremely high levels, up to 6000 nmol/L, have also been reported in very sick babies.[61] To our knowledge, the pattern of glucocorticoid secretion over time in such babies (to determine whether babies with high early output still have above-average output after recovery) has not been studied. There is evidence that preterm babies excrete relatively greater amounts of adrenal steroids other than cortisol (eg, 11-deoxycortisol, 17-hydroxypregnenolone) than do full-term babies,[62] probably because the relevant synthesizing enzymes have not reached mature levels, but there has been little research on this in infants at less than 33 weeks' gestation.

Glucocorticoid Toxicity

Attention has focused on the glucocorticoid steroids as possible mediators of the damaging effects of the stress response. Glucocorticoids are neurotoxic, predominantly to formation of the hippocampus. This is an area of the brain that plays an important role in learning and memory. A consistent link has been demonstrated in humans between structural changes in the hippocampus and impairment of memory. The hippocampus contains the highest concentration of glucocorticoid receptors in the brain and, as discussed earlier, is an important extrahypothalamic inhibitor of HPA axis activity.

Sustained social stress in primates results in marked hippocampal degeneration, multiple gastric ulcers, and hyperplastic adrenal cortices, suggestive of sustained glucocorticoid release.[63] At the extreme of social stress, cerebral atrophy has been described in human torture victims. Exposure of pregnant rats to hydrocortisone for only 3 days affects the long-term development and behavior of the offspring, with precise effects appearing to depend on the time of administration.[64] Rats exposed to high concentrations of glucocorticoids before birth respond to stress in later life with increased glucocorticoid secretion.

In a study designed to mimic clinical practice, treatment of pregnant Rhesus monkeys with dexamethasone resulted in reduced hippocampal cell numbers and pronounced degeneration in the hippocampal CA3 region in their fetuses.[65] Degeneration was dose dependent but occurred even as low as 0.5 mg/kg, which is comparable to the dose used to enhance fetal lung maturation in humans. Long-term effects were studied in rhesus monkeys receiving dexamethasone 5 mg/kg. At 20 months of age, magnetic resonance imaging of the brain showed an approximately 30% reduction in hippocampal volume in treated compared with control offspring.[66]

In animals, including primates, prolonged exposure to high cortisol levels leads to hippocampal cell death and loss of hippocampal volume.[67] Aging is characterized by, among other things, a decrease in glucocorticoid receptors and neurons in the hippocampus and an increase in basal glucocorticoid levels. Exposure to high concentrations of glucocorticoids in the perinatal period results in premature brain aging,[68] but these effects may be attenuated by early postnatal handling.[69] In adults, chronic hypercortisolemia is associated with reduced hippocampal volume and memory dysfunction.[70] Reduction in hippocampal volume has been demonstrated in adults with depression,[71] Cushing's syndrome,[72] and posttraumatic stress disorder.[73] Correlations have been reported between hypercortisolemia and the severity of hippocampal atrophy in patients with Alzheimer's disease.[74] Hippocampal damage sustained in early life was recently described in patients with anterograde amnesia.[75]

In rodent models, a short period of stress or glucocorticoid exposure compromises hippocampal neurons, impairing their ability to withstand seizures and hypoxic insults.[76] After more prolonged exposure, there is permanent loss of hippocampal neurons. Glucocorticoids compromise glucose utilization and potentiate hypoxic-ischemic brain injury,[77,78] which is a major cause of neurodevelopmental impairment in preterm infants, raising the possibility that glucocorticoids may exacerbate other neurological injury.

Glucocorticoids are used extensively for therapeutic purposes in perinatal medicine. They are used to accelerate fetal lung maturation in threatened preterm delivery, and a short course of treatment prior to preterm delivery has undoubtedly beneficial effects on neonatal outcome. On the other hand, recent experience with exogenous glucocorticoids administered immediately after preterm birth in an attempt to reduce the risk of chronic respiratory disease suggests that this exacerbates neurological injury, increasing the occurrence of periventricular leucomalacia,[79] neuromotor dysfunction at 2 years,[80] and, in boys, somatic growth at 2 years. We are currently researching the effects of repeated antenatal glucocorticoid exposure on brain growth and differentiation.

Overall, preterm infants are at risk for substantial exogenous and endogenous glucocorticoid exposure. Areas other than the hippocampus, such as the cingulate gyrus and amygdala, as well as regions of the frontal lobes, are also known to be rich in glucocorticoid receptors. Given the role of glucocorticoids in compromising the ability of neurons to withstand hypoxic, ischemic, and excitotoxic insults, it appears a plausible and worrying hypothesis that glucocorticoids may be neurogenerative to the developing brain and further add to the risk of adverse outcome in these already vulnerable infants.

Current Research

To our knowledge, no study involving extremely preterm human newborns has attempted to influence outcome by reducing the glucocorticoid stress response associated with neonatal intensive care, using nonpharmacologic interventions. We have studied the effects of massage,[81] auditory stimulation (a recording of the uterine bruit),[82] and mother/infant skin-to-skin contact on cortisol responses in infants born at less than 32 weeks' gestation.[83] When performed by an experienced nurse, at times considered suitable for the infant, massage resulted in a significant reduction in serum cortisol.[81] When massage was performed by mothers, without heed to the state of the infant, no consistent pattern of response was seen (unpublished observations). Sound stimulation did not result in a significant change in either cortisol or ß-endorphin.[82]

In our initial skin-to-skin study,[83] both serum cortisol and ß-endorphin fell significantly after the skin-to-skin session (cortisol: geometric mean change 66%, $P=.008$; ß-endorphin: geometric mean change 74%, $P=.002$). There was also a significant fall in cortisol levels during the control session, in contrast to ß-endorphin levels, in which there was no significant change. Analysis of variance showed that the fall in ß-endorphin during the skin-to-skin session was significant compared with the control session but that there was no significant difference in the degree of fall in cortisol between the two sessions (ß-endorphin: F [1,14]=5.70, *P*=.02; cortisol: F [1,14]=0.04, *P*=.8). We have since repeated this study using measurements of salivary cortisol and shown skin-to-skin contact results in a significant reduction (Gitau et al, unpublished data). During skin-to-skin contact, all infants maintained physiologic stability, and in oxygen-dependent infants, a reduced flow rate was required. All the mothers said they found the experience pleasurable. We have therefore chosen this intervention to test in a randomized, controlled trial in infants born at less than 32 weeks' gestation, involving 120 mother/infants pairs. Outcome assessments include both short-term indices of biological well-being and long-term assessments, initially at 2 years.

Future Directions

In the United Kingdom, the environment and nature of neonatal intensive care have changed markedly during the last 2 decades. The limits of viability are now at 22 to 23 weeks' gestation, and infants born at less than 29 weeks' gestation form the major part of the neonatal intensive care workload. Technological and medical advances have meant that physiologic stability is well maintained, even in infants weighing less than 1000 g. Nursery sizes are small and rarely exceed 20 isolettes in total, usually made up of a combination of smaller configurations. Family visiting is open and encouraged. Nursing routines are individualized, and analgesics are used liberally, but the impact this has had on outcome is uncertain. Attempts to improve outcome for extremely preterm newborns through specific environment manipulations have met with only limited measurable success, although the recognition of breast-feeding and nutrition as determinants of cognitive and neuromotor outcome has been a major advance. If interventions are to be better targeted in the future, more research on possible mediators of putative effects of early experiences is necessary. Attention has recently focused on the role of the stress response and on neonatal intensive care as a model of chronic stress. Acutely painful procedures experienced during early development have been shown to result in measurable long-term effects, and adequate anesthesia during surgical procedures clearly improves at least short-term outcome. Concern regarding the provision of pain relief to preterm infants represents a significant change in neonatal intensive care practice; however, the use of opiates and other analgesics and sedatives for prolonged periods during neonatal intensive care is entering into widespread use without evidence of either benefit or harm, although randomized, controlled trials are currently under way. Other, nonpharmacologic methods of stress reduction are also being evaluated. From our perspective at present, it seems plausible that the most potent interventions for enhancing outcome will ultimately prove to be those that not only have direct effects but that initiate a positive feedback loop, such as through enhanced maternal interaction, and so continue to exert their effects after discharge from the hospital, through infancy and childhood into adult life.

References

1. Volpe JJ. Neurologic outcome of prematurity. *Archives of Neurology.* 1998;55:297-300.
2. Volpe JJ. Brain injury in the premature infant: neuropathology, clinical aspects, pathogenesis, and prevention. *Clinical Perinatalogy.* 1997;24:567-587.
3. Barker DJP, Gluckman PD, Godfrey KM, et al. Fetal nutrition and cardiovascular disease in adult life. *Lancet.* 1993;341:938-941.
4. Clark PM. Programming of the hypothalamo-pituitary-adrenal axis and the fetal origins of adult disease hypothesis. *European Journal of Pediatrics.* 1998;157(suppl 1):S7-S10.
5. Nathanielsz PW. Fetal and neonatal environment has influence on brain development. *Lancet.* 1996;347:314.
6. Winburg J. Do neonatal pain and stress program the brain's response to future stimuli? *Acta Paediatrica.* 1998;87:723-725.
7. Huttenlocher PR, Courten C. The development of synapses in the striate cortex of man. *Human Neurobiology.* 1987;6:1-9.
8. Johnston MV. Neurotransmitters and vulnerability of the developing brain. *Brain & Development.* 1995;17:301-306.
9. Singh KD, Hamdy S, Aziz Q, Thompson DG. Topographic mapping of trans-cranial magnetic stimulation data on surface rendered MR images of the brain. *Electroencephalography and Clinical Neurophysiology.* 1997;105:345-351.
10. Hüppi PS, Schuknecht B, Boesch C, et al. Structural and neurobehavioral delay in postnatal brain development of preterm infants. *Pediatric Research.* 1996;39:895-901.
11. Ajayi-Obe M, Saeed N, Rutherfors M, et al. Quantification of cortical folding by magnetic resonance using image segmentation and cortical contour folding (abstract). *Early Human Development.* 1999;1:81-95.
12. Maalouf EF, Duggan PJ, Rutherford MA, et al. Magnetic resonance of the brain in extremely preterm infants: normal and abnormal findings from birth to term. *Journal of Paediatrics.* In press.
13. Meaney M, Aitken DH. The effects of early postnatal handling on hippocampal glucocorticoid receptor concentrations: temporal parameters. *Developmental Brain Research.* 1985;22:301-304.
14. Meaney M, Bhatnagar S, Diorio J, et al. Molecular basis for the development of individual differences in the hypothalamic-pituitary-adrenal stress response. *Cellular and Molecular Neurobiology.* 1993;13:321-347.
15. Sapolsky RM. Potential behavioral modification of glucocorticoid damage to the hippocampus. *Behavioral Brain Research.* 1993;57:175-182.
16. Liu D, Diorio J, Tannenbaum B, et al. Maternal care, hippocampal glucocorticoid receptors and HPA responses to stress. *Science.* 1997;277:1659-1662.

17. Smythe JW, Rowe WB, Meaney M. Neonatal handling alters serotonin (5-HT) turnover and 5-HT2 receptor binding in selected brain regions: relationship to the handling effect on glucocorticoid receptor expression. *Developmental Brain Research.* 1994;80:183-189.

18. Sapolsky RM. The importance of a well groomed child. *Science.* 1997;277:1620-1621.

19. Lau C, Cameron AM, Antolick LL, Stanton ME. Repeated maternal separation in the neonatal rat: cellular mechanisms contributing to brain growth sparing. *Journal of Developmental Physiology.* 1992;17:265-276.

20. Plotsky PM, Meaney MJ. Early postnatal experience alters hypothalamic corticotropin-releasing factor (CRF) mRNA, median eminence CRF content and stress induced release in adult rats. *Molecular Brain Research.* 1993;18:195-200.

21. Ladd CO, Owens MJ, Nemeroff CB. Persistent changes in corticotropin-releasing factor neuronal systems induced by maternal deprivation. *Endocrinology.* 1996;137:1212-1218.

22. Diaz J, Moore E, Petracca F, Stamper C. Somatic and central nervous system growth in artificially reared rat pups. *Brain Research Bulletin.* 1983;11:643-647.

23. Shimoda K, Hanada K, Yamada N, et al. Periodic exposure to mother is a potent zeitgeber of rat pup's rhythm. *Physiology and Behavior.* 1986;36:723-730.

24. Tonjes R, Hecht K, Brautzsch M, et al. Behavioral changes in adult rats produced by early postnatal maternal deprivation and treatment with choline chloride. *Experimental and Clinical Endocrinology.* 1986;88:151-157.

25. Hack M, Klein NK, Taylor HG. Long term developmental outcomes of low birth weight infants. *Future Child.* 1995;5:176-196.

26. Taddio A, Katz J, Ilersich AL, Koren G. Effect of neonatal circumcision on pain response during subsequent routine vaccination. *Lancet.* 1997;349:599-603.

27. Ramsay DS, Lewis M. The effects of birth condition on infants' cortisol response to stress. *Pediatrics.* 1995;95:546-549.

28. Stevenson J, Aynsley-Green A. The long term behavioural sequelae of surgery studied in young twins. *Proceedings of the British Psychology Society.* 1995;3:59.

29. Stevenson J. Long term sequelae of acute stress in early life. *Balliere's Clinical Paediatrics.* 1995;3:619-631.

30. Grunau RVE, Whitfield MF, Petrie JH, Fryer EL. Early pain experience, child and family factors, as precursors of somatization: a prospective study of extremely premature and full term children. *Pain.* 1994;56:353-359.

31. Grunau RVE, Whitfield MF, Petrie JH. Pain sensitivity and temperament in extremely low birth weight premature toddlers and preterm and full term controls. *Pain.* 1994;58:341-346.

32. Lacy JB, Ohlsson A. Behavioral outcomes of environmental or care giving hospital based interventions for preterm infants: a critical overview. *Acta Paediatrica.* 1993;82:408-415.

33. Barnard KE, Bee HL. The impact of temporally patterned stimulation on the development of preterm infants. *Child Development.* 1983;54:1156-1167.

34. Osborn DA, Henderson-Smart DJ. Kinaesthetic stimulation versus theophylline for apnea in preterm infants at risk (Cochrane Review). In: *The Cochrane Library 1999* Issue 2. Oxford, Update Software. CD-ROM.

35. Vickers A, Ohlsson A, Lacy JB, Horsley A. Massage to promote development in preterm and/or low birth weight infants. (Cochrane Review). In: *The Cochrane Library 1999* Issue 2. Oxford, Update Software. CD-ROM

36. Als H, Lawhon G, Duffy FH, et al. Individualized developmental care for the very low birth weight preterm infant. *Journal of the American Medical Association.* 1994;272:853-858.

37. Lucas A. Programming by early nutrition in man. In: Bock GR, Whelan J, eds. *The Childhood Environment and Adult Disease.* Chichester, UK: Wiley; 1991:38-55.

38. Seckl JR, Benediktsson R, Lindsay RS, Brown RW. Placental 11ß-hydroxysteroid dehydrogenase and the programming of hypertension. *Journal of Steroid Biochemistry and Molecular Biology.* 1995;55:447-455.

39. Jeunemaitre X, Soubrier F, Kotelevtsev Y, et al. Molecular basis of human hypertension: role of angiotensinogen. *Cell.* 1992;71:169-180.

40. Lucas A, Morley R, Cole TJ, et al. Early diet in preterm babies and developmental status at 18 months. *Lancet.* 1990;335:1477-1481.

41. Lucas A, Morley R, Cole TJ, et al. Breast milk and subsequent intelligence quotient in children born preterm. *Lancet.* 1992;339:261-264.

42. Morley R. The influence of early diet on later development. *Journal of Biosocial Science.* 1996;28: 481-487.

43. Lucas A, Morley R, Cole TJ. Randomised trial of early diet in preterm babies and later intelligence quotient. *British Medical Journal.* 1998;317:1481-1487.

44. Innis SM. Essential fatty acids in growth and development. *Progress in Lipid Research.* 1991;30: 39-103.

45. Birch DG, Birch EE, Hoffman DR, Uauy RD. Retinal development in very low birth weight infants fed diets differing in omega-3 fatty acids. *Investigative Ophthalmology and Visual Science.* 1992;33: 2365-2376.

46. Sykes DS, Hoy EA, Bill JM, McClure BG, Halliday HL, Reid M. Behavioural adjustment in school of very low birthweight children. *Journal of Child Psychology and Psychiatry.* 1997;38:315-325.

47. Barnard KE, Bee HL, Hammond MA. Developmental changes in maternal interactions with term and preterm infants. *Infant Behaviour & Development.* 1984;7:101-113.

48. Gennaro S, Yori R, Brooten D. Anxiety and depression in mothers of low birthweight and very low birthweight infants: birth through 5 months. *Issues Comp Pediatric Nursing.* 1990;13:97-109.

49. Murray L. The impact of postnatal depression on infant development. *Journal of Child Psychology and Psychiatry.* 1992;33:543-561.

50. Spangler G, Grossman KE. Biobehavioral organisation in securely and insecurely attached infants. *Child Development.* 1993;64:1439-1450.

51. Nachmias M, Gunnar M, Mangelsdorf S, et al. Behavioral inhibition and stress reactivity: moderating role of attachment security. *Child Development.* 1996;67:508-522.

52. Giannakoulopoulos X, Sepulveda W, Kourtis P, Glover V, Fisk N. Fetal plasma cortisol and ß-endorphin response to intrauterine needling. *Lancet.* 1994;344:77-81.

53. Anand KJS, Sippell WG, Aynsley-Green A. Randomised trial of fentanyl anaesthesia in preterm babies undergoing surgery: effects on the stress response. *Lancet.* 1987;1:243-248.

54. Moise KJ, Schumacher B. Anaemia. In: Fisk NM, Moise KL, eds. *Fetal Therapy: Invasive and Transplacental.* Cambridge, England: Cambridge University Press; 1997:147.

55. Schneider M. The effect of mild stress during pregnancy on birthweight and neuromotor maturation in Rhesus monkey infants. *Infant Behaviour and Development.* 1992;15:389-403.

56. Clarke AS, Schneider ML. Effects of prenatal stress on behaviour in adolescent rhesus monkeys. *Annals of the New York Academy of Science.* 1997;807:490-491.

57. Clarke AS, Schneider ML. Long-lasting effects of prenatal stress on emotional regulation in juvenile rhesus monkeys. *Infant Behaviour and Development.* 1996;19:19.

58. Clarke AS, Soto A, Bergholz T, Schneider ML. Maternal gestational stress alters adaptive and social behaviour in adolescent rhesus monkey offspring. *Infant Behaviour and Development.* 1996;19: 451-456.

59. Clarke AS, Wittwer DJ, Abbott DH, Schneider ML. Long term effects of prenatal stress on HPA reactivity in juvenile rhesus monkeys. *Developmental Psychobiology.* 1994;27:257-269.

60. Wittekind C, Arnold J, Leslie G, et al. Longitudinal study of plasma ACTH and cortisol in very low birth weight infants in the first 8 weeks of life. *Early Human Development.* 1993;33:191-200.

61. Hughes D, Murphy J, Dyas J, et al. Blood spot glucocorticoid concentrations in ill preterm infants. *Archives of Disease in Childhood.* 1987;62:1014-1018.

62. Lee M, Rajagopalan L, Berg G, Moshang T. Serum adrenal steroid concentrations in premature infants. *Journal of Endocrinology and Metabolism.* 1989;69:1133-1136.

63. Uno H, Tarara R, Else JG, et al. Hippocampal damage associated with prolonged and fatal stress in primates. *Journal of Neuroscience.* 1989;9:1705-1711.

64. Fuji T, Horinaka M, Hata M. Functional effects of glucocorticoid exposure during fetal life. *Progress in Neuro-Psychopharmacology and Biological Psychiatry.* 1993;17:279-293.

65. Uno H, Lohmiller L, Thieme C, et al. Brain damage induced by prenatal exposure to dexamethasone in fetal rhesus macaques. 1. Hippocampus. *Developmental Brain Research.* 1990;53:157-167.

66. Uno H, Eisele S, Sakai A, et al. Neurotoxicity of glucocorticoids in the primate brain. *Hormones and Behavior.* 1994;28:336-348.

67. Sapolsky RM, Uno H, Rebert CS, Finch CE. Hippocampal damage associated with prolonged glucocorticoid exposure in primates. *Journal of Neuroscience.* 1990;10:2897-2902.

68. Sapolsky RM, Krey LC, McEwan BS. The neuroendocrinology of stress and aging: the glucocorticoid cascade hypothesis. *Endocrine Reviews.* 1986;7:284-301.

69. Meaney MJ, Aitken DH, Bhatnagar S, Sapolsky R. Postnatal handling attenuates certain neuroendocrine, anatomical and cognitive dysfunctions associated with aging in female rats. *Neurobiology of Aging.* 1991;12:31-38.

70. Sapolsky RM. Why stress is bad for your brain. *Science.* 1996;273:749-750.

71. Axelson DA, Doraiswamy PM, McDonald WM, et al. Hypercortisolaemia and hippocampal changes in depression. *Psychiatric Research.* 1993;47:163-173.

72. Starkman M, Gebarski S, Berent S, et al. Hippocampal formation volume, memory dysfunction and cortisol levels in patients with Cushing's syndrome. *Biological Psychiatry.* 1992;32:756-765.

73. Bremner JD, Randall P, Scott TM, et al. MRI-based measurement of hippocampal volume in patients with combat related posttraumatic stress disorder. *American Journal of Psychiatry.* 1995;152:973-981.

74. De Leon MJ, McCrae T, Tsai JR, et al. Abnormal cortisol response in Alzheimer's disease linked to hippocampal atrophy. *Lancet.* 1988;2:391-392.

75. Vargha-Khadem F, Gadian D, Watkins KE, et al. Differential effects of early hippocampal pathology on episodic and semantic memory. *Science.* 1997;277:376-380.

76. McIntosh L, Sapolsky R. Glucocorticoids may enhance oxygen radical mediated neurotoxicity. *Neurotoxicology.* 1996;17:873-882.

77. Tombaugh GC, Yang SH, Swanson RA, Sapolsky RM. Glucocorticoids exacerbate hypoxic and hypoglycaemic hippocampal injury in vitro: biochemical correlates and a role for astrocytes. *Journal of Neurochemistry.* 1992;59:137-146.

78. Stein-Behrens BA, Lin WJ, Sapolsky RM. Physiological elevations of glucocorticoids potentiate glutamate accumulation in the hippocampus. *Journal of Neurochemistry.* 1994;63:596-602.

79. Yeh TF, Lin YJ, Huang CC, et al. Early dexamethasone therapy in preterm infants: a follow up study. *Pediatrics.* 1998;101(5). Abstract.

80. Baud O, Zupan V. Neurological adverse effects of early postnatal dexamethasone in very preterm infants. (Letter) *Archives of Disease in Childhood.* 1999;80(2):F159.

81. Acolet D, Modi N, Giannakoulopoulos X, Bond C, Glover V. Changes in plasma cortisol and catecholamine levels in response to massage in preterm babies. *Archives of Disease in Childhood.* 1993;68:29-31.

82. Giannakoulopoulos X, Murthy S, Modi N, Glover V. Change in circulating ß-endorphin and cortisol in preterm infants: lack of association with intrauterine-like sound stimulation. *Journal of Reproductive and Infant Psychology.* 1995;13:33-39.

83. Mooncey S, Giannakoulopoulos X, Glover V, Acolet D, Modi N. The effect of mother-infant skin-to-skin contact on plasma cortisol and ß-endorphin concentrations in preterm neonates. *Infant Behavior and Development.* 1997;20:553-557.

Effects on Mother and Infant of Oxytocin Released in the Postpartum Period

Kerstin Uvnäs-Moberg, MD, PhD

Introduction

The interactions between a mother and her infant immediately after birth, including breast-feeding, have been shown to cause behavioral and physiologic effects in both of them. These effects may involve activation of endogenous oxytocinergic mechanisms. Consequently, anything that affects this interaction may also affect the development of these oytocin-related adaptations.

Spontaneous Maternal and Infant Interaction

Mammals, by definition, give birth to offspring who receive milk from mammary glands. Parallel with milk production, most mammalian females have an inborn behavioral program to care for their offspring, often referred to as maternal behavior. Of course, humans do not express preprogrammed maternal behavior as do other mammals. However, some innate programs for maternal behavior and attachment may be discerned if the mother is allowed to express them and if they are sought by the infant. It has been found, for example, that a new mother approaches her baby in a very regular way. She starts to examine her baby with her fingertips, speaks in a high-pitched voice, and maintains eye-to-eye contact.[1,2]

Mammalian young are also programmed to approach their mothers' nipples and to start suckling immediately after birth. Newborn human babies (if delivered without anesthesia) may start a sequential, innate behavior to reach the nipple and start sucking when put skin to skin on their mothers' chests. In this "breast crawl" for the first 15 minutes after birth, infants are immobile and slightly unresponsive to environmental stimuli. Thereafter, they start to make rooting and sucking movements as well as hand-to-breast and hand-to-mouth movements, which develop over the first hour until the baby has found the nipple and started sucking. After sucking at the breast, they normally fall asleep.[3,4]

Effects of Early Skin-to-Skin Contact

Maternal Effects

When mothers are put skin to skin with their babies immediately after birth, they report themselves to be warmer, sleepier, and thirstier than mothers without such contact (Widström et al, unpublished data). Surprisingly, such skin-to-skin contact during the immediate postpartum period may also cause long-term effects on the future mother/infant relationship. These effects include such different behaviors as fondling, cuddling, and soothing; time spent with the baby; and other physically affectionate behaviors.[5-7] The duration of breast-feeding has also been observed to be prolonged in some studies.[8] There is reason to believe that suckling immediately postpartum strengthens these effects. In a study in which mothers immediately after birth were either allowed skin-to-skin contact or skin-to-skin contact with breast-feeding, it was found that mothers in the breast-feeding group spent more time and interacted more with their babies than mothers in the skin-to-skin group. The mothers who breastfed and held their infants skin-to-skin also had a different hormonal pattern. Their gastrin levels were lower during breast-feeding, and correlated with the time the infants spent in the nursery. Since gastrin levels are controlled by the vagal nerve, these data indicate that vagal nerve activity and, therefore, digestion and metabolism may also be influenced by contact between mother and baby in the early postpartum period.[9] Each suckling session is followed by a release of oxytocin, prolactin and some vagally controlled gastrointestinal hormones; in addition, cortisol levels and blood pressure fall. After a while, these effects become permanent – thus, breast-feeding is related to lower blood pressure and cortisol levels.[10-13]

The personality profiles of breast-feeding women differ from those of nonpregnant, nonlactating women of the same age. As measured by the Karolinska Scales of Personality, the mothers describe themselves as more open, more interactive, and calmer than nonpregnant, nonbreast-feeding women. This temporary shift in personality begins a few days after delivery and lasts as long as breast-feeding is continued. It is in part dependent on skin-to-skin contact after birth and is reinforced by breast-feeding.[14,15]

A major effect on personality can be seen in studies that documented decreased infant abandonment after the introduction of early contact between mother and baby, rooming in at the maternity ward, and subsequent breast-feeding.[16,17]

Infant Effects

Much less is known about the effects of early skin-to-skin contact on infants. We do know that babies held skin-to-skin cry less than other infants. Also, skin-to-skin contact helps regulate and warm the newborn's skin temperature, particularly distal areas such as the feet. This thermoregulation persists for 2 to 3 days and is mediated by increased cutaneous circulation due to sympatholytic activity.[18,19] Whether the release of gastrointestinal hormones is influenced by skin-to-skin contact is not presently known. However, premature babies kept in the kangaroo position on their mothers' chests have lower levels of cortisol and cholecystokinin than babies kept in incubators.[20] In addition, suckling in infants is followed by a release of gastrointestinal hormones.[21,22]

Together these results indicate that closeness between mother and infant immediately after birth (as well as in connection with breast-feeding) seem to be important to induce certain behavioral and physiologic effects. Both mother and infant become calmer, activity in the sympathoadrenal axis decreases, and some aspects of vagal nerve activity linked to increased gastrointestinal function and anabolic metabolism are enhanced.

Oxytocin

Oxytocin is produced in the supraoptic and paraventricular nuclei of the hypothalamus. The magnocellular neurons send projections to the neurohypophysis, from which the peptide is released into the circulation. In addition, parvocellular neurons from the paraventricular nuclei project to multiple areas within the central nervous system such as the median eminence, amygdala, hippocampus, ventral tegmental area, frontal cortex, brain stem, pons, medulla, and spinal cord.[23]

In addition to causing milk ejection, oxytocin has been shown to facilitate attachment between mother and offspring as well as induce maternal behavior in rats and sheep.[24-26] Oxytocin also promotes social interaction and induces physiologic changes in rats.[27] Oxytocin has anxiolytic and sedative effects and increases vagal-nerve activity, thereby influencing the levels of some gastrointestinal hormones. It has antistress effects (reduces blood pressure and cortisol levels) which can last for more than 1 week, especially after repeated injections.[28-32] In rat pups, the effects induced by oxytocin may become permanent.[33]

It is well established that oxytocin is released during labor and breast-feeding. Oxytocin is also released during the postpartum period if the baby is allowed skin-to-skin contact with the mother. Suckling and the intensity of massage-like hand movements that babies perform on mothers' breasts have been demonstrated to release maternal oxytocin; it is highly probable that skin-to-skin contact by itself stimulates the oxytocin release.[4,34] In support of this, various tactile stimuli such as touch, stroking, massage, and pleasant warm temperature have been shown to cause a release of oxytocin in the central nervous system of animal experiments.[35,36] For the same reasons, oxytocin is also likely to be released in response to skin-to-skin contact in a baby even if it is not detected by increased blood levels. Furthermore, sucking itself may be linked to a release of oxytocin in babies. For example in calves, suckling, but not drinking from a bucket, causes a marked increase in oxytocin levels.[37]

Another factor that may contribute to the effects of skin-to-skin contact is a special kind of sensory fiber that projects from the skin in the mammary gland area to the nucleus tractus solitarius. These vagally mediated sensory fibers use vasoactive intestinal polypeptide as a neurotransmitter. Such fibers have been found to occur in rats and humans. In further support of a functional role of these fibers, suckling in rats increases C-fos activity in the nucleus tractus solitarius.[38,39]

Some correlational data in women also support a role for oxytocin in maternal adaptations. As mentioned above, breast-feeding mothers are calmer and more social than age-matched nonlactating women. When oxytocin levels in response to breast-feeding were analyzed, basal levels were related to calm periods, whereas pulsatile oxytocin levels were related to social interests and the amount of milk transferred to the baby during breast-feeding.[14,15]

It is possible that effects induced by oxytocin during the postpartum period will be augmented by the high levels of estrogen present during pregnancy – estrogen enhances the binding of oxytocin to its receptors. These effects may diminish because estrogen levels drop quickly after the placenta is expelled, and even large amounts of oxytocin will lack the synergistic effects of estrogen and oxytocin.

Influence of Immediate Postdelivery Interactions on Expression of Oxytocin-Related Effects

In the early postpartum period, oxytocin has considerable impact on the immediate and long-term behavior and physiology of both mothers and their infants. It is important to describe and characterize the release pattern and effects of oxytocin in normal mother/infant interaction and identify external factors that may influence oxytocin release. Some clinical situations in which oxytocin release may be influenced by interactions in early life are discussed below.

Rat models. If rat pups are separated from their mothers, they immediately respond by emitting ultrasound distress calls, which cease as soon as they are reunited. When the separation is prolonged, the rats are stressed and their cortisol levels rise (this may even result in permanent overactivity of the hypothalamic-pituitary axis).[40-42] Conversely, extra handling or increased maternal attention has been shown to relieve stress and result in offspring that weigh more, are calmer, and have lower HPA axis activity when they mature than nonhandled controls.[43,44] Rat pups given repeated injections of oxytocin demonstrate a similar response; they weigh more, have higher insulin and cholecystokinin levels, and higher pain thresholds than saline-treated controls.[33] It is reasonable that the effects of extra handling of rat pups are likely to be due to a release of endogenous oxytocin.

Maternal-infant separation. If oxytocin is released in both mother and infant postpartum when they are allowed to stay in skin-to-skin contact, separation most likely leads to reduced release of oxytocin. Such decreased oxytocin concentrations in the postpartum period are likely to induce short- and long-term effects on maternal and infant behavior and physiology.

Interventions. Technical interventions may influence the spontaneous release of oxytocin. Epidural anesthesia given to mothers in labor to relieve pain has been shown to blunt oxytocin release.[45] Mothers who received epidurals also reported themselves to be less calm and less close to their babies the day after birth. These effects may be related to the lower amounts of oxytocin released in these mothers (Uvnäs-Moberg, unpublished data).

Cesarean sections have been shown to influence the development of breast-feeding in mothers which may be related to oxytocin secretion. Mothers who had a cesarean had relatively flat oxytocin levels, compared to the pulsatile pattern observed in the absence of a cesarean. Because the number of oxytocin pulses correlates with maternal social skills and with the amount of milk ejected, the less pulsatile oxytocin pattern may be related to delayed development of breast-feeding following cesarean section. The lower oxytocin levels may have been because the mothers did not experience the second stage of labor and they lacked early skin-to-skin contact with their infants.

The differences between breast-feeding and bottle-feeding may also include the development of oxytocin-related effects in both mother and baby. For example, when a calf drinks its mother's milk from a bucket, it releases only a small amount of oxytocin; in contrast, suckling causes a much larger release of oxytocin.[37] If we assume that similar mechanisms exist in human babies as well, the quality of sucking and the frequency of breast-feeding may influence the physiology and behavior of the baby.

Conclusion

Oxytocin release may be triggered by the interaction between mother and baby in the postpartum period as well as by breast-feeding. Oxytocin released in these situations may have calmative, stress-reducing, and growth-promoting effects in mother and child. These effects may be acute and perhaps also more long-lasting. Professionals attending infants and mothers in the perinatal period should be aware that clinical routines can affect oxytocin secretion and activity.

References

1. Klaus MH, Kennel JH, Plumb N, Zuehlke, S. Human maternal behavior at first contact with young. *Pediatrics.* 1970;46:187-192.

2. Kennel JH, Jerauld R, Wolfe H, et al. Maternal behaviour one year after early and extended contact. *Developmental Medicine and Child Neurology.* 1974;16:172-179.

3. Widström AM, Ransjö-Arvidson A-B, Christensson K, Matthiesen A-S, Winberg J, Uvnäs-Moberg K. Gastric suction in healthy newborn infants. Effects on circulation and developing feeding behaviour. *Acta Paediatrica Scandinavica.* 1987;76:566-572.

4. Ransjö-Arvidsson A-B. *Childbirth Care in Affluence and Poverty. Maternity Care Routines in Sweden and Zambia.* Stockholm, Sweden: Karolinska Institute; 1998. Dissertation.

5. Klaus MH, Jerauld R, Kreger N, McAlpine W, Steffa M, Kennel JH. Maternal attachment; importance of the first postpartum days. *New England Journal of Medicine.* 1972;286:460-463.

6. Grossman K, Thane K, Grossmann KE. Maternal tactual contact of the newborn after various postpartum conditions of mother-infant contact. *Developmental Psychology.* 1983;17:158-169.

7. Hales DJ, Lozoff B, Sosa R, Kennell JH. Defining the limits of the maternal sensitive period. *Developmental Medicine and Child Neurology.* 1977;19:454-461.

8. Salariya EM, Easton PM, Cater JI. Infant feeding. Duration of breastfeeding after early initiation and frequent feeding. *Lancet.* 1978;II:1141-1143.

9. Widström AM, Wahlberg V, Matthiesen AS, et al. Short-term effects of early suckling and touch of the nipple on maternal behaviour. *Early Human Development.* 1990;21:153-163.

10. Amico JA, Johnston JM, Vagnucci AH. Sucking induced attenuation of plasma cortisol concentrations in post partum lactating women. *Endocrine Research.* 1994;20:79-87.

11. Nissen E, Uvnäs-Moberg K, Svensson K, Stock S, Widström AM, Winberg J. Different patterns of oxytocin, prolactin but not cortisol release during breastfeeding in women delivered by caesarean section or by the vaginal route. *Early Human Development.* 1996;45:103-118.

12. Altemus M, Carter CS. Integrative functions of lactational hormones in social behavior and stress management. *Annals of the New York Academy of Science.* 1997;807:164-174.

13. Uvnäs-Moberg K. Neuroendocrinology of the mother-child interaction. *Trends in Endocrinology and Metabolism.* 1996;7:126-131.

14. Uvnäs-Moberg K, Widström A M, Nissen E, Björvell H. Personality traits in women 4 days postpartum and their correlation with plasma levels of oxytocin and prolactin. *Journal of Psychosomatic Obstetrics and Gynaecology.* 1990;11:261-273.

15. Nissen E, Gustavsson P, Widström A-M, Uvnäs-Moberg K. Oxytocin, prolactin, milk production and their relationship with personality traits in women after vaginal delivery or caesarean section. *Journal of Psychosomatic Obstetrics and Gynaecology.* 1998;19:49-58.

16. Buranasin B. The effects of rooming-in on the success of breastfeeding and the decline in abandonment of children. *Asia-Pacific Journal of Public Health.* 1990;5:217-220.

17. Klaus MH, Kennell JH, Robertson SS, Sosa R. Effects of social support during parturition on maternal and infant morbidity. *British Medical Journal.* 1986;293:585-587.

18. Christensson K. *Care of the Newborn Infant: Satisfying the Need for Comfort and Energy Conservation.* Stockholm, Sweden: Karolinska Institute; 1994. Dissertation.

19. Christensson K, Cabrera T, Christensson E, Uvnäs-Moberg K, Winberg J. Separation distress call in the human neonate in the absence of maternal body contact. *Acta Paediatrica.* 1995;84:468-473.

20. Törnhage CJ, Serenius F, Uvnäs-Moberg K, Lindberg T. Plasma somatostatin and cholecystokinin levels in preterm infants during kangaroo care with and without nasogastric tubefeeding. *Journal of Pediatric Endocrinology and Metabolism.* 1998;11:645-651.

21. Uvnäs-Moberg K, Widström AM, Marchini G, Winberg J. Release of GI hormones in mother and infant by sensory stimulation. *Acta Paediatrica Scandinavica.* 1987;76:851-860.

22. Uvnäs-Moberg K, Marchini G, Winberg J. Plasma cholecystokinin concentrations after breast feeding in healthy 4 day old infants. *Applied Animal Behavioral Science.* 1993;68:46-48.

23. Sofroniew MW. Vasopressin and oxytocin in mammalian brain and spinal cord. *Trends in Neurosciences.* 1983;6:467-472.

24. Kendrick K, Keverne EB, Baldwin BA. Intracerebroventricular oxytocin stimulate maternal behaviour in sheep. *Neuroendocrinology.* 1987;46:56-61.

25. Keverne EB, Lévy F, Poindron P, Lindsay DR. Vaginal stimulation: an important determinant of maternal bonding in sheep. *Science.* 1983;219:81-83.

26. Pedersen CA, Ascher JA, Monroe YL, Prange AJ Jr. Oxytocin induced maternal behavior in virgin maternal rats. *Science.* 1982;216:648-649.

27. Witt DM, Winslow JT, Insel TR. Enhanced social interactions in rats following chronic, centrally infused oxytocin. *Pharmacology, Biochemistry and Behavior.* 1992;43:855-861.

28. Petersson M, Alster P, Lundeberg T, Uvnäs-Moberg K. Oxytocin causes a long-term decrease of blood pressure in female and male rats. *Physiology and Behavior.* 1996;60:1311-1315.

29. Uvnäs-Moberg K. Antistress pattern induced by oxytocin. *News Physiol Sci.* 1998;13:22-26.

30. Uvnäs-Moberg K. Oxytocin-linked antistress effects – the relaxation and growth response. *Acta Physiologica Scandinavica.* 1997;161(suppl 640):38-42.

31. Uvnäs-Moberg, K. Physiological and endocrine effects of social contact. *Annals of the New York Academy of Science.* 1997;807:146-163.

32. Uvnäs-Moberg K. Oxytocin may mediate the benefits of positive social interaction and emotions. *Psychoneuroendocrinology.* 1998;23:819-835.

33. Uvnäs-Moberg K, Alster P, Petersson M, Sohlström A, Björkstrand E. Postnatal oxytocin injections cause sustained weight gain and increased nociceptive thresholds in male and female rats. *Pediatric Research.* 1998;43:344-348.

34. Nissen E, Lilja G, Widström AM, Uvnäs-Moberg K. Elevation of oxytocin levels early post partum in women. *Acta Obstetrica & Gynecologica Scandinavica.* 1995;74:530-533.

35. Stock S, Uvnäs-Moberg K. Increased plasma levels of oxytocin in response to afferent electrical stimulation of the sciatic and vagal nerves and in response to touch and pinch in anaesthetized rats. *Acta Physiologica Scandinavica.* 1988;132:29-34.

36. Uvnäs-Moberg K, Bruzelius G, Alster P, Lundeberg T. The antinociceptive effect of non-noxious sensory stimulation is partly mediated through oxytocinergic mechanisms. *Acta Physiolica Scandinavica.* 1993;149:199-204.

37. Samuelsson B. *Importance of Milking and Feeding Routines in Dairy Cattle.* Uppsala, Sweden: Swedish University for Agriculture: 1996. Dissertation.

38. Eriksson M, Lindh B, Uvnäs-Moberg K, Hökfelt T. Distribution and origin of peptide-containing nerve fibers in the rat and human mammary gland. *Neuroscience.* 1996;1:227-245.

39. Uvnäs-Moberg K, Eriksson M. Breastfeeding: physiological, endocrine and behavioural adaptations caused by oxytocin and local neurogenic activity in the nipple and the mammary gland. *Acta Paediatrica.* 1996;85:525-530.

40. Hofer MA. Early relationships as regulators of infant physiology and behaviour. *Acta Paediatrica.* 1994;397(suppl):9-19.

41. Hofer MA, Shair H, Murowchick E. Isolation distress and maternal comfort response of two-week-old rat pups reared in social isolation. *Developmental Psychobiology.* 1989;22(6):553-566.

42. Levine S. Plasmafree corticosteroid response to electric shock in rats stimulated in infancy. *Science.* 1962;135:795-796.

43. Wakshlak A, Weinstock M. Neonatal handling reverses behavioral abnormalities induced by prenatal stress. *Physiology and Behavior.* 1990;48(2):289-292.

44. Carden SE, Hofer MA. Effect of social companion on ultrasonic vocalizations and contact responses in 3-day-old rat pups. *Behavioral Neuroscience.* 1992;106(2):271-279.

45. Goodfellow CF, Hull MGR, Swaab DF, Dogterom J, Buijs RM. Oxytocin deficiency at delivery with epidural analgesia. *British Journal of Obstetrics and Gynaecology.* 1983;90:214-219.

Section 6:
Discussion

Abstract From Section 6. Discussion

Nathan Fox, PhD, Betsy Lozoff, MD, Lewis Leavitt, MD,
Ronald Barr, MD, Ann C. Stadtler, MSN, CPNP,
Rosemary White-Traut, DNSc, RN

Discussions at the Pediatric Round Table conference covered a spectrum of issues related to the role of early experience in infant development. The consensus of those exchanges is presented in this final chapter.

Discussion

Nathan Fox, PhD, Betsy Lozoff, MD, Lewis Leavitt, MD,
Ronald Barr, MD, Ann C. Stadtler, MSN, CPNP,
Rosemary White-Traut, DNSc, RN

The faculty of the *1999 Johnson & Johnson Pediatric Round Table: The Role of
Early Experience in Infant Development* are among the world's leaders in the
field of infant development. Each brought to the table years of experience
from a variety of disciplines. Together with a discussant in clinical practice,
presenters from each session were charged with summarizing the most salient
issues for healthcare professionals and parents, and identifying directions for
future research. The highlights of these discussions are presented in the following chapter.

Salient Findings

Brain development. In many ways the neurologic underpinnings of brain
development in infancy set the stage for an infant's development in all other
realms: cognitive, social, perceptual, language, and motor. Recent technical
advances have made it possible to analyze the developmental progress of neurons in the central nervous system under a variety of conditions. This new
information is expected to clarify several misconceptions that have evolved in
the popular "science and medicine" press. For example, the eloquently stated
concept that "…the years 0 to 3 is a critical period, and if you do not stimulate your child in precisely the correct way, at exactly the right time, his brain
is toast…" was soundly refuted by the faculty for a number of reasons.

Human brain development is an asynchronous process with different brain
systems becoming competent at different times. Sensory systems tend to
develop earlier than most other brain areas, so incoming visual, auditory, and
tactile information will have effects sooner rather than later. "Sensitive periods" or "critical periods" do exist within the overall envelope of brain development, but these periods differ for different functional systems, and persist
beyond 3 years. For example the critical period for binocular vision ends at
about 6 months of age, but the period for learning a second language accent-
free ends years later.

Brain development also entails dendritic arborization and the creation of an excess number of synapses, which is followed over a number of years by selective pruning and loss of synapses. The process of synapse loss is normal and necessary. Synaptic pruning can be regarded as the body's way of fine tuning the wiring of the nervous system to best meet the needs imposed by the environment. In fact, deficient pruning (or excessive synapses) has been linked to pathologic conditions such as fragile X mental retardation. Thus attempts to preserve synapses at all costs are ill-advised.

Synapses form and persist in greater numbers in the context of a rich environment than in a stimulus-poor environment. These observations indicate that the structure of the brain is modified by experience. This neural flexibility is greatest in the very young, but synaptic plasticity is a lifelong process in which learning and recovery from injury can occur throughout life. The brain's inherent plasticity is such that the same experience will cause an injured brain to react differently from an intact brain, creating the possibility for experience-based therapy following brain trauma.

Language development. The auditory system is mature at birth and ready to process signals that are important for language development. During the first year of life infants interact with their parents and caregivers to develop important language-related skills, such as the ability to identify native from non-native speech, recognize word segmentation, and distinguish stress-based cues. Continued interaction with language input during the first several years is associated with developing skills needed to "find" words in the language stream and learn the grammar of a language.

Experience with language molds the developing nervous system. These experiences modify an infant's ability to perceive and produce speech, as they become more fluent in their native language. For example, Japanese infants actually lose the ability to distinguish the sound of "r" from "l" and also forfeit the ability to pronounce distinct "r" and "l" sounds because they never hear an "r" sound in the Japanese language. However, the brain's speech center is sufficiently adaptable that children growing up in a bilingual environment are able to achieve typical development in two languages while keeping the language skills separate.

Language production in the first 3 years is clearly related to the amount of language input; the more one speaks to a child, the greater is the child's vocabulary. This effect is proportional to the amount of speech, not the size of the parent's vocabulary. However, the content of what caregivers say is related to growth in syntax; greater syntactic growth is observed in the children of parents who frequently expand on what their infants say. Nonetheless, children can achieve typical language development across a wide range of input, although the precise boundaries of that range are presently unknown.

Research on deaf, blind, neurologically atypical, and neglected children has shown that early experience is very important for language development. In children with language impairments, some remediation is possible through intervention, due to the brain's inherent plasticity, even after the first several years of life. Research in these populations and on sign language development suggests that there are special mechanisms common to communication skills that are a fundamental part of the human nervous system.

The faculty also advocated mandatory hearing screening for infants and school-age children as a clinically important and cost-effective method of preventing learning disabilities that may stem from undiagnosed hearing problems.

Cognitive development. Cognitive development does indeed depend on experience; while many remarkable examples of that experience have been described in the literature, simply hearing words, moving around in an ordinary physical environment, and interacting with people are sufficient for normal cognitive development for most infants. Infants who are exposed to this experience can benefit from it much earlier than is often assumed, expected, or imagined. However, it is clear that well-intentioned caregivers can push infants excessively in an attempt to advance the experience-learning curve, and that these experiences can be frustrating (and even counterproductive) for the infant. For this reason, people who interact with infants should be attentive to the infants' cues to engage and disengage; with careful observation, an infant can literally tell you what sorts of activities are within the boundaries that they are ready, willing, and able to experience and benefit from.

Human beings pass information from generation to generation in a social context; we learn from the experience of others. We are more imitative than other species, and a substantial portion of our learning comes from observing and imitating the actions of others. Infants understand the intentions of adult actions and can "smooth over" mistakes or incomplete actions. In so doing they can extract from imperfect experience the important points of that experience for their own benefit. For example, by about 18 months, children who observe an adult unsuccessfully attempt an action are able to successfully perform that act without ever having seen it done correctly.

Cognitive development can be affected in very specific ways by generalized insults to the entire body. For example, children with phenylketonuria, a genetic defect that alters tyrosine and phenylalanine levels throughout the body, perform within the normal range on global IQ tests, but show impaired working memory and inhibitory control. Measurement of these and other changes are being made possible by a new generation of specific cognitive tests. Although currently research tools, these evaluations may have broader clinical application in the near future.

Perceptual development. Infants are energetic people that enter the world with the tools they need to interact with the world around them. They are born with the ability to perceive human facial information, enabling them to rapidly recognize parents and caregivers. Face processing originates in specific cortical regions and follows an established developmental pathway. Yet the brain is plastic, and if this path is blocked by deprivation or brain lesions, other pathways are activated that are less efficient, but still facilitate face recognition.

Infants perceive spatial relationships in simpler terms than adults, and their understanding of space develops rapidly in the first several months of life. Changes in their perception of space coincides with periods of rapid development in the cerebral cortex. The specific role of experience in development of spatial perception is not precisely known, but there is little reason to doubt that everyday visual experiences are sufficient for normal development.

Infants are sensitive to predictability and regularity of their environment at an early age; infants can form expectations of what comes next as early as 2 months of age. Experience with predictable events fosters the development of expectations and future-oriented thinking. Parents can facilitate forward thinking by including in their usual discourse with their children comments about what they will be doing, rather than what they are doing.

Biosocial development. To maximize the potential development of each infant, including those born preterm or otherwise challenged, the postnatal environment should be designed to facilitate optimal development. This is because an infant's experience within that environment has the potential to alter development.

The effects of experience are mediated by the nervous system. Sensory pathways that provide input from environmental stimuli are capable of either promoting or inhibiting growth, restoration, and development, depending on the type of stimulus and the behavioral and physiologic state of the infant. Many experiences are context dependent, and each infant is unique, therefore caregivers must be sensitive to the infant's cues and the overall setting in which the infant receives care. Among these experiences, breastfeeding is a powerful example of how behavior influences biology with a wide range of long-term beneficial effects.

Research Perspectives

Exciting research is ongoing in many aspects of infant development beyond those discussed at this *Pediatric Round Table*. In the area of developmental neurobiology, investigation at the molecular level of neurotrophins, and the substrates of synapse addition and loss, will add to the understanding of brain dynamics. Noninvasive imaging techniques will continue to add new information about brain metabolism and its relation to synapse arborization and pruning. Additional resources should probably be allocated to develop animal models that mimic relevant human clinical conditions. And, observing that more research has been performed on sensory systems than some other relevant systems, the faculty suggested that further study is needed on the effects of experience on other functional brain systems.

Newer imaging techniques also offer a richer understanding of the relationship among language skills and brain structure and function. Longitudinal studies are needed to discern the implications of individual differences in language reception and production, as well as to reveal the effects of differences in language input. Both cross-sectional and longitudinal studies should be performed to gain insight into special populations such as children with Williams Syndrome, Down's Syndrome, autism, deafness, and blindness. Similar studies would also be beneficial in addressing issues related to bilingual language exposure as well as the development of dialectical differences.

Understanding individual differences is also one of the growing areas of interest in cognitive development. Ongoing research will lead to a better appreciation of the boundary conditions that define meaningful experiences for individual infants. This research will involve careful observation of behavioral phenomena from which robust definitions of infant competencies can be drawn. Such information should lead to more effective interventions for cognitive, perceptual, and other developmental challenges.

The faculty proposed several unanswered questions in the area of perceptual development that were ripe for additional research. For example, how does early passive experience while being carried influence an infant's perception of space? What is the effect if infants are carried facing outward or inward? Does early experience make a difference in how a child understands and constructs the future through planning and problem solving?

In the area of biosocial development, the faculty recommended that further investigation be directed toward defining the components, mechanisms, and processes associated with healing, especially for preterm infants.

Summary

Early experience has a profound impact on infant development and the very structure of the human brain. The extent of the impact has very often been documented by extreme outliers in terms of normal experience, such as deprived Romanian orphans, those with congenital cataracts, or those raised in the absence of language input. Fortunately for parents and others who care for children, the range of "normal" is quite broad, and as long as infants are supplied with affectionate social interaction, an environment containing objects to see, touch, and manipulate, and caregivers who speak to them, most infants will develop normally. And although windows of opportunity and critical periods do exist, most normal environments contain enough keys to open those windows without special toys or enrichment classes.